MBAZO

FOOTPRINTS THROUGH THE KRUGER NATIONAL PARK

Lynn van Rooyen

Order this book online at www.trafford.com
or email orders@trafford.com

Most Trafford titles are also available at major online book retailers.

Mbazo Image Courtesy: Ronnie & Nicole Rogoff

Printed in the United States of America.

ISBN: 978-1-4907-2132-3 (sc)
ISBN: 978-1-4907-2131-6 (hc)
ISBN: 978-1-4907-2133-0 (e)

Library of Congress Control Number: 2013922584

Trafford rev. 03/26/2014

 www.trafford.com

North America & international
toll-free: 1 888 232 4444 (USA & Canada)
fax: 812 355 4082

Although the contents of this book is factually correct, the incidents are not necessarily chronologically presented

-Lynn

ACKNOWLEDGEMENTS

The purpose of this book is not to present a complex philosophical thesis on conservation ecology, but it is merely a means of giving expression to some campfire stories, which provided me with some cherished memories, which I have never shared with anyone else. I have always held the view that these were my private memories and that it was of no concern to anyone else.

Having retired from the South African National Parks (SANParks) on 28 February 2006, my wife and I preoccupied ourselves with building our dream retirement home. In September 2007, through the convergence of various circumstances, I became involved with the development of a 'Big Five' nature reserve in the north-eastern corner of the Gauteng province. The 'Dinokeng Game Reserve' is a Public/Private initiative to address poverty alleviation in that area. This information is relevant as it was in this work environment that I *inter alia* met Emelia who practically forced me to start writing this book.

I first of all want to give humble thanks to my Creator who not only created everything, but who also allowed a small portion of His creation to remain practically unscathed by man for us to work in, to spend time in, and to enjoy.

Secondly, I wish to thank my family: Liza, Mela, Morné, Magnus, Henrie, and Liezel who travelled this journey with me, through all of its ups and downs, and who made this the wonderful experience that it was. To my parents, Gert and Sannie, and my in-laws, Dassie and Bettie, many thanks for all your love, support, and understanding.

Thirdly, I would like to express my appreciation to all my mentors, colleagues, and friends during my stay in the Kruger National Park (KNP). I would like to mention a couple by name, who with their purposeful inputs made major contributions in shaping who I am today: Oom Tol, Oom Johan, Dirk, Sollie, Flip, Ted, Oom Ampie, Louis, Vossie, Ian, Merle, Oom Albert, Oom Jan, John Mnisi, Simeone Mujovu, and William Ngobeni. If I were to continue with the list, I would have to mention everyone in the KNP. Please be assured that you have all contributed in one way or another to an unforgettable KNP experience.

Thank you, Emelia, for your continued pressure to complete this book and for doing all the typing. To Memories SA who proved that one can have a book (the Afrikaans version) print ready and published in an unbelievably short period of time.

Thank you, Liza and Lorraine, for your hard work to complete the English version.

Place names referred to in the book.

Limpopo river

Northern Kruger National Park

Luvuvhu river   **Pafuri**

Madzaringwe spruit   **Nkovakulu**

Tshipudza   **Xantangalani**

N'waxitsumbe

Dongadziva   **Punda Maria**   **Xirhombe picket**

Punda Maria Gate   **Dzundzwini hill**

Vlakte Plaas

Marithenga fire break crossing   **Xingomeni picket**

Wik en Weeg dam

Mooigesig dam

Mafunyane   **Awie se Dam**   **Shingwedzi**

Shangoni

Dipeni picket

Maxokwe dam

Kostini picket

Xipandani spruit   **Hlamvu dam**

Mopanie Rest Camp

Makhadzi

Ramiti pan

Letaba Rest Camp

Klip Koppies

Phalaborwa   **Letaba river**

Olifant Rest Camp

Olifants river   **Houtboschrand**

Southern
Kruger National
Park

Satara

N'wanetsi

Kingfisherspruit

N'waswitsontso river

N'wamuriwa

Tshokwane

Xiteveteve Windmill

Leeu Pan

Nkumbe

Munywini

Paul Kruger Gate

Skukuza

Nkuhlu Picnic Site

Msimuku spruit

Mlondozi dam

Tree House

Numbi Gate

Lower Sabie

Pretoriuskop

Makohlolo dam

Stolsnek

Crocodile Bridge

Wolhuter
Trails Camp

Crocodile river

Malelane

Nsikazi

PREFACE

In hindsight, I wish to make an apology, especially to my wife, children, and parents, if I disappointed them with my silence through all the years. Through this book, however, I will attempt to make up for this by sharing, especially, the joys of my work environment and experiences in the KNP with you. My work was 'work' but at the same time was my 'hobby/passion' and gave me a great measure of satisfaction. I hereby wish to dedicate this book to all of you.

One of my personal work ethics was never to try and impress anyone else but myself with anything that I accomplished; after all, I could fool others but not myself. Self-satisfaction was only achieved after I met the very high demands that I placed on myself. If my seniors were satisfied with my work performance, they could deploy me within the KNP as they pleased, and I would tackle the challenge to the best of my ability. I had a very good work relationship with all my colleagues, of whom only a few were real friends. I never misused friendships for self-promotion. The ill-informed could very well interpret the above and come to the conclusion that I had no ambition. My ambitions, however, were founded in a self-analysis that occurred in a bizarre way for me.

An annual helicopter census was required for the proper ecological management of the elephant and buffalo populations in the KNP. Elephants were counted individually with special attention to the identification and counting of calves younger than one year. This enabled us to calculate the annual percentage growth of the population. For the buffalo, we adopted a different method. Lone bulls were counted individually. The large herds of buffalo were split into smaller groups by expert flying by the helicopter pilot. Such smaller groups were photographed and counted from the photographs after the completion of the census surveys. Numbering and record-keeping of the films and individual photos was not child's play. The elephant census numbers usually varied between 7,000 and 8,000 animals, while the buffalo added up to approximately 30,000 animals. I do not wish to delve deeper into the management aspects of these censuses. The elephant and buffalo censuses, however, will later clarify who and what I am and why I did things the way I did during my period of service.

During the elephant and buffalo censuses, Letaba Rest Camp played a major role. Census teams, including the helicopter pilots, were accommodated and rotated there. The photographer/archivist, unfortunately for him, had to participate in the entire census. This amounted to 125 flying hours for the whole KNP. No need to state that these occasions ended up in an evening barbecue of ten to twelve people. Later, after the first few beers, everyone became very talkative, and they described or rather 'bragged', about what each one had achieved and what each still wanted to achieve in life.

Examples of such bragging were:

'I have apprehended so many poachers.'
'So many wounded/injured lions have attacked me, and then I shot them at 5 m distance.'
'I had to shoot a huge elephant bull at 10 m with a single shot as it charged at me.'
'The largest barbell/tiger fish I have caught was . . .'
'The most beers I have had to drink at one party were . . . and then I was really sick.'
'At one stage in my life, I had five girlfriends.'
'I still want to row the Duzi Marathon/Orange River.'
'I still want to climb Kilimanjaro.'

That was the content of 'campfire talk'. I never drank any alcoholic beverages, and I never became talkative around the campfire. Others must have thought that I was a rather dull sort of character.

The different groups would then retire to bed. I was usually the last one to leave as I would see to it that all had reached their beds safely, and I would tidy the mess left behind.

I will return to the above story shortly. The photographer/archivist of the elephant and buffalo censuses and his wife were dear colleagues and friends. Discussions with his wife were always special. Before the barbecues started, we used to speculate on who would be 'bigger, better, and stronger' than anyone else that evening. During the barbecues, she sat opposite the fire from me. Time and again during the narration of one or other big story, she formed her mouth as if to say 'Wow', while looking at me to confirm our discussion before the barbecue.

Once in bed, after a long and tiresome day, I would fall asleep quickly. I seldom dreamt, but on one occasion, the discussions around the fire must have stuck in my subconscious because I then dreamt of the lady mentioned above, and I remember we were involved in a heated argument. At one stage in my dream, she asked me: 'Who the hell do you think you are?'

I replied with the following:

'Who I am?'
I have never wanted to climb the highest mountain
I have never wanted to swim the deepest sea.
I have never had to shoot a raging elephant bull
Nor have I been stalked by a pride of lions
But even if it were so
Nobody else but I need know.

I have never wanted to fly to the furthest horizon
Nor have I hurled the biggest cat
I am not a computer fundi
Nor am I a financial giant
But nowhere will you ever find
A more loyal and committed KNP subject around.
I have always believed in a gracious God, not above us, but down here amongst us.
I have always showed dignity towards all humankind.
I am committed to righteousness and self-discipline
All year round
But most of all, I am utterly content
Just being little old me.

Having uttered the last line, I woke up and realised it was a dream. I grabbed pen and paper and jotted down what I had declared in my dream.

That was the first and last time I ever did a self-analysis.

The silences on my experiences in the KNP are based mostly on the following two declarations in my self-analysis, i.e.:

'Nobody else but I need know.'

'But most of all, I am utterly content just being little old me.'

*   *   *

We, the four brothers, and our four cousins (three brothers and a sister) made contact with Mother Nature at a very early stage. We four brothers grew up on the farm 'Rustenburg' in the district of Greytown in Natal (now Kwazulu-Natal). The four cousins grew up on a farm in the district of Hluhluwe (Zululand) in Natal. By coincidence, we were all together during 1954 and 1955 on the farm 'Rapids' in the district of Letaba in the Transvaal (now Limpopo). The farm was situated on the Letaba River, approximately 70 km upstream from the Kruger National Park (KNP). As youngsters, we went to school in Gravelot and were boarded in the school residence. Most importantly, we spent weekends and school holidays fishing in the Letaba River, shooting vervet monkeys and birds in the orange and pawpaw orchards and tomato fields and cycled until we were totally exhausted. Our weaponry consisted of a .22 Brno rifle, a 1912 BSA model airgun, and a Daisy pellet gun, which were carried on hunting trips in order of our seniority. My eldest brother carried the .22, I carried the airgun and my eldest cousin carried the Daisy pellet gun. The rest of the hunting group had either catapults (ketties) or home-made arrow guns.

On one occasion, the hunting group came upon the tracks of a large cat. After much arguing, we concluded that these were the tracks of a lion. The lion most probably came from the KNP. That, however, was of no concern to us as we were sure that the lion was after our cattle. That could not be tolerated, and the lion had to be put down. After thorough deliberation, it was decided that we would follow the tracks and that the potential cattle thief should be put down. My brother, with the .22 rifle, led the hunting expedition; I followed with the airgun, followed by our cousin with the Daisy pellet gun, with the intention of killing anything that moved at the first attempt. The rest with their catapults and toy arrow guns would provide backup fire, should it be necessary. At that stage, my eldest brother must have been about 11 years of age, my eldest cousin and I, were 9 years old, and the rest were all younger, with the youngest being approximately 4 years old.

I can still recall the pathetic hunting expedition of eight 'heavily armed members' following the lion tracks on a forlorn game path in the hazy late afternoon sun. Fortune smiled upon the lion as the hunting expedition commenced about 1 hour before sunset. One of us was either very sharp or too scared and warned after half an hour that if we did not turn around, we would walk home in the dark after sunset. It so happened that we were all more scared of the dark than we were of the lion. Later on in life, I often wondered what would have transpired had we come across the lion. I am not one to attach human characteristics to animals but wondered what the lion would have thought observing a 4-year-old charging at it with a toy arrow gun. I now thank the Lord that we did not cross paths with the lion nor confront it. I do not recall that any of us brothers or cousins ever boasted about that failed hunting expedition. Was it perhaps that we never came across the lion, or was it because none of us would inherently 'brag' about such an occasion? I believe the latter was the correct reason.

During 1956, we moved back to Greytown from the farm 'Rapids' because the fruit and vegetable markets could not sustain the two Van Rooyen families on one farm. My father was a motor mechanic by trade. With our return to Greytown, he returned to the trade. He had participated in motor racing events in his younger days, and I, therefore, grew up in a mechanical environment where motor vehicle engines were taken out and repaired. My childhood dream was to become the first South African Grand Prix world champion driving my own designed and built racing car. We, however, maintained contact with the farm 'Rapids'.

The farm was situated next to the farm 'Eiland', a provincial nature reserve with hot water springs, tourist accommodation, and game drives. During one of our holiday visits to Rapids, the nature conservation staff of Eiland were in the process of planning game-reduction operations. The operation consisted of the game being herded on horseback into catchment enclosures. It was a time-consuming and complicated process. Amongst others, they had a crazy mare that would never run in front but rather in the bunch or at the back. She was crazy because, on seeing another horse in front jump over a trench or barricade, she would also jump right there where she was. By the time she reached the trench or barricade, she would have no more jump in her. She would go straight into the trench or barricade, much to the consternation of the rider. Needless to say, each new member of the game-catching cavalry was given the privilege of starting off on the crazy mare, much to the delight of the colleagues.

My father was a creative designer and built all kinds of technical gadgets. All the frustrations associated with capturing the game at 'Eiland' triggered his creative mind to develop a better method or apparatus to improve the catching of game. That was the commencement of the crossbow-and-dart era which later would develop into a very sophisticated chemical (muti) method of catching game.

Back in Greytown, the development of the crossbow and dart resulted in my father leaving the motor mechanic trade to attend full-time to perfecting and building the crossbow and dart equipment. During this period (1961-1963), I often joined my father in his workshop, calibrating crossbows, testing darts, and developing an intense interest in micrometers and tolerances of 1/1,000 of an inch (2.54 cm), setting lathes, and sharpening chisels and drill bits, etc. This resulted in me joining my father when he had to demonstrate crossbows and darts to potential buyers, obviously all from the nature conservation fraternity. As a result, we met many KNP staff who later became very close friends, particularly Dr U de V (Tol) Pienaar (Oom Tol to me), who at that stage was head of the Research Section of the KNP. Also Messrs. Johan Kloppers (Oom Johan), Dirk Swart, Mike English, Solomon Joubert, and others (all Section Rangers). I have to explain the 'title' 'Oom'. When you were a kid, any male person who was 10 years older than yourself was addressed as 'Oom' as a token of respect. Your father's brother was also addressed as 'Oom' in family context. The appropriate English equivalent would be 'uncle', which is not the same as 'Oom' in the first mentioned context.

One of our visits to the KNP stemmed from the desire of KNP Management for more information on the movements of elephant bulls, particularly in the northern regions of the KNP. My father and I overloaded our 1959 Morris 1000 with all the necessary camping equipment to join Oom Tol at Skukuza. From there, we moved to Shingwedzi and further on to a camping site at N'waxitshumbe. There, Oom Johan Kloppers (District Game Ranger at Punda Maria), Dirk Swart (Section Game Ranger at Shingwedzi), and Mike English (Section Game Ranger at Shangoni) awaited us at the campsite. Oom Chris Lombaard was Oom Tol Pienaar's right-hand man at Skukuza, being the Chief Technician in the Research Section. For the above expedition, Oom Chris acquired a small Honda generator to provide lighting around the campfire and during the preparation of meals.

During the first sunset – and what a beautiful one it was – Oom Chris 'started' the generator for the first time; I observed some grumbling among the field staff, who were not content with the loud *'prrrrr . . .'* disturbing the silence or the night sounds. After the second or third round of drinks, Oom Johan, Dirk, and Mike invited me to join them and excused themselves from the campfire to go and relieve ourselves of all the liquid. They enquired whether I liked the noise of the generator. I responded negatively, and they invited me to join them. We stalked the generator, and Oom Johan instructed me to take off the petrol cap and to urinate into the petrol tank. Who was I to argue with the adults or to refuse his instruction? Within a few seconds, the generator produced a *'pr . . . pr . . . puff'*, and everything was clothed in darkness, and the quiet of the nightlife fell on us.

With a *'Tsk . . . tsk'*, Oom Chris took a flashlight and walked off to inspect the generator. After half an hour, he had cleaned the generator's carburettor of all the water in the float chamber. His explanation was: 'It was probably water from the petrol jerry cans.' We field staff (I was now one of them) had Oom Chris take the carburettor apart to clean another three times before he capitulated, and at last, we had quiet around the campfire. As a school kid, I was impressed with this desire for quiet around the campfire in the bush as well as the camaraderie amongst the field staff.

* * *

After my military service (1964), I moved to the University of Stellenbosch to study Mechanical Engineering to give expression to my childhood dream of becoming the first South African World Champion racing driver that designed his own Grand Prix car. I sometimes questioned the need for the subjects Physics, Mathematics, Applied Mathematics, and Chemistry, but it was new to me and did contribute to my education. Engineering Drawing, Strength of Materials, and Building Science were interesting, developmental, and applicable. During a Mechanics lecture, we were exposed to the theory of a braking system – the application was based on the brake shoes of ox wagons – I became rather despondent. At that stage, I was already familiar with the theory and application of disc brakes, how it was developed for aircraft, then adapted for racing cars and later for high-performance sports cars. During engineering vacation work,

I soon realised that qualified engineers, having practiced the engineering profession for 5-7 years, were promoted to the levels of human resource management, and their hard-earned engineering qualifications were no longer of any relevance in their new posts. To say the least, I was rather disgusted with this state of affairs. I concluded, however, that in order to fulfil my childhood dream, I had to pursue my Mechanical Engineering studies.

By the end of my second year at university, my father's crossbow-and-dart business had grown to the extent that he was manufacturing darts for cross bows already in service on a full-time basis. He no longer had time to manufacture new cross bows in order to expand his business. I wanted to take a break from my studies, and we decided that I would take leave of my studies for a year to manufacture darts on a full-time basis in order for my father to manufacture more cross bows. For the next 9 months during 1967, my father manufactured cross bows on a full-time basis, and I concentrated on the manufacturing of darts. This mainly entailed working on the lathe. At the beginning of September 1967, I received an important telephone call from Oom Tol Pienaar. He enquired whether I would be interested in becoming the first full-time game capturer in the National Parks Board (later the South African National Parks or SANParks) stationed in the KNP. They were looking for a young person who was familiar with the cross bow and who was prepared to stay in the bush. I requested 2 or 3 days to consider, after which I would call and confirm. They wished to fill the post as from 1 October 1967.

This was a life-changing call. I was sitting torn between two irreconcilable fields of interest. On the one hand, Mechanics: cold, clinical, exact (secure), and predictable. On the other hand, the natural environment: alive, 'messy', not governed by man-made rules. For the first time in my life, I was dictated to by my heart and not my head. It did not take long to make the decision. Within half an hour, I called him back and very excitedly confirmed that I would love to become the game capturer. After a while, however, the hard reality hit me. I did not possess a vehicle; in fact, I had nothing to register on my list of assets. I merely had the conviction that I wished to go to the Kruger National Park.

My parents came to my rescue. My mother would provide all the kitchen utensils, and my father promised that if I paid for the parts, we could repair the 1959 Morris 1000, to be my first mode of transport. What a pleasure! There was nothing to stop this aspirant game capturer. I could now earn my daily keep with my father's masterpiece. I departed early on the morning of 26 September 1967 from Greytown on the long journey to Skukuza. Accommodation was arranged in the rest camp, and the next day at 08.00, I had an appointment with Oom Tol Pienaar. As was to be expected of a young man, I arrived at the Nature Conservation's offices too early. Oom Tol formally welcomed me at 08.00 and gave me a broad outline of what my work would entail. I did not pay much attention to what he was saying to me. I could not help staring at all the maps of the park on the walls of his office and all the bottles of scorpions, snakes, frogs, etc. He handed me over to Oom Chris Lombaard, who accompanied me from office to office and introduced me to all my potential/future colleagues. From there, we proceeded to the Administrative stores where I was kitted out with khaki (still my favourite colour) uniforms, Parks Board epaulettes, shoes, and a metal pocket logo informing all that I was a Game Ranger/Game Capturer, and I was proud of the fact. I had to sign a document in triplicate to indicate that I was now in possession of a six-bed Sprite caravan.

Oom Chris would later help me park it under a tree in the rest camp—my home for the next few weeks.

The next day, I was summoned to the Mechanical Workshop, where Oom Jan van Achterberg, again with the signing of the necessary forms in triplicate, introduced me to a cream-coloured one-and-a-half-ton Chevrolet LDV – how lucky can a pipsqueak be! During the next few days, I was informed that I would be stationed at Tshokwane. I was to build animal-holding pens there for the housing and selling of zebras. Those in the know informed me that zebras could not contract foot-and-mouth disease as they did not have cloven hooves. I was further informed that I would earn R150.00 per month, that I was to pay R2.00 per month rent for the caravan, and that I would not receive any 'S&T' as Tshokwane would be my permanent base. I was to report to Dirk Ackerman, the Section Ranger at Tshokwane. The two of us were to determine where the caravan would be parked, where the holding pens would be built, and how water was to be installed to the holding pens. I had to commence by designing the holding pens, ordering the materials, and appointing a team of six labourers, one cook, and one driver. I was thrown in at the deep end, but here and there, a helping hand would appear to rescue the drowning youngster.

I was ready to depart with the caravan to Tshokwane, when I was instructed by Mister (to me) Dolf Brynard to spend December at Skukuza as the Section Ranger, Ben Pretorius, was going on leave, and Skukuza could not be left without a Section Ranger. So within 2 months, I was now also a Section Ranger albeit in a temporary capacity. How fortunate can one be?

I will always remember two incidents that took place during my stay at Skukuza as acting Section Ranger. First, there was the annual 'end of year' staff function, and the second was the episode that took place on 16 December. In the South African context, 16 December is a public holiday. In the old South Africa, this was a holiday commemorating a battle between the indigenous Zulu people under King Dingaan and the early Afrikaner settlers. In the new South Africa, it is still a holiday to commemorate reconciliation between all the peoples of South Africa. With Oom Chris's approval and with a twinkle in his eye (he knew what lay ahead for me), I was handed over to the whims of the ladies of Skukuza who were to arrange the year-end function. I was sent all over to collect chairs and tables which I had to transport to the Skukuza Restaurant (closed for tourists during this important function). I was ordered to pick branches and flowers from veldt trees for the decoration of the venue. I was so exhausted that I did not even attend my first year-end function. I knew that operation clean-up was to follow the next day.

The unfolding of the following incident started when Oom Chris handed me a list of budget categories, with budget numbers, which I was to use to declare, by the 20th of each month, the kilometers travelled during the month. I could determine a budget category from the list for all the other kilometers travelled, except for the kilometers travelled for the year-end function. The most appropriate category I could find for this purpose was 'Chief Director's Public Relations Fund', number HK0004. So determined and done, the logbook was completed and handed in – it was very neat, and I was proud of it. A week later, a very concerned and wide-eyed Oom

Chris informed me that the Head of the Park, Mr Brynard, urgently wanted to see me. 'What have you done?' was Oom Chris's concern. I replied with shrugged shoulders and nervously proceeded to the office of Mr Brynard. I knocked on his door, and he replied rather annoyed: 'Who is there?' I identified myself, and he let me in. 'Be seated,' he said, and he continued with whatever he was occupied with. The longer I waited, the more anxious I became. I figured: 'Not yet 3 months in service and already in the dog box.' Eventually, he looked up, and I thought I noticed a well-hidden smile, with a twinkle in his eyes. 'Who gave you permission to use the budget category which is only available for the exclusive use of the Chief Director? Even I am not allowed to use it.' I was stunned and confused. What was he talking about? 'How do you utilise a category of budget?' 'I am sorry, sir, I do not know what you are talking about,' I stuttered. 'How do you use a category of the budget?' flashed through my mind. I am convinced Mr Brynard could see by my perplexed expression, that I had no idea what he was talking about. He explained that I had to complete a logbook in which kilometers travelled had to be reported against suitable budget numbers to facilitate financial management. It dawned on me that Oom Chris Lombaard had provided me with such a list of numbers with cryptic wording next to each number. But how was I at fault? 'What made you decide to use number HK0004 – Chief Director's Public Relations Fund?' Mr Brynard enquired. 'Oh that!' I replied and explained about the staff year-end function and all the travelling I had to do for that function. With the completion of the logbook, I studied the list of numbers, and the most appropriate one was the one that now had me in trouble. 'If I were in your position, I probably would have made the same choice,' Mr Brynard responded. 'Remember that number is for the exclusive use of the Chief Director.' That concluded the matter.

Needless to say, I immediately called in the help of one of the more senior officials to explain the use of the budget numbers. I have often wondered if Oom Chris had not found out how we had sabotaged his Honda generator at the camp and that he purposefully wished to get back at me by not guiding me through the full list of budget numbers.

The second incident that took place as acting Section Ranger at Skukuza occurred on 16 December 1967 (for me, this was an exceptional Dingaan's Day). Early morning, I was summoned to the office of Mr Brynard.

'Have you ever shot a lion?' I could feel in my bones that here was trouble brooding. 'No, sir, but firearms are not foreign to me.' I had, after all, spent my childhood days shooting birds with an airgun and done target shooting for the shooting team of my school with a .22 calibre rifle and, occasionally, with my father's Commando .303. 'Tourists continually report a sick lion on the Skukuza/Lower Sabie tarred road, about 12½ km from Skukuza. Go and shoot the lion, if it is necessary. Here are the keys to the firearm vault. Get yourself an appropriate rifle.' I was again left alone at my own discretion. 'What calibre rifle is used to shoot a lion? Where do you shoot a lion? How sick is a sick lion? Will it charge or run away?' While I mulled over these thoughts in my head, I proceeded to the firearm vault, 'You wanted to be/play Section Ranger,' I contemplated. This did not appear to be child's play any longer but deadly serious and nerve-wracking work. I unlocked the vault and was amazed by the rows and rows of .303 and other firearms. Eventually, I decided on a Mannlichter .3006 with a telescope.

Little did I realise that a rifle with a telescope was the most inappropriate piece of equipment for the task at hand; although, it was of the correct calibre. In ideal circumstances, one would be able to take accurate aim by resting the rifle on something stable – if the animal were to be standing or lying still and was not hiding behind leaves or branches. I took the rifle and ten silver-tipped .3006 rounds from the vault and then returned the keys to Mr Brynard. I proceeded to the rubbish dump, put a beer can up at 50 m, sat down, and took aim. My target-shooting experience kicked in; I pressed the rifle firmly against my cheek bone, put the trigger finger firmly around the trigger; took a deep breath, aimed, and 'squeezed' the trigger with a uniform motion. The rifle fired, and the can toppled over. 'Sick lion beware, this rifle shoots where I aim,' the thought flashed through my mind. I tried another practice shot to confirm that the first one had not been a lucky shot. Another hit, and I departed self-assuredly. 'This rifle shoots where I aim!'

Back at the office, I bumped into one of the more senior colleagues who enquired what the rifle was intended for. Having informed him, he mentioned that it was SANParks policy that when dangerous animals were to be encountered, two officials should work together for each other's safety. I was not in the mood to take someone along to witness my failures.

Two hours before gate closure, I enquired at Skukuza Reception whether the sick lion was still being reported. They confirmed it, and I departed in search of the sick lion. Approximately 12½ km from Skukuza, I came across a group of vehicles parked in and alongside the road. I concluded that the sick lion was the attraction. I slowly approached and saw the lion lying with its back towards us. The lion was evidently starved and in a weak condition.

'What are you going to do?' passengers in every second or third vehicle enquired.
'We will monitor the animal and then decide,' was my response.
'But the animal has been lying in the same spot for the last hour!'
'Thank you for the useful information,' was my only response.

To understand the rest of the ensuing drama, I have to provide a description of the terrain. Anyone who has travelled the Skukuza/Lower Sabie tarred road would have noticed that there are several drainage lines from the south towards the Sabie River. As the road surface was level, large Armco pipes had to be installed in the drainage lines to take the floodwaters under the road during the rainy season. The lion was lying downstream (the northern side) of the tarred road, between the tarred road and the Sabie River, in the bed of the drainage line. At this point, ground fill was approximately 6 m high. As gate closure time forced the tourists away from the scene, I approached to better inspect the lion and the terrain. Approximately 40 m from the lion, there was a fallen tree, which would provide a good stable platform to aim from. I could feel the excitement of what lay ahead eating at my nerves. My plan of action was formulated. I would wait until all the tourists had departed, and then I would go down the ground fill on the upstream side of the drainage line to the same level as the lion. Then I would slowly move towards the lion through the Armco pipe and towards the fallen tree. The distance from the fallen tree to the lion was approximately 40 m – fortunately more or less the same distance that I had tested the rifle from.

I glanced at my watch; it was 18.00, the official gate-closing time at Skukuza. I would wait another 15 minutes to ensure that there were no more lost tourists on the road. Dusk was falling, and my nerves were gnawing at me. After the 15 minutes, the plan of action unfolded. Step by step, I moved up to the fallen tree that would provide the stable platform to fire from.

My heartbeat accelerated, and my mouth became very dry. With increased adrenaline secretion, everything is intensely observed and experienced. About 2 m from the fallen tree, I heard a vehicle approaching. 'Should I first shoot and then hide in the Armco pipe? What if I only wounded the lion in the hurry?' flashed through my mind. I decide to rather retreat into the Armco pipe. Just as well. The tourist vehicle stopped next to mine, probably to see what was going on. The lion was still lying with its back towards me. When the tourist vehicle departed, I started stalking again. My body was full of adrenaline; my nerves were almost shot. My heartbeat was sky high, and I didn't know that one's mouth could become so dry, and it was becoming darker. As I again arrived at the fallen tree, I stepped on a twig with an ensuing loud 'crack'. Suddenly, all my meters were running in the red. Everything was now happening at great speed. I noticed the lion jumping onto its feet and staring in my direction. With the rifle in my shoulder, I just noticed a brownish movement through the telescope. I 'squeezed' the trigger and I heard the shot hitting the target. Instinctively, I reloaded. Through the telescope, I saw the lion attempting to move away from me, using only its front legs. Its back was obviously broken as the back legs were lame. I could now take dead rest on the fallen tree, and it took all my concentration to hold the rifle still. I again took aim at the head of the lion and fired; the bullet hit home, and the lion lay still. Another round was chambered, and I slowly and very carefully approached the still lion. I was breathing heavily, and my heartbeat was over the limit. When I finally realised that the lion was dead, I lost all control of my body, and I started shaking like a leaf in a strong wind. I attempted to say thank you but could not utter a word. At least it crossed my mind. Had I not used the rifle as a crutch, I would probably have fallen over from the shakes.

After having calmed down to an acceptable level, I was thankful that no one had come along to observe me shooting my first sick lion. The most important lessons learnt from the lion experience were that one could formulate the most perfect plan of action but that it could go horribly wrong in the blink of an eye. One then had to think fast and implement an emergency plan. With experience, the so-called emergency plan becomes instinctive reaction. Between you and me . . . the second lesson was that one should never use a rifle fitted with a telescope when negotiating a potentially moving target. With an open-sighted rifle, one can observe the entire scene and still place an accurate shot. Telescopes are for dead-rest positions and stationary targets . . .

*   *   *

After the acting functions at Skukuza, I could finally start with the actual function I was appointed for. The zebra-holding facilities were planned; treated creosote poles and zinc roof plates were ordered and delivered. A team of six labourers were selected and appointed, amongst whom were four Mozambique citizens and two 'Transvalers'. All six were Shangaans (Tsonga). The Mozambicans were from the Gaza Province in Mozambique and the Transvalers from the Gazankulu Homeland. One would be the cook of the team, and the other five would assist me in building the zebra-holding pens. Our language of communication was iSizulu. Having come from the Natal midlands, I could communicate in iSizulu. All the team members had worked on the mines at some stage, where they were taught to communicate in Fanagalo (a universal mine language), and iSizulu is the language which Fanagalo is based on. We could, therefore, more or less communicate, even though we had to include some sign language.

The Sprite caravan was moved with great care to Tshokwane. The caravan would be my base/house/office for the next couple of years. The caravan was parked under and on the southern side of a large Maroela tree in order to maximise the little shade the tree provided. I had wonderful experiences while staying in the caravan at Tshokwane.

An area of approximately 10 m^2 in front of the caravan was cleared of all plant material. In the centre of this area was the heart of the hot water system consisting of half of an old 200-l petrol drum raised from the ground in order to make a log fire under the drum. An old 5-l petrol can was used to scoop hot water from the big container for dishwashing, washing of clothing, and replenishing shower water.

The shower structure consisted of two forked branches planted into the ground with the forked section being at a specific height above ground level. The two forked sections kept a 50 mm steel pipe in a horizontal position. The shower itself comprised of an old 20-l paraffin drum with a shower head and a tap fitted to a hole made in the centre of the bottom end of the drum. An s-bent piece of reinforcing rod was the connection between the horizontal steel pipe and the shower drum.

To make the shower five-star quality, the horizontal steel pipe was placed at such a height that I could stand under the shower without bumping my head against it. The down side of this was that one could not stand on 'terra firma' to hook the steel pipe because it was too high! One now had to stand on an overturned 10-l milk bucket and still jump up a further 30 cm with a shower drum full of hot water to hook the s-bend onto the horizontal steel pipe before one could enjoy a hot shower. This was the best open-air shower in the world. Fortunately, there was nobody within 500 m to spoil a wonderful open-air shower.

While describing the hot water system and shower facilities, the urbanites amongst you must have wondered what the arrangement was regarding the toilet facilities. This was spelt out as follows (and suppress a smile at your indignation): Walk a minimum distance of 200 m from the camp in any chosen direction, armed with a spade. The spade was both for self-defence and to dig a hole at least 20 cm deep. A sudden attack of diarrhoea could complicate matters if the soil was hard and dry.

To illustrate the above, I have to tell the following story of Mr Eric Marthinesen (Oom Eric to me). During the early years of elephant-and-buffalo monitoring, SANParks did not have their own helicopters or pilots. These services were contracted in from a firm, AUTAIR, that had regional offices in Johannesburg. The Managing Director was Mr Eric Marthinesen. He was besotted by the bush, and his forte was cooking. During his official visits to the KNP, he also worked in a couple of days staying over with me in the caravan at Tshokwane. Oom Eric was a huge, somewhat over-weight man. He was duly informed of all the dos and don'ts including the strict toilet arrangements. By mid-morning one day, he took the spade, and as befitting a true urbanite, he set of in a northerly direction and extended the 200 m minimum to approximately 260 m. I was out catching zebras and so was not at the caravan. On my return to the camp, I found a very upset Oom Eric sitting at the fireplace, poking a stick into the embers.

'What is the matter?' I enquired.

'Why did you not inform me of the tourist road?' he pointed in the northerly direction.

The story unfolded as follows. Nature called; he took the spade and walked the minimum of 200 m, but he could still see the caravan. He added another 60 m. As he was a little apprehensive of being so far from the caravan, he chose an open spot to do his thing and still be able to see any wild animals approaching him. Just as he was nicely occupied relieving himself and enjoying it, he heard and saw an approaching vehicle.

What Oom Eric did not know was that he had chosen a spot approximately 40 m from a tourist road. How was he going to resolve this predicament to everyone's satisfaction? He could run away with his pants on his ankles, but what if he got entangled and tripped over? Or he could try and crawl from the open spot that he had chosen with the same embarrassing end result; these thoughts had flashed through his mind. He had, however, rejected all of the above options and chosen to make a 180° turnaround with his blunt end facing the tourist road and his identifiable end looking away from the road.

'Can you imagine how humiliated I was? I heard the vehicle stop right opposite me, and I could have sworn I heard the click of a camera.' The vehicle had then driven off.

'Oom Eric, it was entirely your own fault,' I countered. 'Had you stuck to my instructions, you could have enjoyed the tourist vehicle driving by in the knowledge that they were not even aware of you. Now they have a beautiful picture of your blunt end.'

'I am going to kill you if you tell anybody else. Do you hear me?'

One cannot, however, do justice to such a wonderful story, especially with Oom Eric demonstrating, in detail, how he had successfully accomplished jumping up and turning around without losing his dignity.

*   *   *

After the caravan tent was pitched, the tent floor was covered with a 12 cm layer of river sand. This area was the workshop and store facility for the capture equipment and 'mutis' (drugs or medicine) I would be using during the game-capturing period. In the tent panel furthest from the caravan, there were two openings, one on the left and one on the right-hand side due to the tent zips not being zipped, providing entry to the tent and caravan from either side. The caravan site and the zebra-holding facilities were approximately 80 m apart. The one corner post of the fence around the holding facility was approximately 25 m from the caravan. Next to this corner post stood a tank stand supporting a 4,500-l water tank. The caravan and supporting 'infrastructure' consisting of the fireplace and shower facilities were not fenced. The caravan site was approximately 500 m from the resident Section Ranger Dirk Ackerman's house. Tshokwane was one of the first Section Rangers' houses built in the KNP. This house and the caravan site were joined by a two-track road. The junior staff quarters were approximately 200 m away from the Section Ranger's house. The above terrain layout information is for better understanding of future incidences.

We commenced with the construction of the zebra-holding facilities with only the most basic pieces of equipment. In fact, it comprised of two hatchets (small axes). (The isiZulu name for these is 'Mbazo'), an empty 200-l petrol drum, which served as a stepladder and workbench, and a tape measure which started at the 3-m mark (the first 3-m section had disintegrated through years of hard work). The gradient of the chosen terrain to build the holding pens necessitated the pens having a split level. The use of a spirit level was, therefore, inevitable. In the whole of Tshokwane, we could not source a spirit level, and I had to be very inventive to devise one. We got hold of a 50 mm diameter plastic pipe 12 m in length. The pipe was filled with water. One end of the pipe was held at a predetermined height on a planted pole. The other end of the pipe was then slowly lifted until the water was just about to flow out. The water levels at both ends would then be at the same horizontal height. A marker peg was then driven into the ground with its top end at that level to serve as reference height. From this marker, the other levels could be determined to proceed horizontally with the holding pens. I was very proud of this simple but very effective large spirit level.

The hatchets were used as multipurpose tools. The blunt end served as a hammer head, and the sharp end was used as a chisel to make dowels. The sharp ends of the hatchets were kept sharp by sharpening these on a piece of sandstone we scored from the veldt.

Some say that my cultural name 'Mbazo' originated from the extensive use of and my constant calling for a 'Mbazo' (hatchet) during the construction of the holding pens. Whatever the origin might have been, I am very proud of my name 'Mbazo'.

Many incidents occurred during the construction of the holding facilities and in and around the caravan, and I would like to share a few with you.

The vertical corner posts of each holding facility were planted in concrete and were later cut off at the correct height. The horizontal poles that would carry the IBR roof plates were secured to the vertical corner posts by means of a 2 mm thick by 60 mm wide galvanised metal hoop nailed on the one side of the vertical posts, placed over the horizontal beam, pulled tight, and nailed down on the other side of the vertical post. To achieve this, holes had to be drilled through the metal hoops at appropriate sites with a blunt drill bit and a hand drill. No grinding stone was available to sharpen the drill bit, and this was the only drill bit available at Tshokwane, with no general dealer around the corner to buy a new one if it were to break. We, therefore, battled on slowly and circumspectly to drill the holes.

At that point in time, Dirk Ackerman came around for inspection and enquired why progress was so slow. After we explained our dilemma to him, he questioned why we did not just punch holes through the metal hoops with a nail. I explained to Dirk that I had already tried that route without success. I noticed how his facial expression changed to: 'I will show him. Who is this pipsqueak to tell me that my brilliant plan cannot work?' He grabbed a nail and held it upright on the metal hoop, between the thumb and forefinger of his left hand. He held the hatchet with his right hand, blunt end down. He tapped the nail softly once or twice . . . took aim . . . withdrew the hatchet as far as possible . . . 'The pipsqueak did indicate that it would not work . . . would therefore apply a little extra downwards force.' The withdrawn hatchet flew forward and down and hit the nail dead centre on the head. The point of the nail must have been at a slight angle as there was sufficient force to drive the nail through two pieces of hoop. Lo and behold, the tip of the nail slipped on the metal hoop, and the blunt end of the hatchet crushed Dirk's thumb onto the hoop with blood squirting from it. He looked up at me, and when our eyes met, I could clearly read the message: 'Bastard, just laugh, and you are dead.' I turned my back on him and walked away to get some distance between us and for Dirk to take control of his pain and emotions. Needless to say, I had to stay out of Dirk's way until the pain in his thumb, as well as his hurt ego, had abated.

We later often referred to the incident; if one wished to convince the other of a good plan, the question that arose would be: 'Whose thumb will get in the way this time?' This question only had significance for the two of us.

* * *

The construction of the zebra-holding pens was accompanied by much blood, blisters, and litres and litres of perspiration. Construction duration was from January 1968 to February 1968. This is midsummer in the KNP, and ambient temperatures at midday touched on the 40°C mark.

The team of labourers and I toiled from early morning (07.00) to late afternoon (17.00) without any grumbling over the number of hours worked per day, lunch breaks, overtime, etc. It was a great pleasure to labour and perspire together and on a daily basis to see the transformation of a bare piece of land into zebra-holding facilities comprising of six individual bomas. Each boma consisted of three sections. The rear section was roofed over and walled with vertical creosote poles. The front section was closed with horizontally slated creosote planks housing a feeding rack and drinking trough. Each boma had three doors: one at the front end to gain access for cleaning purposes, one in the middle to be able to separate different zebras in each boma, and the third door opening into a crush pen/passage at the back that connected each boma to a loading ramp and sorting facility. From the sorting facility, zebras could then be chased back to each separate boma. The holding facilities had concrete floors and channels for washing purposes. The loading ramp and sorting facility had river sand bedding.

When zebras were in residence, each individual boma would be cleaned and washed on a daily basis. The zebra in each pen would be herded down the crush passage to the sorting facility in order to clean the boma and then returned to the clean boma. By the third day, the zebras had learnt the routine. When the door was opened, they would move down the crush passage to the sorting facility on their own accord and similarly would return to the boma once the boma was cleaned just by opening the appropriate gates. This learnt behaviour or conditioning obviously assisted greatly when zebras had to be loaded onto trucks or into crates as the same crush passages were used for this purpose.

Just to the east of the holding bomas, we built a roofed store facility consisting of an open half to store zebra crates and other equipment and an enclosed section to store a supply of lucerne. Water was piped from a borehole to the water tank on the tank stand and from there was gravity-fed to the drinking troughs in each individual boma and to different taps on the site. The borehole water had a very high salt content. When I took a sip of this water, I imagined that I was taking a dip in the sea somewhere. The zebra, however, readily drank this water, and this, together with the change in diet to lucerne, lead to diarrhoea for the first day or two in the boma, after which they adapted and flourished.

We later addressed this problem by cutting natural veldt grass for hay and gradually changed the hay/lucerne mixture to a feed of lucerne only.

As with human beings, zebra 'personalities' also differed, and one had to carefully select those that could safely share a boma. If not done correctly, one zebra could seriously hurt another by kicking and biting another zebra should the sexes and age groups not adequately match, especially in the confined space of a boma. In the natural environment, there would be enough space to avoid a 'nasty' zebra. I was amazed at the power that could be generated by a male zebra's kick. On occasion, we had to replace some of the horizontal planks of the boma after they were broken by such a kick. If one on occasion had to work on or with a zebra without sedating it, it was wise to give it a piece of plastic pipe to bite or chew on. I can assure you, it would be less painful than having the zebra grab hold of some human flesh.

To be able to load zebra into crates on top of the load bed of a truck, a suitable drive through excavation had to be made at the end of the crush passage so that the zebra could walk into the crate at ground level. The zebra would experience the crate as an extension of the load passage. Each zebra crate had an up-and-down sliding door at each end. When zebras were loaded into the crate, an operator had to stand on top of the crate, holding the sliding door in the open position. As soon as the zebra was in the crate, the door had to be quickly lowered before the zebra realised it was at a dead end and would attempt to turn around or reverse. If the door was successfully lowered in time, the zebra would inevitably let fly and kick the door with resounding force. Should the sliding door not be closed in time, the following would result: the zebra would be halfway into the crate, and the door would be pressing down onto the back of the zebra. Inevitably, the zebra would start jumping up and down as if it had a rider on its back. Under these circumstances, the person on the crate had to have a good sense of balance to remain on top of the crate, and additional hands would be required to keep the crate upright. It once occurred that the crate and zebra toppled over with the zebra halfway in or out with very limited space between the crush passage door and crate. There was no way that the zebra would be allowed to go free, and it took a lot of pleading to get the crate and zebra in an upright position with the doors closed and the crate still on the truck.

I am getting a bit ahead of myself. We are already loading zebras, and the holding facilities have as yet not been completed. After each tiring day toiling in the sun, building the holding facilities, I was too exhausted to go jogging or to do some physical exercises. After sunset, I would sit in the middle of the cleared area in front of the caravan with a glass of Oros mandarin flavoured water in my hand. I sat on one of those green steel-framed folding chairs with wooden slats screwed onto the steel frame that I scored from the Tshokwane Picnic Area. With a good sense of balance, one could turn the chair into a rocking chair, balancing oneself on the two rear legs of the chair. After a long day in the sun, this was my favourite meditation position while I reflected on what had materialised during the day and what was to be done the following day. On my second day at the caravan, I was instinctively rocking backwards and forwards on the chair, planning the next day. I was very deep in thought and totally oblivious of what was happening around me. Suddenly, I heard a strange snorting noise. Frightened out of my wits and adrenaline pumping, I disturbed the fine balance of the chair's rocking motion, and I toppled over backwards and landed on my back with mandarin flavoured water raining all over me. I had barely landed on my back when I found myself standing in the caravan door with my heart pounding in my throat. Then I noticed the animal that had produced the snorting noise. It was a Blue wildebeest bull standing about 40 m from where I was balancing on my chair. It again snorted to inform me that my presence would not be tolerated in its territory. Great was the surprise of the Blue wildebeest when I ran from the caravan tent shouting and gesticulating at it for disturbing my meditation in such a rude manner. The wildebeest jogged off in typical wildebeest fashion, swinging its backside from left to right while glancing at me over its left shoulder and then over the right shoulder. The Blue wildebeest bull and I became good neighbours (or was I the squatter?) in its territory. It would, henceforth, regularly visit and talk, or was it rather snort, at me and I would listen and enjoy it. After this episode, the snorting of a lone Blue wildebeest bull became one of the typical sounds of the KNP for me.

The construction of the zebra-holding pens and the erection of the fencing progressed slowly but surely to a point where only minor finishing touches were required to complete the work. I was itching to get zebras into the holding bomas to test the functionality of the facilities. The carpenters at Skukuza were busy building six wooden crates to individually transport the zebra in. The crates had slat floors to ensure that the zebras would not slip on these. Lengthwise on the side of the crate, there were two air-vent openings, the upper and lower openings being separated by a solid section at eye level of an adult zebra, preventing it from detecting people or movement on the outside of the crate. The crates had split doors at each end that opened upwards. The crates, therefore, had no defined front or back end. One of the equestrian colleagues taught me a halter knot that could be tied around a zebra's head to guide it into a crate while manual labour pushed from the rear. Once inside the crate, with the doors closed, the tension on the rope and knot would be released, and the knot would become loose and fall off.

*   *   *

Living in a caravan in the bush had its pros and cons. On the one hand, the space to keep tidy and clean is small and easily done. On the other hand, however, the space at one's disposal is small as the caravan served as living space as well as storeroom. During the summer months, it became a 'sauna' as day temperatures soared to the 40°C mark and higher, especially if one had to light the gas stove in the caravan to make coffee or prepare food. The caravan refrigerator was never put into operation due to the heat it generated when on. At one stage, my meals consisted of one 'Steri Long Life Milk', a box of 'Eat-sum-more' biscuits, and a tin of canned fruit. Fortunately for me, Dirk and Antoinette Ackerman had sympathy with my disposition, and whenever we were together at Tshokwane, I had a standing invitation to dine with them, a gesture I would forever be thankful for. One of the other cons of living in the caravan was the use of gas-powered lights. Apart from the heat generated by the lamps, these did not last very long before a moth or another insect flew in through the lampshade and destroyed the lamp 'sachet/bag' that generated the light. Therefore, if one wished to do some reading or office administration after sunset, this was very short-lived as the Lowveld is notorious for its insects, especially those of the flying type. This particular disadvantage of caravan-living in the KNP most probably resulted in a custom I still have to this day, and that is, to go to bed early. I have never been one for late nights. The non-availability of caravan gas lights resulted in the need to complete all reading or writing matters before sunset. Bible reading and prayer were usually the last items on the agenda before or during sunset. This was my favourite time of day, and I often experienced the presence of God in the quiet of dusk when every diurnal being came to rest, before the nocturnal ones became active.

Sitting at the smouldering embers of the campfire, looking in wonder at the stars above and wondering about Creation, from elephant to mosquitoes, from Baobab trees to the smallest algae, I realised that there had to be a Mastermind that had fitted all these things together to create Mother Nature. I could not help but believe that a divine Hand of Creation was involved. In my view, random occurrences could not have formulated all the natural laws responsible for the orderly coexistence of the natural environment. Furthering my studies, in later years, I had the opportunity to view Creation through a microscope and a telescope, and this reaffirmed to me that the hand of a Creator God was ever present.

As was expected of a boy of 16 years old growing up in a Christian Protestant home, I completed the expected Catechism in the Dutch Reformed Church. At this stage of my life, I had book knowledge that

Jesus Christ had died for my sins, and I confessed this to the congregation and to myself. After school, I did my compulsory military training at the Air Force Gymnasium at Swartkops. Every Sunday evening, we attended church parade. Every Church denomination formed up in a platoon, and we were marched off to each church hall. At one of these Sunday evening sermons, the clergyman dealt with Paul's sea voyage to Rome and more specifically with their experiences surrounding the storm near the island of Crete. The crux of the sermon, however, dealt with the safety and surety we can have, if Jesus Christ is the helmsman of our life's boat. After the service, we did not have to fall back into a platoon again and were allowed to wander back to the barracks. The next thing I knew, I was standing in the middle of a rugby field, engulfed in my own thoughts. I instinctively knew this was the moment that I had to invite Christ into my life and to be the helmsman of my boat. I experienced a great calm come over me as I made the request, and I knew this heralded a change in my life. At future stages in my life, I often stepped out of my boat even in high seas and tried to swim in my own direction just to be brought back to the safety of the boat by Someone bigger than me Who would keep my boat on course.

I knew I was destined to stay in a caravan at Tshokwane, to build the zebra-holding facilities and, by means of my father's crossbow and darts, to capture and sell zebras as part of the game reduction policy of the KNP, but most of all, to have meaningful interaction with people around me.

*   *   *

It was with great excitement when we loaded and tied down the zebra crate for the first time onto the Chevrolet 'bakkie' (the Afrikaans name for a one-and-a-half-ton truck or smaller). The five Shangaan game capturers squeezed themselves into the limited space between the crate and the side of the bakkie. We also had to find space for two 20-l plastic 'jerry cans' full of water. I kept the crossbow, the cocking lever for the crossbow, and preloaded darts in the front with me. I had to be able to use both the left- and right-hand windows to shoot through. Apart from the crossbow and darts, the other most important piece of equipment in the bakkie was the range finder. The weight and length of the dart gave it a flight trajectory that made it very sensitive to distance errors of more than 5 m. Needless to say, before this big day had dawned, I had already made many practice shots with darts loaded with water. The range finder was operated by looking through an eye piece and by adjusting a calibrated disc to place two split images over one another to make a single image. The striped markings on a zebra skin worked perfectly for this method.

Eventually, the safari departed in search of zebras. As we drove along, it played in my mind that the game farmer had ordered one adult and one subadult stallion and four adult mares. As we slowly approached the first group of zebras, I knew we had a problem. How does one successfully determine the sex of a zebra at a distance of 60-80 m? With the first zebra, this would not matter, but as the zebra order neared completion, one would have to determine the sex and age class of the animal to be darted more accurately. With all these thoughts flashing through my mind and the excitement of actually going to dart the first zebra, it is needless to say that the first shot missed the target. I had aimed at the left-hand rump of what I thought was an adult stallion. I could have sworn that as I 'squeezed' the trigger, the zebra jumped forward. This, however, could not explain why the dart fell short. The only obvious explanation was that the wrong zebra markings were matched on the range finder, and the wrong setting was used on the crossbow's sights. Fortunately, the guys on the back of the bakkie had keen eyes, and we could recover the dart. Unfortunately, a few rand's worth of 'muti' had been injected into the ground, fortunately without any harmful consequences. I was forewarned that the M99 'muti' we were using to catch zebras was lethal if it got into the bloodstream of human beings.

Now for the second attempt to capture a zebra. We came upon a group of five zebras standing in the shade of a Knob-thorn tree. I was tempted to take a pot shot into the group, hoping one would be hit. Having slowly driven around the group – they were reluctant to move out of the shade due to the heat – I selected one of them. The range finder indicated a distance of 68 m. I then heard the little voice in my head: 'Make sure, take your time. They are quite calm.' The second reading confirmed the distance to be 68 m. I quickly cocked the crossbow and put the dart in the slot and adjusted the sight to the 68-m mark. I took careful aim and 'squeezed' the trigger. The dart hit the zebra on the right shoulder, exactly where I had aimed. 'Who cares whether it was a mare or a stallion?' the thought flashed through my mind.

Nobody was prepared for the ensuing moments. The zebra scattered in all directions. I had to put the crossbow on the seat next to me and start the bakkie. When I looked up, the zebras were gone. 'Which one did we dart?' I asked, shouting in isiZulu. The foreman pointed in a direction, and I sped off in that direction, negotiating a passage between trees, rocks, fallen trees trunks, warthog hollows, etc. 'Left, left!' shouted the foreman from the back. They could see better from the back of the bakkie and so could shout directions. Eventually, I could also see the group of five zebras, so that meant the darted one was still in the group. Then I realised that I had forgotten the exact time that the zebra was darted. The researchers at Skukuza had requested that I take note of the reaction time of the 'muti' to bring the zebra down. I guessed that almost half an hour had lapsed since darting the animal. Everything that had happened since the darting could not have been fitted into less time. I noticed that the darted zebra was beginning to show effects from the drug. It raised its front legs like a horse that was trotting. The zebra tripped over a fallen tree trunk, clearly affected by the drug. The next time it tripped over something, the zebra went down head over heels in a cloud of dust. In their excitement and inexperience, everyone on the back of the bakkie jumped off and swarmed all over the zebra, grabbing here, there, and everywhere but carefully avoiding the sharp end – the biting end – of the zebra.

The zebra, at this stage, however, was so far gone from the effects of the drug that there was no real danger to any of us. We offloaded the crate and manoeuvred the forequarters of the zebra into the crate. A rope with the special slip knot was tied around the zebra's head and passed on to someone at the front of the crate who would have to pull from the front at a given signal. Another rope was placed around the rump of the animal and would serve to pull the animal into the crate once the antidote took effect. I injected a long-lasting antibiotic into the rump and disinfected the dart wound. I then filled a syringe with the correct amount of antidote and injected this intravenously into an artery on the inside of the rear leg after making sure that the needle was correctly inserted into the artery by pulling the syringe plunger back and seeing blood mixing with the antidote in the syringe. I slowly administered the antidote. We were all surprised by how quickly the antidote took effect. The zebra tried to get up. All the ropes were pulled tight. As the zebra was getting up, it had only one way to go, and that was straight into the crate. When the zebra was completely

28

in, I shouted 'Vala, vala!' (close the drop doors) to the person on top of the crate. Nothing happened. I looked up and saw that there was no one on top of the crate to operate the drop door. Everybody in their excitement to get the zebra into the crate had forgotten the most important person and function, namely to close off the crate once the zebra was crated. I scrambled up the side of the crate, placed the drop door in its slots, and lowered the door. The zebra was already retreating when the door closed on its back. The irritation caused the zebra to jump and kick backwards. The more I pushed down on the door, the more the zebra jumped and kicked. The door flew up and nearly took me off the crate. With all the jumping, the zebra fortunately had some forward momentum, and I was fortunate enough to get the door closed. The tension on the rope around the zebra's head was slackened, and the special knot came loose as it should. For a moment, everybody stood back and stared in amazement at the zebra in the crate, and I wondered what the zebra thought of the spontaneous applause. We had actually successfully caught and crated a zebra. The zebra was then drenched with water to keep it cool. Only then did we determine that it was a mare. I positioned the bakkie to load the crate. The rear hatch was opened, the team lifted the crate, and I reversed in under the lifted portion of the crate. The team then lifted the backside of the crate and shoved it onto the load bed of the bakkie. The crate was then tied down with ropes.

How long had it taken from when the dart hit the zebra till the crate was loaded onto the bakkie? I tested the team's time judgment. Their estimations varied from half an hour to one hour. My own estimate was about 40 minutes. 'No! You are all wrong,' exclaimed one of the team members with a wrist watch. 'It was 25 minutes. I wanted to check the strength of the 'muti', and I checked the time when the dart hit the zebra. The zebra was on the ground in 8 minutes, and it is now 25 minutes from when the dart hit.'

I jotted down the following details in my notebook:

Number: 1
Date: 5 May 1968
Place: Ntlhomorwana spruit

Muti:	2 mg M99
	2 cc Azaparone (tranquiliser)
Antidote:	3 cc intravenous
Target:	Right shoulder
Reaction:	First reaction approximately 4 minutes – lifting front hooves. Tripped over a fallen tree trunk, and zebra on the ground in 8 minutes.
General:	Injected antibiotic into the dart wound and some intramuscular. Zebra crated and loaded in 25 minutes and released into boma in 55 minutes.

Having arrived at the holding facility, I reversed into the offloading ditch in order to have the crate level with the ground and in line with the crush pen. The crated zebra was dragged halfway into the crush pen. I stood on top of the crate and slowly opened the sliding door after the correct boma gate had been opened. The zebra, still under the influence of the tranquilliser, calmly walked out of the crate with a little nudge from us. It calmly walked down the crush pen into the boma specifically reserved for it. 'Vala, vala!' was the instruction to close the boma door once the zebra was inside. Number one was safely in the boma. Prior to offloading, we had ensured that there was lucerne in the feeding shelf and water in the trough. The zebra had five-star accommodation. The next day, we discovered that the change in diet from dry veldt grass to lucerne in combination with the salty drinking water resulted in serious diarrhoea. This, however, stabilised within the next 2 days.

We were fortunate enough to successfully capture, crate, and offload two more zebras on the first day without having to worry about the sex ratio of the animals. We had one adult mare and one adult and one subadult stallion in the holding facility. The first game farmer had ordered two stallions and four mares of different age groups. What now? The stallions in the bomas were of the correct sex and age structure. The rest of the zebras to be caught all had to be mares.

The team and I had an emergency conference in an attempt to solve the 'sex at a distance' problem – unsuccessful! The next day, we started off early as it promised to be another one of those scorching hot days. We came upon a group of ten zebras, and I slowly encircled them, coming closer and closer to have a good look at body size, build, shape of neck and head, etc. The adult stallions and pregnant mares were easily distinguishable with the above criteria. The problem lay with the non-pregnant mares, subadult animals, and fouls. The more I circled them, the more they calmed down, and the more they continued with their normal activities. Two subadult zebras stood grazing with their backsides turned towards us. They were lustily swinging their tails to ward off the flies as if declaring: 'Look, are you blind?' Suddenly, I saw the solution. Under the tail of the zebra, there was a small round black mark indicating the anus of the animal. The other zebra had an oblong marking indicating the anus and the opening of the female genitals. Fortunately, the two zebras were standing next to one another, and the difference was easy to spot. 'I've got it!' I exclaimed to the team, pointing to the zebras and explaining the difference. We carefully inspected the rest of the group and could tell the sex of every animal wagging its tail. This was a solution to a major problem. What a relief! The atmosphere in the team changed immediately after the 'discovery'. If one could call it a discovery. It had always been so, but we had noticed it only now. Any game farmer could in future order any combination of age and sex, and we would be able to deliver as requested.

Although each and every episode of catching, loading, and offloading a zebra was different in its own way, it became a routine. During the next 2 years, we were able to successfully capture and sell more than 500 zebras. We were particularly proud of the fact that our losses were less than 5 per cent, especially if one took into consideration that these zebra were caught throughout the year in all climatic conditions, varying from a mild 20°C maximum ambient temperature during extremely cold winters to 40°C during summer. Currently, game capture is mainly conducted during the cooler months of the year with similar losses.

During these 2 years, I had many experiences, which nobody else was aware of. I would like to share some of these with you as 'stories around the campfire'.

*   *   *

In the KNP, we refer to N'wamuriwa as a 'mountain'. It is situated approximately 10 km to the east of Tshokwane and towers out above the surrounding area. A tourist road winds its way to the top of the mountain, with a turning circle around a trigonometric beacon at the top. From up there, one has an unrestricted view of 360° from Mozambique in the east to the Drakensberg Mountain range in the west with Mariepskop clearly visible. On a clear day, the Swaziland Mountains can be seen to the south and Satara Rest Camp and the rest of the KNP up to the Limpopo River to the north.

Once, an Israeli army general visited South Africa by invitation of the government of the day. As Dirk Ackerman, the Section Ranger at Tshokwane, was on leave, I was instructed, by head office in Skukuza, to meet the general at the Tshokwane Tea Room and to demonstrate to him the whole zebra-capturing operation and to show him around (whatever that meant). We met the general at the Tshokwane Tea Room/Picnic Site early on the appointed day. First, we drove to the zebra-holding facilities, and I explained to him the functioning of the crush pens, sorting facilities, and gate systems. I could not tell whether he was impressed or not. He was probably more accustomed to bomb shelters in Israel! Fortunately, the zebra capturing, crating, and offloading demonstration went according to plan. He showed more interest when we demonstrated the functioning of the holding facility to him with the 'in-house' zebras. These performed like circus zebras; they ran down the crush passages to the sorting facility and back with little encouragement from any of us.

Having successfully demonstrated the whole zebra exercise, I wondered how next I could entertain the general. I had not come across anybody who I had taken up to the top of N'wamuriwa who had not been impressed by the unhindered view from up there. I hoped that the general would also be impressed. Arriving at the top of N'wamuriwa, I showed the general the 360° view and tried to impress on him the number of square kilometers of the KNP that were visible from this vantage point. The general became quiet and twice slowly turned through the 360° to take in the extent of the area in front of him.

'What is the total area of the KNP?' he enquired. Fortunately, I knew the answer. 'Approximately two million hectares,' I responded. The general became pensive, and then he exclaimed: 'Do you realise that the KNP is larger than the whole state of Israel? Your game park is larger than Israel!'

he reiterated. Now it was my turn to be surprised. My only knowledge of Israel consisted of Bible stories that I had read, and I had always imagined Israel to be much bigger. The general sat down on a rock and drank in the view in front of him. I got the impression that the zebra operation had had a lesser impact on the general than the view from the top of N'wamuriwa.

I drew his attention to the east and indicated where the international border was between Mozambique, RSA, and the KNP as well. As the Israelis were involved in continual border clashes, he expressed the wish to see our border with Mozambique. I did not wish to cause an early disappointment by verbally describing the border setup to him, and so we departed for the border. The seasonal N'waswitsontso River that flows past Tshokwane exits the KNP directly east of where we were on top of N'wamurima. There was a Field Ranger picket on the southern embankment of the N'waswitsontso, comprising of two traditional thatched mud huts and an enclosed cooking shelter. The picket was manned by two Field Rangers armed with pre-World War One .303 rifles. They had heard the vehicle approaching and were standing outside on the clean-swept terrain when we arrived. They promptly came to attention and saluted us as was the custom. I began questioning them on their well-being and work activities. One of the Field Rangers was very curious about my companion with the smart uniform with all the shiny stuff on his shoulders and chest. On completion of my debriefing session with the Field Rangers, I explained the gist of the discussion to the general. He promptly came to attention, saluted the two flabbergasted men, and shook hands with them. The two men obviously had no idea where Israel was, and I wondered what they would tell their folks back home about this very important man they had met.

After completion of all the formalities and niceties, we departed from the picket. I explained the functioning of the picket system in the KNP and more specifically the Tshokwane ones on the eastern boundary of the KNP as well as the duties and responsibilities of the Field Rangers. There were three pickets on this section of the KNP boundary situated approximately 20 km from one another. The Field Rangers did daily foot and bicycle patrols in the immediate vicinity of the border and further into the KNP to establish any signs of poaching or untoward human activity. Once a week, they would meet the Field Rangers manning the other pickets to exchange information. They were also tasked to make ecological observations such as big game numbers and sex and age structures of these, carcasses found, and obvious cause of death; they also had to take blood or marrow smears of these for analysis by the Veterinary Department at Skukuza. They were also the first line of defence against accidental fires from across the Mozambique border or fires that were caused by lightning in their immediate vicinity. At the end of the month, all the picket staff would come to Tshokwane to give their reports, to receive salaries, to do private purchases at the Tea Room, and to receive their dry ration for the month ahead. All these actions took place by prior arrangement as there were no radios, landline telephones, cell phones, or computers in those days.

'But where is the border?' the general enquired. I stopped at a spot where the firebreak road was closest to the border. From there, we had to walk approximately 500 m to the actual border. I could see that the general was ill at ease approaching an international border without any firearms or support. As we reached the border, I indicated a 'kaplyn' 5 m wide, disappearing into the distance to the north and the south. ('Kaplyn' is the Afrikaans term for veldt that has been cleared of woody vegetation to demarcate a boundary line.) The general was flabbergasted at the sight of the international border. During my military training, we had an instructor who had imprinted into us that we had to surprise the enemy during an ambush and not amaze them. On our way back to the bakkie, I could not help but wonder whether I had surprised or amazed the general with the international border between Mozambique and the RSA.

What I do know, however, was that the general went back to Israel with a completely new notion of how two neighbouring states with a common border of approximately 400 km can coexist in contrast to what they were experiencing in Israel. The calm 'atmosphere' on the Mozambique-RSA border would, however, not remain so as was later experienced during the *Frelimo-Renamo* civil war in Mozambique.

*   *   *

During December 1968, the Section Ranger at Shingwedzi was critically ill after having had a heart attack while on leave. During this time, KNP Management received information from the Military that the first terrorists had crossed over the Zambezi River, presumably to infiltrate the RSA through Rhodesia (Zimbabwe) and Mozambique. KNP Management was requested to safeguard the northern border, along the Limpopo River, with Rhodesia as well as the eastern border with Mozambique from Pafuri to the Olifants River. How does one go about achieving this almost impossible task? The above mentioned borders were divided up into sectors, and the Field Personnel would patrol these and would pass on any untoward activities to the military.

Sector one stretched from the KNP western boundary on the Limpopo River further along the river to the confluence of the Limpopo and Luvuvhu Rivers at Pafuri and southwards along the eastern boundary to the Xingomeni picket. Oom Johan Klopper, the District Ranger at Punda Maria, would take charge of this sector. The next sector stretched from the Xingomeni picket southwards beyond the Shingwedzi River to the Kostini picket. In the absence of the Shingwedzi Section Ranger due to his illness, I was instructed to take charge of this sector. Sector three stretched from the Kostini picket southwards to the Olifants River and was manned by the Section Ranger stationed at Klip Koppies.

On my way to the Xingomeni picket (my temporary base), I picked up Field Ranger Corporal Phineas at Shingwedzi and all our equipment, including a .375 Winchester rifle that would be my constant companion during our boundary safeguarding campaign. Phineas, and I did vehicle and foot patrols along the KNP boundary, and every second day, we met with Oom Johan at his temporary base in the Nyandu bush close to the Xirhombe picket and with Fanie Botha, the Section Ranger from Klip Koppies, to exchange relevant information. After 2 weeks of no action, I asked Phineas how close the nearest human habitation in Mozambique was to the Xigomeni picket. He indicated that there was habitation close to seasonal pans a fair way into Mozambique when these had water. I argued that terrorists were human beings and that they would be dependent on food and water like the rest of us and that these commodities would be available from the local inhabitants. Why couldn't we go and sniff out the enemy in Mozambique where they would be at ease and not suspecting anything? The fact that the terrorists carried AK-47 automatic rifles and that I was armed with a bolt action .375 rifle and Phineas was only armed with a short-handle stabbing assegai did not bother me. I asked Phineas how far into Mozambique these dwellings were. His answer was that it was far but not so far. Distance in kilometers meant very little to Phineas. He also probably did not know how fast I would walk or by which route.

Under Phineas's guidance, I was none the wiser; we stopped on the eastern boundary firebreak road directly west of the intended destination in Mozambique. As was to be expected from any outdoor man, I could determine north with my wristwatch. I had decided to draw a sketch map, on a 2 cm per km scale, updated every half an hour by determining north and on the assumption that we were walking at a pace of 2 km every half an hour. This might seem very slow to you, but remember, we were illegally in enemy country. After the first hour, I could determine that we were not walking in a straight line. Phineas was most probably guiding us from one known beacon to another. After walking for approximately 3 hours, Phineas indicated that we were now very close to the seasonal pans. We crept-stalked closer very carefully until we could identify four clay and thatched huts close to the water pans. For the next half an hour, we carefully scrutinised the surrounding area before deciding that there were no other people in the vicinity. There was only a little muddy water left in the pans, and only game spoor could be identified. The huts were empty, and all signs confirmed that these had not been inhabited for at least a month; therefore, there were no signs of any terrorist either. Fortunately for them . . .

At this stage, the sun had already started dipping towards the western horizon. My map indicated that we had walked a sickle-moon-shaped route from the vehicle to the pans. When I asked Phineas to give directions to the vehicle, he instinctively pointed in the direction we had come from as was their custom. I referred him to my map and indicated the direction of the shortest route back to the vehicle. He gave me a very sceptical look which left no doubt in my mind that he did not agree and that he didn't trust my map. I took the lead on my shortcut route followed by a very reluctant Phineas. Every half an hour, I still plotted our position on the map and made slight directional changes when necessary. After approximately 2½ hours, we suddenly came upon the eastern boundary 'kaplyn'. This meant that the eastern boundary firebreak road had to be approximately 200 m directly west of our position now. Phineas was very surprised when we got to the firebreak road and saw the vehicle approximately 300 m to the north of us. I heard him mumble something to the effect that it was nothing but a fluke.

Inspired by the above expedition into Mozambique, without a passport, Phineas and I were south of the Shingwedzi River between the Dipene and Kostini pickets when I again asked where the nearest habitation was to the KNP boundary. He indicated the crest of a hill approximately 5 km into Mozambique and said that if one stood on that crest, one could see habitation at the foot of the hill. Again, we were on our way to go and flush out the enemy in its den. There was not a cloud in the sky and already very hot. After an hour's walk, we were three quarters of the way up the hill when suddenly Phineas and I heard something rumble that resembled thunder. We both looked up simultaneously for any sign of a storm, but there was none! It flashed through my mind that the terrorists must have seen us and were in hot pursuit with their tanks. I looked at Phineas in bewilderment and shouted, 'Run!' We turned around and headed for the safety of the KNP as fast as the terrain would allow us to. We didn't even stop to hear whether the tanks were still following us. Out of breath, we reached the vehicle. Only now did I look at Phineas. 'What was that?' 'Mtagati!' (witchcraft) he exclaimed, agitated. I don't believe in witchcraft, but I couldn't think of a logical explanation.

I had my scheduled meeting with Oom Johan at his camp in the Nyandu bush early the following morning. I warned Phineas beforehand that mum was the word about yesterday's experience. When we arrived at Oom Johan's camp, Field Ranger Corporal Wilson Dinda was still preparing Oom Johan's breakfast. Phineas and I were cordially invited to join them for breakfast. 'Did you feel the earthquake yesterday?' Oom Johan asked. 'What earthquake?' I enquired. Oom Johan had a little transistor radio that he used to try and listen to the daily Afrikaans news on SABC through the heavy static background noise. On the news that morning, it was reported that, at approximately twelve o'clock yesterday afternoon, an earthquake registering 3 on the Richter scale was recorded. It was felt down in Natal and most probably originated from the Great Rift Valley in East Africa. Oom Johan had not experienced it as he had been in his vehicle at that time. 'No, Oom Johan, I didn't feel anything,' I lied. I could not tell him about Phineas and my illegal expeditions into Mozambique. I knew it, I said to myself, I did not believe Phineas's 'Mtagati' (witchcraft) explanation, but this was certainly a logical explanation. I somehow got the feeling that the Big Boss up there was telling me to stop my illegal expeditions into Mozambique. After another 2 weeks of unsuccessfully 'hunting' terrorists, the whole campaign was temporarily stopped. This, however, heralded the beginning of a different work and lifestyle for all field personnel in the KNP.

*   *   *

At this stage, historically, almost 80 per cent of all the Field Rangers of the KNP were from Mozambique. They possessed excellent bush skills and a good knowledge of the veldt. They had a very good work ethic and were very well disciplined due to the Portuguese rule in Mozambique at the time. All the Field Rangers at Tshokwane were of Mozambiquen descent.

When I started working in the KNP, the so-called Mafourteen system had just been phased out. The 'Mafourteen' name was derived from an arrangement whereby the gold mines on the Reef (Gauteng) could employ labour from Mozambique on the condition that they worked in the KNP for 2 weeks as 'payment' for the registration and passport documents needed to enter the RSA. The KNP Management also used these 14 days to select candidates for permanent appointment in the KNP. Field Ranger Corporal Elias Nzima and Field Ranger Lance Corporal Maxim Chauke at Tshokwane were recruited and appointed as Field Rangers many years ago as a result of this 'Mafourteen' system.

Section Ranger Dirk Ackerman at one stage noticed that there was unease amongst the Field Ranger Corps at Tshokwane. After many hours of questioning, it came to light that Maxim Chauke was apparently using witchcraft to get rid of his immediate senior, Elias Nzima, as he wanted the Corporal's position. It also transpired that Maxim Chauke was one or other tribal leader of the Chauke clan in Mozabique and that the Lance Corporal position was not worthy of his standing. We tried everything possible to resolve the issues at hand. Maxim Chauke, of course, denied all the allegations. Elias eventually insisted that the matter be resolved by a Sangoma (Witch doctor/Clairvoyant in their culture). Maxim reluctantly agreed to this. They knew of a Sangoma living approximately 10 km in Mozambique, directly east of the Munywini picket on the eastern boundary.

So as not to give the 'Impimpis' (spies) the opportunity to spread the information, we left early the next morning for the Munywini picket, and from there, we proceeded on foot into Mozambique. The party consisted of Dirk, Maxim, Elias, and me, six other Field Rangers, the Storeman, and two labourers. The Sangoma was taken aback by our unannounced arrival (not the custom at all), especially by two white males in the visiting party. The spokesperson of our party formally introduced us to the Sangoma and requested the Sangoma to tell us what the purpose of our visit was. Fortunately for me, the Sangoma spoke isiZulu, and I could follow everything she said. Initially, she was very reluctant to help us. Our spokesperson, however, made a convincing plea and emphasised that the life of one of the group was at stake if she did not intervene. She eventually picked up her 'dolossak' (bag of witchcraft bones and 'goodies'), which she used to 'see' the problem and to predict the outcome of the problem. She swung the 'dolossak' in front of her, uttering (to me unintelligent gibberish) strange words before eventually throwing the contents of the bag in front of her on the reed mat she was kneeling on. I could not decide whether the 'bones' had made her any the wiser as she picked up the contents and placed them back in the bag. She swung the bag in front of her again with more intensity. She seemed to go into a trance, her eyes rolling backwards and her whole body emphasising the swaying of the 'dolossak' while uttering the witchcraft gibberish first softly and then louder in an effort to communicate with the spirits of the forefathers. She again threw the contents of the 'dolossak' onto the reed mat in front of her. Again, it seemed to me that the 'bones' hadn't told her anything. The contents were again returned to the bag. The third swinging of the bag became more intense, and I noticed the overwhelmed expression on the faces of the watching group. The contents of the 'dolossak' were again thrown onto the reed mat in front of her, and I detected a slightly relieved expression on her face. In a whispered voice, I translated to Dirk that someone in the group was using witchcraft to try and eliminate another one in the group in order to get his job. She, however, did not reveal the identity of the two individuals. When our spokesperson asked her to be more specific, she stood up with a pained expression on her face and entered the hut behind her. Our spokesperson indicated to us that we should remain seated and remain silent. After approximately 10 minutes, she reappeared out of the hut and again knelt on the reed mat and repeated the whole ritual. While putting the contents back into the bag for the second time, she looked straight at Maxim and said that he was the one using witchcraft. Maxim kept staring at the ground in front of him, and I detected an expression of relief on Elias's face. The Sangoma addressed Maxim and asked whether he had anything to say. In a soft, quivering voice, Maxim promised never to 'kataza' (to bother his soul) Elias again and to live and work in peace with him in the future. She looked at Elias, who only nodded his head in acceptance.

The group was in a jovial mood on the way back to the Munywini picket. Dirk and I tried to make sense of all the happenings of the past 2 hours. I personally am convinced that the 'brotherhood of Sangomas' has an information network second to none and that the rituals are just for the show. Who will ever know?

*   *   *

One mid-afternoon in autumn, we saw smoke from a veldt fire to the east of Tshokwane. We loaded all the necessary firefighting equipment plus twelve helping hands onto the bakkie and drove up to the top of N'wamuriwa from where we could get a better idea of where the fire was and the extent thereof. We estimated that the fire was still in Mozambique but very close to the border. It was an annual habit of the Mozambiquens to light veldt fires in autumn for two specific reasons: firstly, to have short green grass available for their cattle during winter and secondly, to entice the game from KNP into Mozambique in order to poach them. These fires often spread into the KNP, fuelled on by the south-easterly winds associated with cold fronts at the change of the season.

We tried to get to the eastern boundary as quickly as possible as there was a light south-easterly wind blowing. The chances were good that the south-easterly would pick up in intensity during the late afternoon, and we were going to try and have a wide enough firebreak in place before then to prevent the fire from entering the KNP. First of all, we had to determine where the head of the fire would strike the eastern boundary. At this point, we divided the manpower into two teams to prepare a firebreak along the eastern boundary firebreak road. After 3 km, the northbound team came upon a section where fire had already burnt up to the firebreak road. We could now utilise this team to strengthen the southbound team. As the fire gods would have it, we were very fortunate to complete the firebreak before a near-gale-force south-easterly wind hit us. Our back burn now had to be systematically checked and made safe. All burning tree trunks and logs as well as smouldering elephant and buffalo dung had to be dragged deeper into the burnt area to prevent the strong south-easterly wind from blowing these potential firelighters into the unburnt areas to the west of the firebreak road. At about 18.30, this was safely achieved, and so everyone could take a breather and relax.

We again took stock and loaded all the firefighting equipment onto the bakkie with twelve very weary bodies trying to get the best vantage point for the trip back to Tshokwane. We had no sooner left than the bakkie's engine cut out for no apparent reason. The engine refused to fire up regardless of all my mechanical knowledge. We had to make a quick decision to either battle on in the semi-dark to try and get the bakkie mobile or to walk 20 km back to Tshokwane. Fortunately for us, there was a sickle moon in the western sky that would provide a very faint light for the next 5 hours. Armed with two 1-l plastic water bottles and ten hatchets, we started the journey back to Tshokwane.

At first, the group was spread out and conversed in normal voice tones. However, the darker it became, the closer together the group became, and the louder the voice tones became. This was a natural survival tactic in the dark to ward off anything that could harm the group. As time went by, the distance to Tshokwane diminished, 10 km, 5 km, 2 km, and eventually, we were at the Tshokwane Tea Room/Picnic Site. Now we had to cross the N'waswintsontso Spruit with its dense reed bed to the staff living quarters. For the last kilometer to the caravan, I was on my own. The sickle moon had dipped below the horizon, and only the stars provided enough light to detect the road. In the dark, I walked into two buffalo bulls sleeping in the road. They fortunately saw me first and ran off snorting into the bush. At this stage, my nerves were on edge, and my heartbeat was sky-high due to adrenaline saturation. Another 100 m, and I would be safely in the caravan. It felt like an eternity. Then I saw the glowing embers under the water drum. The Storeman had fortunately filled the drum with water and stoked the fire when he realised that we would probably only be returning late from the firefighting. First of all, I wanted to enjoy the safety of the caravan and sent up a silent prayer for getting home safely. The shower water was still very hot, and I felt like a new sixpence after the shower. I was still busy towelling myself off under the star-studded heaven when I heard the roar of a lion in the distance. It was already past midnight, and I was sitting next to the fire and reflected on the day's happenings. Again, I heard the lion roar. It was markedly closer. I was busy getting ready for bed when the lion roared again – closer still. Again, the lion roared. I estimated it was at the Tshokwane Tea Room/Picnic Site. When it roared again, I placed it near the staff quarters. The next two roars were louder as it neared the caravan. There was a 5-minute silence; then it roared at full blast next to the caravan. The magnitude of the roar was so intense that the cutlery on the shelves rattled. I wondered if the cutlery could hear my heart beating 'doef-doef' as well. The lion roared twice more, and the sound actually hurt my ears. It was evident that the lion had picked up our trail earlier that evening and had tracked us all the way back to Tshokwane, the staff quarters, and then to the caravan. With the last roar at the caravan, it warned us that we were very lucky to have escaped his attentions earlier and that we would not be so lucky next time around. I was overcome with fatigue and fell asleep waiting to hear the next roar as the lion moved away.

Early the next morning, armed with the right mechanical tools and the Section Ranger's vehicle, we went back to my vehicle to get it mobile again. Along the way, we saw the evidence that the lion had started following our spoor from about 5 km out. On the way, I tried to imagine the chaos that would have transpired if the lion and the group had walked into one another, we armed with ten hatchets and the lion armed with five sharp ends (mouth and four clawed paws). What a nightmare!

*   *   *

A story to illustrate the huge difference between day- and night-time behaviour of lions. During the day, lions are normally very passive and sleep practically most of the day. Although lions normally hunt during the evening, there are many reports of daytime hunting. Lions are extremely opportunistic and will not let an opportunity to kill a prey go by.

The zebra-holding facility was full of animals ready to fill the next batch of orders. Late afternoon, we captured the last subadult zebra mare to complete the order for delivery in 3 days' time. This specific animal was very strong-willed and gave us all a hard time trying to capture her. I was worried that the animal might have overexerted itself during the capture, and I would have to monitor her very carefully until the next morning. If the animal were to show any abnormal signs by the following morning, I would have to capture a replacement animal. Just after sunset, I walked over to the boma where this animal was held. The animal was, however, still under the influence of the sedative that was administered after the capture and was very calm. At approximately nine o'clock that evening, the animals in the holding facility were very restless; they were barking, and I could hear them kicking one another.

For you to understand the ensuing happenings better, I need to recap the layout of the surrounding terrain. The zebra-holding facility was fenced with a 1.8-m high fence with ten strands and an additional diamond mesh section from ground level up to 1-m high. An ordinary cattle gate gave access to the fenced-off area. The one corner post of the fence was 25 m away from the caravan. The water tank stand also stood within these 25 m and close to the fence.

For one reason or the other (call it premonition if you will), I did not only take the six-cell torch but also the 9 mm revolver that I had in the caravan with me to go and see what was causing all the commotion in the bomas and to check on the condition of the mare. Without putting on the torch, I walked to the corner post and then along the fence line to the cattle gate. It was easier to jump over the gate than to climb over the fence at the corner post. I proceeded further to the holding facility and used the torchlight to inspect the animals in all the bomas. I could not see any apparent reason for the previous reaction of the animals. To my relief, the mare that we had captured earlier that afternoon was very calm. As a precautionary measure, we could put her through her paces in the crush passages to see if there was any stiffness in her legs.

I walked back in the dark from the holding facilities to the inside of the fence and then along the fence to the corner post. While walking on the inside of the fence, I heard a rustling sound on the other side of the fence. I switched on the torchlight and shone the torch in the direction of the rustling sound. I saw a young lioness less than 3 m away. She lay ready to pounce and glared at the torchlight. I felt relatively safe behind the fence line but still needed to reach the safety of the caravan. To frighten the lioness away, I decided to fire two shots with the revolver, one to the left and the other to the right of her within 1 m of where she lay ready to pounce. I was very surprised by her reaction. She pulled her ears flat, crouched lower in the jump position, and growled softly at me. What now? I did not want to kill the lioness. I kept the torchlight focused on her and slowly, centimeter by centimeter, started moving towards the corner post. Fortunately, the torchlight was very powerful, and the lioness could not see how uneasy I was behind the torchlight. The lioness, on the other hand, wasn't scared of anything as was very evident from the reaction when I fired the two shots in close proximity to her. When I reached the corner post, I slowly started climbing up the post, still keeping the lioness blinded by the strong torchlight. At this stage, there were 25 m between me and the lioness and 25 m to the safety of the caravan. I realised that when I had to jump down from the corner post, I would not be able to keep the torchlight focused on the lioness. I also realised that I could land awkwardly and stumble after the jump and even fall flat on my face. If this were to happen, my days would be numbered. 'You have to take a chance to have a chance,' the thought flashed through my mind when I switched off the torchlight and jumped from the top of the fence and took ten massive strides to the safety of the caravan, with my heart thumping in my throat.

Why hadn't I jumped over the cattle gate as I had previously done and walked back to the caravan on the outside of the fence? This was the least physically challenging route. Was it premonition? Was it a sixth sense? Or was it fate? I don't know! 'It' saved my life!

During the following morning's post-mortem of the previous night's events, it was evident that the lioness had not chased after me when I had made a run for the caravan. The marks where she had prepared to jump at me were, however, clearly visible. From this spot, the spoor did not follow me to the caravan but moved away in the opposite direction. Some nerve-racking questions without answers again flashed through my head. Had the lioness watched me when I walked to the holding facility on the outside of the fence? If so, how far was the lioness away from me, and why did she not attack me? Was it because she was a young animal? Were there other lions in the vicinity? The restlessness of the zebras had most probably been due to the proximity of the lioness/other lions in the vicinity. Did all the unanswered questions add up to the fact that it just wasn't my day?

*   *   *

It was usually on moonlit nights that I experienced wonderful and sometimes amusing incidents. I don't know how many similar experiences I had missed during the dark-moon periods.

After a very tough cricket match at Skukuza, I arrived back at Tshokwane one Saturday evening, exhausted from the heat of the day and physical exertion. I decided to lie down before taking a shower. As fate would have it, the little lie-down resulted in deep sleep, and I only woke much later that evening – still dirty. The shower water in the drum was still lukewarm. I previously described the construction and functioning of the primitive but five-star shower at the caravan. I filled the 20-l shower drum with lukewarm water and climbed onto the overturned bucket in order to hook the shower drum onto the cross pipe by means of the s-shaped hook. When I jumped up to hook the drum, still half asleep, I slipped on the bucket, missed the cross pipe, and fell down into the spilt water of the shower drum. Now I wasn't only sweaty and sticky from the cricket match, I was covered in mud as well. Fortunately for me, there was still a little lukewarm water in the drum on the dead embers. The shower process started all over again, and this time, I successfully hooked the s-hook onto the cross pipe, and I started soaping myself. While showering, I noticed movement out of the corner of my eye, and approximately 3 m away, I saw a hyena eying me with ill intent.

Without a moment's hesitation, I took the initiative and charged the hyena. It immediately ran off, tail between the legs and uttering their typical laughing sound. I could hardly suppress my own laughter. How long had the hyena been watching me? It had most probably watched the first unsuccessful shower attempt as well. If the hyena had had a sense of humour, it most probably would have burst out laughing at that stage. After this incident, I could not help but wonder how many times and by what I had been watched while showering.

One evening, I was awakened by a very deep rumbling sound very close to the caravan which was unfamiliar to me. I very slowly and quietly got up from the caravan bunk bed and moved to the window closest to where I thought the sound had come from. Through the window, I saw a big elephant bull towering above the caravan, picking Marula fruit from the tree under which the caravan stood, and he was uttering the rumbling sound. I was later told that elephants communicated over long distance with one another by means of this stomach-rumbling sound.

On another occasion, I was awakened by the caravan moving gently back and forth. I lay silently and debated what was causing the movement. Without any logical answer, I again very stealthily got out of the bunk bed and moved to the window to see a big male lion rubbing his ribcage against the corner of the caravan. It most probably itched on a spot where it could not reach by means of its normal devices.

On another occasion, I was awakened by soft sounds emanating from the caravan tent. At closer inspection, I saw four lion cubs, playing as only cats can, on the layer of sand I had put on the tent floor to suppress dust. Both the zip openings of the tent always remained open and had given the lion cubs access. The cubs were not mischievous and left my private belongings alone as they ran in and out of the tent playing 'catch me' and rolling on the sand. Two lionesses peacefully lay next to the heat of the glowing embers of the campfire, watching the shenanigans of the youngsters.

In all the above-mentioned incidents, all the strange objects and smells in and around the caravan did not deter the animals from getting close to and even entering the caravan tent. Wild animals and especially predators react very atypically and unpredictably during night-time.

On one occasion, Section Ranger Dirk Ackerman took a squad of labourers to the Xiteveteve windmill to camp there in order to dig a furrow from a newly built animal drinking trough to the reservoir. They had to lay a 50 mm plastic water pipe to connect the two. Fortunately, the labourers elected to pitch their tent close to the windmill structure. The next day, Dirk and I were on our way to Skukuza and so decided to drive via Xiteveteve to check on the work in progress. We arrived early in the morning only to find the whole squad clambered up into the windmill tower with the tent flat on the ground next to the tower. After coaxing the squad members down from the windmill tower, the squad foreman came to grips with himself and gave Dirk and me the following description of what had transpired.

'At about midnight, a pride of lions had announced themselves with loud roaring and grunting and started to drag the picks and shovels that we had parked against the windmill tower all over the show. The lions had even started gnawing on the handles. During the early hours of the morning, six lions had turned their attention on the tent. They had started hitting their claws into the side of the tent and pulling back and forth with the whole tent swaying backwards and forwards. The whole squad had protested, and we had shouted at the top of our voices without any effect on the lions. It had rather seemed as if they had been encouraged by our screaming. We had even hit at the paws where the nails penetrated the tent material, with the hatchets inside the tent. Alas, it had been to no avail. At one stage, the lions had lost interest in the tent and had gone and laid down approximately 20 m away. We had then all fled from the tent and clambered up the windmill tower to relative safety. With all the commotion, the lions had run off but had later returned to flatten the tent. They had then left us alone and later moved off with their roars, disappearing in the distance.' Needless to say, four out of the six labourers had immediately resigned and had been adamant to be taken to Skukuza to receive their outstanding remuneration. After relating their experience to the pay clerks, they had sympathetically obliged.

To my knowledge, this was the first and only occasion that lions had reacted aggressively (or was it playfully?) to people sleeping in a tent. I spent many peaceful hours camping out in a tent after that. On several occasions, lions were in the immediate vicinity of my tent, with one or two of them roaring to high heaven. I must say that one cannot help but be filled with awe and respect when there is only a thin piece of tent material between yourself and the so-called king of the animals.

During a capturing and marking research project of Blue wildebeest in the Bangu windmill area, we arrived back at the windmill at dusk one day and saw a lioness at the drinking trough. A colleague and I were on the back of the bakkie, with a further two up front in the cab. We drove closer to inspect the lioness. Big mistake! On closer inspection, we saw that there were two cubs with the lioness. The lioness charged at the vehicle without any provocation or warning. Fortunately, the driver kept his cool and changed direction and skirted past the drinking trough and picked up speed with our encouragement. The lioness also accelerated and was trying to clamber/jump onto the back of the bakkie. I grabbed the spade at the back of the bakkie and hit the lioness's paws off the rear lid every time she tried to clamber onto the back. At the third unsuccessful attempt, the lioness lost interest and returned to the cubs patiently waiting at the trough. Don't ever interfere with a lioness that has cubs in attendance. You will come second!

Volumes have been written about the grit, determination, and bravery of the honey badger. Black people are convinced that a honey badger can kill a buffalo bull. The badger supposedly achieves this mean feat by grabbing hold of the buffalo bull's scrotum and systematically damaging the scrotum until the buffalo bull dies from blood loss. I cannot vouch for this as I have not experienced it. What I can vouch for is the badger's grit, determination, and courage. On one occasion, driving back to Tshokwane after successfully combating a fire caused by lightning, we came across a badger trotting down the road in the same direction as we were going. I slowly increased speed, keeping up with the badger until the front of the bakkie was level with the small animal. I was extremely surprised when the badger turned towards the adjacent front tyre and tried to bite it. I could not believe my eyes. This small animal was attacking this big, smelly, rumbling contraption, completely foreign to anything it had ever experienced, to protect its own life. Maybe there is an element of truth in the buffalo story. Another example of a predator's (albeit a small one) change of attitude and aggression during the evening.

*   *   *

I don't know if the following story is a reflection of my courage or of utter stupidity. It might even look as if I am blowing my own trumpet. You be the judge! Nonetheless, near the end of my zebra-catching career by means of the crossbow and darts, an individual by the name of Jannie Oelofse from the Natal Parks Board began capturing game by means of nets and plastic curtains that were erected in the veldt in the shape of a funnel with a holding facility at the end. A helicopter was used to herd the animals into the funnel. As the animals entered the mouth of the funnel, longitudinal curtains were drawn closed to prevent the animals from escaping. As the animals progressed down the funnel, with the helicopter hot on their heels, other longitudinal curtains were closed off behind them until all the animals were enclosed in the holding facility at the back of the funnel. The holding facility at the back was strengthened by nets. This methodology revolutionised game capture, and large numbers of game could now simultaneously be captured at the same time. The holding facility also had a crush passage and mobile-loading ramp in order to mass load the captured animals onto special large transport vehicles.

The National Parks Board (SANParks) invited Jannie Oelofse to come and demonstrate his capture method in the KNP. On the prearranged day, Jannie arrived at Tshokwane, and I took him to see the large concentrations of zebra and Blue wildebeest congregated on the Lindanda flats between Tshokwane and N'wanetsi. He immediately started looking for a suitable terrain with lots of trees and shrubs to successfully hide the legs of the funnel. The plastic curtains had to be well camouflaged so that the game would not notice them when being chased into the funnel by the helicopter. It took us 2 days to complete the erection of the funnel, holding facility, loading crush passage, and loading ramp. We planned to chase a herd of zebras into the capture facility by late afternoon the following day if wind and weather conditions were favourable.

A herd of approximately forty zebras was isolated from the rest of the zebras and wildebeest by the helicopter and was herded towards the capture facility. When the front movers were about 100 m from the opening of the funnel, the helicopter picked up the herding speed. By the time the front runners became aware of something strange, it was already too late. The first curtain was already almost closed. The helicopter swooped down on them and remained on their backsides. There was only one way . . . forward. Systematically, all the other longitudinal curtains closed behind the zebras until they were all milling around in the holding facility. Incredible! In less than half an hour from the helicopter becoming airborne, approximately forty zebras were herded and successfully captured in the holding pen. The plan was to allow the zebras to calm down overnight and to load and transport them the following morning. Full of excitement and joy at the successful capture operation, we left for 'home'. Jannie and his team left for Skukuza, and my 10-year-old friend, 'Klein Jan', and I went home to Tshokwane. Tomorrow, we were going to load forty zebras!

The following morning, before sunrise, Klein Jan and I were at the capture facility. I clambered up the netting of the holding facility to inspect and do a proper count of the animals. My high spirits disappeared when I saw three zebras lying dead on the ground in the holding facility. The rest of the zebras were congregated to the left of me, up against the side of the holding facility. I noticed some movement out to the right, and I was horrified to see three lions feasting on a zebra's carcass inside the holding facility. We had underestimated the ingenuity of these predators. During the evening, they had dug under the netting and chased the zebras around in the holding facility and in the process had killed four of them. They were now feeding on one of the zebra carcasses. And to think that we had wanted the captured zebras to calm down during the night!

I climbed down from the holding facility, numbed by what I had seen, and went and sat in the bakkie to formulate a plan to get the lions out of the holding facility before the big shots from Skukuza arrived. Klein Jan asked, 'What are we going to do?' 'I don't know!' I could not go into the holding facility by myself or with the vehicle to chase the lions out. I could imagine the chaos. There was only one solution, and Klein Jan would have to be the only witness. I parked the bakkie close to the holding facility and instructed Klein Jan not to leave the bakkie under any circumstances. I got out of the bakkie and walked towards the holding facility with Klein Jan pleading in the background, 'Oom Lynn, please don't do anything stupid!'

When I reached the holding facility, I started rolling up the outside netting to a height of approximately 2 m at its highest point. The rest of the netting draped at an angle towards the ground, forming an opening of approximately 4 m wide at ground level. I then cut the plastic section on the inside of the holding facility and tied it down to the side to create a complete opening into the holding facility. While I was tying down the plastic material, the lions in the holding facility saw me and moved away slightly from the carcass. My plan of action was to antagonise the lions sufficiently from the inside of the holding facility so that they would charge at me. At the last possible moment, I would turn around, run through the opening, and clamber up the side of the netting to be out of reach of the lions once they had exited the holding facility through the created gap, in the hope that the lions would carry on charging into the bush. Now to initiate the plan, I walked through the opening into the holding facility and started jumping up and down, shouting at the lions. After a while, one of the lions did not like my performance and charged. Now the decision was mine! Where was the point of no return where I would still have sufficient time to turn around, run through the opening, and clamber up the netting to safety? 'Now!' I triggered myself, turned around, ran through the opening, and clambered up the netting. I was about 1.5 m up the netting when the lion burst through the opening. The lion was bemused when it couldn't detect me. It looked around in bewilderment and then ran off into the bush.

I had hoped that all three lions would charge simultaneously. Now I would have to face the ordeal a second time, I thought to myself while catching my breath, trying to control the adrenaline levels in my bloodstream, and calming my nerves, all the while hanging from the netting. Fortunately for me, the second lion did not take a lot of convincing to make it charge, and it also disappeared into the bush. The high level of adrenaline in my bloodstream affected my clear thinking, and I started to doubt the wisdom of my plan and my ability to decide on the point of no return.

For the third time, I entered the holding facility and saw the third lion immediately going into a crouching position. This lion was not as manly (maybe it was a lioness) as the other two had been, and I had quite a struggle getting it to charge at me. I threw a log at it. By doing so, I had entered the holding facility further than was originally intended. When the log struck home, the lion charged with intent. I almost missed the point of no return, and I also misread the speed of the charge. I did not have sufficient time to clamber up the side netting by the time the lion emerged through the hole in the holding facility. It immediately stopped and started growling at me where I stood. I immediately took the initiative and charged at the lion, all the while shouting and screaming at it. The lion chose to flee from this maniac and ran off into the surrounding bush. I there and then fell on my knees, first of all to mutter a thank-you prayer and second of all because my legs refused to support me any longer. After a couple of minutes, I shakily got up and walked up to a completely fogged-up cabin of the bakkie. When I opened the door, Klein Jan greeted me with: 'Is Oom dan mal?' (Are you insane?). I forbade Klein Jan there and then to tell anyone what he had witnessed.

By the time the big shots from Skukuza arrived, all the zebra carcasses were disposed of in the bush, and the plastic and netting was back in place as it should be. The loading of the zebras through the crush passage, through the loading ramp onto the transport vehicles, went very smoothly, and these valuable goods were quickly on their way to the zebra-holding facilities at Tshokwane. These holding facilities were, however, not designed to simultaneously house so many zebras; although, we had made short-term modifications to them. Long queues of game farmers pitched the following day to load their animals.

*   *   *

On occasion, I also had the opportunity to ask one of my colleagues: 'But, Louis, are you mad?' The story unfolded as follows: At that stage of his career in the KNP, Louis Olivier was attached to the NPD ('Newe Produkte Depot') or Factory where all the culled carcasses of elephants and buffaloes etc. were maximally utilised. On a rotational basis, Louis drove the big culling transport vehicle from the culling terrain to the NPD loaded with the culled carcasses. Culling was normally done during the late afternoon in order for the carcasses to be transported to the NPD during the cool of the evening so the carcasses were delivered in a good and fresh condition. Where the culling of the day took place determined at what time during the early morning of the following day the carcasses would arrive at the NPD.

One cold winter morning at approximately 02.00 I was rudely awakened by somebody trying to break down the caravan door. When I, frightened out of my wits and not fully awake, eventually opened the door, I found a very frightened Louis Olivier standing in the tent of the caravan. Louis immediately started explaining his predicament. I could, however, see that he was very tensed up. I indicated to him to be quite, sat him down on the side of the bunk bed, and poured him a glass of coke. After Louis had calmed down a little, the following story unfolded. The culling transport vehicle, with thirty-five buffalo carcasses on board, had run out of diesoline near Leeu Pan (Lion Pan). Louis had a very high regard for NPD Manager Oom John Marais's strong discipline and unapproachable attitude towards waste of any kind. When the culling vehicle, therefore, had run out of fuel approximately 30 km from the NPD with thirty-five buffalo carcasses on board, Louis could imagine the consequences as this could have been avoided by better planning.

Leeu Pan is situated approximately 12 km from Tshokwane, towards Skukuza, and it is known for its high density of lions that roam the area. Louis found himself caught between the devil (Oom John Marais) and the deep blue sea (lions), and he had to make a plan to save thirty-five buffalo carcasses. The only solution was to walk back to Tshokwane where he was sure he would get hold of diesoline. To keep the lions and all other animals with ill intent at bay, he decided on the following modus operandi: He would take one of the slaughtering knives and place its blade down between his sock and leg for a quick draw. In his left hand, he held a box of matches (of course made by the Lion Match Factory) and a bundle of dry grass that he had collected. In his right hand, he had a single match which he would use to light the dry grass to provide light in the event that he heard or became aware of anything that meant him harm. He would then draw the knife to protect himself against any danger that threatened him. All his planning was, however, futile in that he was blinded by the light created by the burning grass. The light period was also of very short duration as the grass was very dry and burnt out quickly, also burning his fingers in the process. At one stage, he almost lost the box of matches when the box in his hand fell out of his hand and onto his boot, when the grass caught fire, kicking it further into the grass. Going down on his knees, he felt all over and eventually found the box. All the while, he could hear lions roaring in the distance as the distance between Leeu Pan and Tshokwane slowly but surely grew less, and the adrenaline level in his blood grew more.

With great relief, he pushed open the gate to the Section Ranger yard. He got the fright of his life when three barking dogs charged at him. He eventually got them under control without suffering any bite wounds. His courage hit rock bottom when he realised that Dirk Ackerman would have been awakened by the commotion and would have come to investigate. But there was nothing! Dirk wasn't at home! He went to the front door and knocked on the door . . . again . . . and again . . . nothing! Dirk wasn't at home. Now he had to proceed to Lynn's caravan, another ½ km through lion country. Louis confirmed that this last section was the most nerve-racking half a kilometer of the whole journey. The adrenaline levels were very high, and his heart felt like it was jumping out of his chest. This was the Louis whom I found in the caravan door. After Louis had told his eventful story, I said to him: 'Louis, are you mad, thinking that thirty-five buffalo carcasses are worth more than your own life?' After Louis had calmed down sufficiently, we went and loaded enough diesoline for him to get to Skukuza and took it to Leeu Pan to get Louis on the road again. On our way to Leeu Pan, we encountered two hyenas that could have been the cause of the rustling in the grass that had triggered the grass-lighting by Louis. Who would know? I must say, I admired Louis's commitment.

* * *

I often, especially during a full-moon period, took one of the bunk bed mattresses from the caravan, loaded it onto the back of the bakkie, and drove into the veldt or to a special place and slept under the star-studded heaven. The only protection was the old .38 Smith & Wesson revolver and a broomstick as one was relatively safe on the back of the bakkie. I can recall the one occasion that I drove out to Leeu Pan just after the first spring rains to go and enjoy the first frog-chorus performance. What an ear-numbing experience. I could identify at least ten different frog calls. There was, however, no question of falling asleep. At about midnight, I returned to the caravan to catch up on a little bit of sleep.

During similar excursions, I often slept over at various game-watering points whether these were natural or artificial. Big herds of elephants and buffaloes as well as groups of rhinos and lions came down to drink. What was again very noticeable, even though the whole area was lit up by bright moonlight, was the difference in behaviour of all of these animals during the evening and during the day. They were much calmer and restful during the evening than during the daytime.

On one occasion, I just drove off a firebreak road into the veldt for approximately half a kilometer to sleep there. As there were no natural pans in the near vicinity, I did not expect to hear any animal activity or night sounds. Early evening, I could hear the distant call of a Pearl-spotted owl. The owl later stopped calling. There was no breeze to rustle the tree leaves. I couldn't even hear a mosquito. This kind of silence was to be cherished and was very dear to me. I heard a very faint sound and decided it was the sound of the blood flowing through my arteries/veins. At a later stage in the Kalahari Gemsbuck National Park, I walked to the middle of a large pan and experienced the same silence and the sound of blood flowing through my arteries/veins. Exceptional! I enjoyed this utter silence for a while and then decided to lie on the back of the bakkie.

Late evening, I was awakened by a faint rustling of the grass in the vicinity of the vehicle, or was it a sixth sense? I supported myself on one elbow and peered over the side of the bakkie and saw a hyena prowling around the bakkie. The hyena looked up at the rear lid of the bakkie, stalked closer, and put its two front paws on the lid. I could smell the rotten breath of the animal while it breathed with an open mouth, peering into the load bed. The hyena went down to ground, and I could sense that its investigation had not been completed. I very silently felt for the broomstick and took a good grip on it. My premonition that the hyena would continue with its investigation to inspect the content of the load bed proved to be correct. The hyena stood up on the left side (my right-hand side) of the load bed with its rotten breath about 1 m from my face. I let fly with my best broom-handle backhand and connected the hyena on the side of its snout. I haven't since heard that sound that came out of the hyena's innards as it fled off into the bush. Going back to sleep again was quite difficult with all the adrenaline in my bloodstream. At one stage, I burst out laughing recalling the weird sounds the hyena had uttered as it had run away.

*   *   *

Earlier in the book, I introduced you to my pride and joy: the 1959 Morris Minor 1000. My 'ge-Morrisie' and I understood one another, and I could perform miracles with her. Long before she became solely mine, it had been my imposed duty every workday morning to take the 'ge-Morrisie' out from under the lean-to garage to the front of the house, from where my parents would then drive to work with her. As my dad was a motor mechanic by trade, he had early on imprinted in us that the weakness of a petrol engine exhaust system lay in the stop-start motoring over short distances done by many townsfolk. By this method, water condensates and accumulates in the exhaust system, causing severe rust. The access road to our house, at Greytown, went past the golf clubhouse and along the side of the golf course. From the house to the clubhouse was just over a kilometer's distance. Every morning I, therefore, would take the 'ge-Morrisie' out from under the lean-to garage, drive down to the clubhouse, and only then park her in front of the house, the engine and exhaust system nice and hot. On these early morning escapades, the 'ge-Morrisie' and I had become accustomed to each other and come to respect each other's capabilities, especially after the rains when the two-track road became very slippery in places. I could easily do a 180° spin on the slippery surface at approximately 40 kph without any sweat. At one stage, I had tried a 360° spin but only got as far as 270°. I had unceremoniously left the two-track road and landed up on the golf-course fairway, fortunately without any damages to the car. My dad was a very observant individual and very little slipped his notice. I, on the other hand, had been very sure that nobody knew about my shenanigans with the 'ge-Morrisie'. In retrospect, I was sure that he had noticed the many skid and broadside tyre marks on the two-track road. However, as long as the Morris was parked in one piece in front of the house, he didn't say a word. In all probability, he had done the same sort of thing in his youth.

In the KNP, the bond between the 'ge-Morrisie' and me became even stronger. She was now mine. During the summer/cricket season, I drove to Skukuza every Tuesday and Thursday afternoon for cricket practice. I always tried to leave Tshokwane at around 16.00 to travel the 40 km to Skukuza at 60 kpu (the official speed limit for KNP staff) to get in a decent cricket practice and to be back at Tshokwane by 20.00. Driving in the KNP after sunset was frowned on. Dirk Ackerman, however, relented after considerable nagging from my side and gave me grace up to 20.00. On occasion, the zebra capturing prevented me from leaving at 16.00. I then had to transgress the 60 km per hour speed limit to be able to fit in a decent practice.

The tourist road to Skukuza (the tar road only came later) had a few classic curves that the 'ge-Morrisie' and I thoroughly enjoyed practicing oversteer and understeer cornering techniques on. (The uninformed called them broadies.) I had to be very circumspect adjusting my own speed in the vicinity of tourist traffic on the road lest I be reported to higher authority for speeding. Dirk would immediately retract the privilege of night driving, and that would put paid to my cricket practice.

There was one specific corner in the vicinity of the Orpen Memorial rock that provided the 'ge-Morrisie' and me great pleasure. From the Tshokwane side to Skukuza, it presented a long curve to the left with long thatch-grass plumes bending the thatch grass into the road. One could, therefore, not see around the corner, and vision unfolded as one progressed around the corner. The road was gravelled with fine granite material that provided an ideal loose driving surface. If one negotiated the corner at the right speed, the front left headlight would clip the overhanging thatch grass out of the way with the 'ge-Morrisie' negotiating the corner in a perfectly controlled four-wheel drift. For the ill-informed: during a four-wheel drift, the front end of the car would be pointing into the veldt on the inside of the corner, while the rear wheels would be following a longer route around the corner with all four wheels in a sliding mode.

If in the nature of one's activity one is obligated to drive around this corner twice a week, it is understandable and quite natural to see if the corner can be negotiated at a higher speed than the previous time. It so happened that on one Thursday afternoon, I was behind schedule, and the official speed limit was tested on every suitable occasion. The 'ge-Morrisie' and I were in the process of showing our favourite corner who was actually boss when . . . What happened next is going to take quite a lot of words to describe but actually played out in fractions of seconds.

Halfway through the corner, I became aware of one of these old round-bodied Mercedes-Benzes on our side (the inside) of the corner, looking directly at us with its round glass eyes (head lamps). I could have sworn I saw the Mercedes's eyes enlarge in shock. The two elderly people in the Mercedes were watching a herd of Sable antelopes approximately 60 m off the road on our side of the road. They had parked there to have a better view of the Sable. The lady was the first one to see the car speeding down towards them on a collision course. Her eyes got very big, and she screamed. (At least that is what I deducted) I did not hear anything. Maybe she could not utter a sound. I now had to make a very quick decision on how to avoid the head-on collision. Without thinking, I instinctively threw the 'ge-Morrisie' into a 180° slide by turning the steering wheel sharply to the left and immediately neutralising the slide. The 'ge-Morrisie' reacted immediately as we had practiced so many times before. The rear end of the car swung out to the right and dragged the front end with it. We were now travelling backwards towards Skukuza, slipping past the Mercedes with 1 m to spare between us. The backwards movement wasn't a pleasure anymore. I turned the steering wheel sharply to the right and immediately back to the neutral position. The 'ge-Morrisie' reacted accordingly and completed another 180° slide, now facing the original direction we'd been travelling in. As there was still forward motion, I put the 'ge-Morrisie' into third gear and continued towards Skukuza and cricket practice.

Seeing that the 'ge-Morrisie' and I had regularly practiced the above manoeuvres under controlled circumstances, the above was not a very stressful experience for either of us. The elderly couple in the Mercedes was, however, frightened out of their wits, judging by their facial expressions as we skidded by. I was quite sure that they wouldn't have been able to remember any details, and I preferred it that way.

*   *   *

I would like to tell you of two incidents where two separate zebras, one a male and the other a female, almost caused me grave bodily harm. During my zebra-catching days, negotiations were being conducted between the then Department of Native Affairs and the National Parks Board concerning the transfer of a piece of land in the south-western corner of the KNP to the department of Native Affairs. After the conclusion of the negotiations, the KNP was mandated to chase out the game from the demarcated area back into the KNP before the new boundary fence could be closed.

The KNP Department of Nature Conservation got approximately 200 men together who would walk through the area in a line abreast with approximately 10 m spacing between individuals. Some of the team members were given empty paraffin drums to beat on to make as much noise as possible. The other members had to clap hands, shout, and whistle to add to the hubbub. The plan was that all the game would slowly move in front of the noise to a predetermined opening in the fence. Not all game, however, takes kindly to being chased from their known and favourite haunts. This was the case with a group of seven zebras that had been moving in front of my section of the drive since we had started. Initially, this group of zebras was very calm and restful and moved off in front of the slowly advancing line of noisy men just within visible distance of us. After about 1 km of being forced into a strange area, I could detect that the stallion was beginning to get restless. The stallion would come to a standstill, facing the advancing line of noisy men, and then it would snort and run towards the line of advancing men and at a safe distance veer off at an angle to join the rest of the group. The intervals between testing the line became more frequent, and sometimes, others of the group accompanied the stallion on its testing charge. The counter reaction of the advancing line was to kick up a louder racket to make the charging zebra group turn around. As we continued with our operation, the whole group of zebras eventually took part in the charge towards the advancing rowdy line and only stopped in a cloud of dust approximately 20 m from us and then ran back.

At each charge, I became more and more apprehensive about the ability of the rowdy advancing line of men to herd this group of zebra towards the opening in the new fence. Again the zebra stallion followed by the remaining group charged the line. This time, however, it identified me as the weak link in the chain. When it resolutely sped past the 20-m mark without stopping, I knew I was in for bigger trouble than what I could handle. The distance was 10 m, then 5 m. I started to sidestep the stallion and the rest of the group. The stallion also made an effort to take evasive action. Then I felt the right shoulder of the stallion hit me square in the chest. I was flung through the air like a rag doll and landed about 5 m back amongst some rocks. When I opened my eyes, I saw the belly of the zebra mare jumping over me. Helping hands quickly surrounded me. I was severely winded, but fortunately, there was no blood to be seen. The end result was a bruised body . . . and ego. I think the zebras in the Tshokwane area had sent a message to these zebras to take me out for what I was doing to their brethren during the capture process. Why else would they have targeted me?

Then there was the zebra mare that almost castrated me. During the zebra-capturing process with the crossbow and darts, it very seldom happened that not all the muti in the dart was delivered into the bloodstream of the darted animal or that the dart struck home in an area with slow blood circulation. These animals had the tendency to go into a drugged trance with a deliberate trotting gait with raised hoofs and short steps. The only way to stop this trotting animal was to try and get a rope across its path of movement. The rope across the animal's chest or neck, with two or three people on either side of the animal, hanging on for dear life, heels digging into the ground, was the only way to try and stop the forward momentum. This was a tug-of-war match second to none. Eventually, the zebra would be brought to a standstill. This was the ideal situation. If the bakkie and rope were too far away from the semi-drugged animal, the only way was to try and grab hold of the animal's tail.

This resulted in a tug of war of a different kind, resulting in scratch marks of all kinds, blue and purple knobs and bumps on the shins, etc. as one was dragged through shrubs and branches and over fallen tree trunks.

On one such occasion, Eduardo Livasse and I were the only ones who could get close enough to the zebra mare that had fallen into the drugged trotting gait. The other guys could not get close enough as the rope was getting tangled in the thick vegetation. I eventually could get close enough to grab hold of the mare's tail and dug in my boots. The extra resistance gave the mare further impulse, and I was thrown around like a rag doll. I had clearly underestimated the drugged status of the animal, and the animal was stronger than what I had anticipated. I, however, did not want to let go of the tail and encouraged Eduardo to catch up and assist. Eduardo eventually caught up and grabbed hold of the tail with one hand. He was just to the side of me. When the mare experienced the additional tension on her tail, she did something that I had not experienced up until then and that was totally unexpected. While jogging along, she kicked with both rear feet and caught me somewhere down below; that was very painful. Once again, a zebra caused me to fly through the air like a rag doll. In this instance, however, I was in a jackknife position. I was completely winded long before I hit the ground about 5 m back. I felt as if I had been cut in half. Eduardo was quickly at hand. 'Sorry, sorry, Mbazo.' I was completely winded and could not communicate. After I had eventually forced myself into an upright position, my first reaction was to pull down my pants and inspect the damage. It felt very painful. Fortunately, I did not see any blood or water (my bladder could have burst). With the clothing out of the way, I could only see two perfectly matched zebra hoof prints on my pelvis. I was extremely relieved that the mare had not aimed 5 cm lower because then I could have lost or damaged my crown jewels.

*   *   *

On one occasion, I had to take six zebras to the Golden Gate Highlands National Park. I don't know how many of you have been there during winter. It is a bloody cold place! The sort of place where you don't just take all your warm clothes along, but rather all the clothes you own and more. I am not shy to admit that two pairs of pantyhose that I hijacked from my girlfriend's wardrobe saved the day and night during this trip. Hendrik Thola was the appointed driver of the vehicle to Golden Gate and back. Hendrik was a remarkable old man. He had been a batman during World War II and served in North Africa and Italy. Hendrik spoke seven languages fluently. His Afrikaans was exemplary. This was the language we communicated in on the trip. Hendrik was also an elder in the Dutch Reformed Church of Africa. He was an esteemed member of his community, and I had great respect for him. On many occasions, I requested and even instructed him to call me Lynn or Mbazo. He, however, point blankly refused, and I was always addressed as 'Basie' Lynn, and that was final. The trip to Golden Gate took more than 8 hours. After Hendrik and I had laid out our family trees for one another and discussed all kinds of things, I could sense that Hendrik was beginning to take me into his confidence more. At a stage, he turned to me and said: 'Basie Lynn, there is something that bothers me and that I am very concerned about.' 'Yes, Hendrik,' I responded. 'It is better for two people to share a problem than to leave it up to one. What is it that concerns you?' Hendrik started in a roundabout way, emphasising the wonderful technological advances that the Americans had made, for example, being able to send spacecrafts into space. The original ones were called sputniks. I can remember when the Russians had launched their first sputnik; I think I had been in standard four or five (grade six or seven today), and I had been on holiday with a school friend at the Tugela River mouth on the North Coast of Natal (Kwa-Zulu Natal). What impressed Hendrik the most was that the Americans had developed the technology to bring these sputnik contraptions safely back to Earth. Within the next 2 weeks, the Americans were to launch a manned mission into space, encircle the moon, and bring the men back safely to Mother Earth. This troubled Hendrik as he was a devoted Christian and heaven (his understanding thereof) was God's domain, and he interpreted the manned spaceship as a breaching of God's holy domain. He could not accept that God would allow the desecration of His sanctum by man, and he was convinced that God would not allow the safe return of these spacemen to Earth.

Hendrik could not understand that these clever (technological) Americans could not see the stupidity (theological) of their effort. How was I going to explain this to Hendrik? Hendrik was convinced that the space mission would end in a great tragedy for man. If, on the other hand, the space mission were successful, and the spacemen were to return back safely, Hendrik's understanding of a divine God and his belief would suffer irreparable damage. We drove on in silence for quite a while, me contemplating on how I would approach the delicate subject at hand. After a long silence, Hendrik eventually asked: '*Basie* Lynn, do you agree with me?' I could not postpone any longer. 'Hendrik, it is not a question of whether I agree with you or not but rather your understanding of the issues at hand.' I had to start somewhere, and the beginning is always the best place to start. I started with Genesis and worked my way through the creation narrative (my understanding thereof). How was I going to explain the words *forever* and *eternity*? How was I going to explain how big Heaven is, that our solar system is one of millions, how big Heaven/the Universe is in reality, how far a light year is, what the speed of light is, and the fact that the sun's rays takes approximately 8 minutes to reach Earth, etc., etc.? I used all the above examples to explain to Hendrik that we have an all-knowing, omnipresent, and Almighty God for whom nothing is impossible. This Almighty God, who nurtures every flower in the veldt and looks after the smallest bird, is always in control, and nothing happens without His knowledge. The fact that Hendrik and I were on our way to Golden Gate to deliver zebras was his doing. The fact that Hendrik and I were discussing God was his will. God is always with and amongst us here on Earth. He doesn't stay in heaven. His throne might be up there somewhere, but he works with and amongst us here on Earth. The one thing we as human beings must never do is try and hem God in because we cannot fathom the greatness of God with our limited human brain.

'Hendrik, did you listen and understand what I was trying to share with you?' I asked him whether there were other issues that he was doubtful about or did not understand. Hendrik nodded his head in agreement to having a better understanding of most of the things I had shared with him. I again wanted to know: 'Do you still want to know whether I agree with your previous statements?' Hendrik remained silent for a very long time without answering, and I did not wish to discuss these sensitive issues with Hendrik any further. I concluded our discussion by saying to Hendrik, 'You must please promise me one thing. If the Americans do go to the moon and come back safely to Earth and because of this you start doubting the existence of God, we must have another discussion.' Hendrik promised me he would, and we travelled on in silence for quite a while.

Hendrik never reopened this specific discussion even though we had many other informative discussions regarding other matters. I, therefore, deducted that Hendrik had found acceptance and that my small input had contributed to this. Until Hendrik went on pension, he remained an elder in the Dutch Reformed Church of Africa.

*   *   *

During the early winter of 1969, we received instructions to capture two young hippopotami (approximately 2 years old), a male and female, for the Addo Elephant National Park. There was only one old bull left in the Ceaser dam at Addo. In between all the zebra capturing, we started building a hippo-holding facility at Tshokwane. Up until then, nobody had any experience or knowledge as to what was required to successfully keep hippos (even small ones) in captivity for more than a month. The State Veterinarian at Skukuza insisted that the hippos would have to remain in captivity for at least a month in quarantine for fear that the hippos might spread the foot-and-mouth virus from the KNP (foot-and-mouth endemic area) to Addo. After the quarantine period of a month, throat samples were to be taken for analysis at the Onderstepoort Veterinarian Research facility in Pretoria. If the test results were negative, the hippos could then be relocated to Addo.

The hippo-holding facility had to have a dam that was deep enough for the hippos to submerge themselves in. The dam also had to be drained and cleaned regularly because hippos don't have any sense of decency and defecate in the water. In order to clean the dam in safety, the hippos needed to have a feeding area that could be closed off from the rest of the facility. The holding facility also had to have an offloading and loading ramp. I also made provisions for a platform/walkway over the top of the facility to be able to persuade the hippos in a direction by means of long, light poles. It took just over a month to complete the hippo-holding facility. Would it, however, with human planning and insight, work for hippos? Only time would tell. I personally have a very high regard for hippos, especially if they are out of the water. Hippos feel very safe and at ease when they are in water, and one can approach them with relative safety. During the hippo capturing, we as humans would have to venture into this safe environment. There was no way that a hippo could be captured chemically on dry land with the aid of the crossbow. How could we solve this problem? After a long brainstorming session, it was decided to make use of graders. The person who would be doing the darting, the grader operator, and somebody with a heavy-calibre rifle to ensure our safety would be the only people on the grader.

The hippo pools in the Olifants River that were identified for the capture project were relatively small and shallow – or so we thought. The plan was for the grader to slowly drive into the water to get the hippos moving and to herd them towards the shallow water, to identify a young hippo of the right size to dart. Selecting the sex of the young hippo was potluck. When, after successful darting, the hippo was sedated, it would have to be coaxed to shallower water where it would be roped around the neck to prevent it from drowning. It all sounds very easy, doesn't it? If one intervened too early, the hippo might still have enough savvy to attack to defend itself. If one were to leave it too late, the real danger of the hippo drowning came in to play.

The first hippo to show its head above the water to take a breather appeared to be of the correct age group. I had to take quick aim and fired and in passing had to make adjustments for the distance. There was no time to determine exact distances. The dart struck home in the thick skin just behind the ear. The first signs of intoxication began showing after 3 minutes. The capture process went according to plan. The female calf was, however, too small and too young. The young calf was given the correct antidote and was reunited with the rest of the herd in no time. We fortunately now had a measure to use to select the right size/age group. We again started the whole process. This time around, I had to hit a quick-moving target when the grader operator pushed the herd into shallow water. The dart struck home high up on the shoulder, and the drug quickly showed its effect. In anticipation, the ground crew came nearer as the 'muti' took effect, to prevent the darted hippo from drowning. The herd bull, however, had the same intensions and charged out of the water directly at the advancing ground crew. Consternation broke loose. The ground crew turned on their heels and headed for the safety of the vehicles which were about 50 m away. The herd bull followed in full pursuit, with its wide mouth gaping open. The large-calibre rifle which was supposed to provide safety could not be fired as the charging hippo bull and retreating ground crew were all in direct line of fire. The ground crew fortunately reached the vehicles in time. The crew entered the vehicles from the side, the back, and even the top. The bull stopped charging about 5 m from the closest vehicle and turned back towards the relative safety of the water, its big jaws still flapping. After all of us had come to our senses, we remembered that there was a darted hippo in the water busy drowning, and we focused our attention on that. Fortunately for us, there was a length of rope on the grader, and seeing that the ground crew were not very eager to leave the safety of the vehicles, the grader team had to do the best they could. After the third attempt, we successfully secured the rope around the young hippo, and slowly but surely, the grader managed to pull it to shallow water and safety.

After lots of gentle persuasion, the ground crew were persuaded to leave the safety of the vehicle to come and assist us on the condition that the grader was positioned between themselves and the herd of hippos that were now in the safety of deeper water. The young hippo was a female and of the right age group. The hippo crate which had been specially made was brought closer while the youngster was injected with the correct long-term antibiotics. With all the helping hands, the young hippo was safely crated and loaded onto the back of the bakkie. I left for Tshokwane late that afternoon with the precious cargo on board. Fortunately, there was a fair amount of moonlight, so we could offload the hippo safely into its new enclosure.

We grabbed a couple of hours' sleep, and very early the next morning, we were on our way back to the hippo pools in the Olifants River. Seeing that we could not identify another suitable hippo in the hippo pool we had used the previous day, we moved on to a hippo pool upstream where we identified a hippo of similar size to the previous one. The grader and ground crews sorted out their equipment, and the next capturing attempt commenced. There were no rocky ridges or rocky plates near this hippo pool, which created the impression that the pool was quite shallow and well suited for the purpose at hand. The grader crew gingerly moved into the water, and the hippo herd became suspicious and started grunting and snorting at the grader invading their territory. I spotted the hippo we were looking for. I couldn't get an open shot. The young hippo was hidden behind the big cow and just showed its head above water to take a big gulp of air. At my request, the grader operator went deeper into the water to force the hippo herd to shallower water. The front wheels of the grader became submerged in the water and kept on sinking. I gesticulated to the grader operator to stop and reverse. Something just didn't seem kosher to me. Alas, it was all in vain. It was too late! With the grader in reverse gear, the rear tandem wheels just kept spinning, and the grader slowly kept sinking into the water. Trying to go forward was also not an option. The grader slowly sunk deeper into the water. At first, we all thought that it was a big joke being stuck in a hippo pool on a grader. The mood quickly changed as the grader gradually sank deeper and deeper into whatever was underneath. As the water level rose up to about 30 cm below the grader's cabin, emergency evacuation plans were made. There was no boat available, and it took all our efforts to get a rope from the land crew to the crew that were stranded on what was left of the grader above water. In the mean time, the hippo herd was sharing the same pool with us. The rope was tightly secured over the top of the cabin of the grader, and the other end was tied to a vehicle on the bank and pulled tight. Now we had a 'foefie' slide without the slide. One by one, the grader team abandoned the grader with all the valuables strapped to our bodies. Upside down and hand over hand, like lemurs, we slowly proceeded one by one to the eager hands of the land crew which helped us to safety. Looking back, we saw the grader continuing its downwards movement into the quagmire below. When the water level had risen (it sounds better than to say the grader sank deeper) to the point that only the yellow hood of the cabin was visible, everything came to rest. What now? We had one hippo in the holding facility, but we also had one drowned grader, one very agitated Roads Dept. Foreman who did not want to lend us another grader after the drowned grader had been recovered, one very angry Workshop Foreman who had to strip the drowned grader to drain all the water from its innards, and one very grumpy Financial Manager who had to motivate and release funds to pay for the mess. All these problems in exchange for just one very young female hippo in the holding facility. After a couple of days, when the dust had settled and all the frayed egos had been soothed, the second hippo project began on the condition that all the necessary guarantees and precautions were strictly adhered to. In this line of business, there are no guarantees.

The capturing of the second young hippo went without a hitch, and soon, the young male hippo was on its way to Tshokwane. The two strangers adapted well to one another. The conditioning ability of the two hippos surprised me. During the first two attempts that we had to drain the dam to clean it, we had to coax the hippos into the crush pen with long sticks and then rewarded them with lucerne. After that, as soon as the water started draining from the dam, the two hippos would walk out of the dam and straight to the crush pen to be rewarded with lucerne while the dam and the boma were being cleaned. This process was diligently adhered to for the rest of the quarantine period. After a month, the State Veterinarian arrived to dart and immobilise the hippos. Small containers attached to the end of a flexible iron rod were inserted into the mouths of the hippos and shoved up and down the throat to collect throat samples from each hippo. These throat samples were packed in coolers with ice, to be transported to the Onderstepoort Research Facility to be tested for foot-and-mouth virus. After a week, the results were received, and because the results were negative, we could finalise the planning to transport the two hippos to the Addo Elephant National Park. It was crucially important with the loading of the hippos into the crates and onto the bakkies that the hippos were loaded in the crate back-to-front, with their backsides facing towards the cabin of the vehicle. The impact during emergency stopping would be far greater than during acceleration. During braking, the hippos' rear ends would absorb the impact and not their heads.

Two other colleagues plus the State Vet and I would take the hippos to Addo in two separate vehicles, each loaded with a hippo crate. The trip was planned to commence late in the afternoon and would continue through the cool of the evening and into the cool early morning of the next day. Close on every 2 hours, we stopped to take in petrol and to wet the hippos with water. The whole trip was uneventful and went very well. As the vehicles started moving after each stop, the hippos would lie down on the crate floor. The Park Manager and his staff eagerly awaited our arrival at Addo. We immediately set off for Ceaser dam. The bakkies were parked with the backsides towards the water. The crates were offloaded by many eager hands, the heads of the hippos facing the water approximately 10 m from the water's edge. After all the inquisitive bystanders were safely hidden away, the crate doors were simultaneously opened, and with a little encouragement, the two hippos walked out straight into Ceaser dam, their new home, away from home. We were only then informed that there was a lone hippo bull in the dam. 'Trouble!' flashed through my mind. The bull was most probably still out grazing when the two youngsters had been offloaded. The Park Manager convinced us to give the docile and very friendly bull a chance to adopt the two newcomers into his domain. After the long trip, we fortunately decided to sleep over at Addo and commence our journey back early the next morning. The following morning, before coffee time, we were informed that the young male had been seen outside the park boundary. The big, docile, and very friendly bull had in all probability chased it out of the dam and park. The State Vet and I immediately started tracking the young bull, and we found it on the boundary fence, trying to re-enter the park. Fortunately for us, there was a dart gun and darts at Addo. We quickly loaded two darts. In less than half an hour, the youngster was again crated and on its way back to the Ceaser dam. In the meantime, our other two colleagues fetched the Park Manager's .375 rifle, had a couple of practise shots, and returned to the Ceaser dam to get rid of the big, docile, very friendly bull. A single well-placed shot was sufficient to dispose of the big bull.

When a hippo is killed by rifle or any other means, the carcass immediately disappears/sinks into the water. After a while, the fermentation process in the stomach releases gases that accumulate and make the carcass buoyant to the point that it rises above the water level and can easily be retrieved. The big bull was skinned and the meat distributed to the locals. The young bull was released back into the safety of the Ceaser dam. The following morning, we returned to Skukuza with everything calm and peaceful at Addo.

*   *   *

I have always been very meticulous about personal/physical and mental fitness. I, however, have never been fanatical about it. I have always been of the opinion that the human body, as we know it, wasn't designed to run 100 km, to swim 20 km in arctic waters, to lift 200 kg above one's head, etc., etc. If a human being was not capable of getting safely away from

68

danger threatening it within 1 to 6 km, one would have to succumb to the law of nature: Survival of the fittest. This implied that any animal/human being had to be clever enough, agile enough, strong enough, etc. to be able to survive.

Due to the nature of my work and my participation in various forms of sports, I had to be reasonably fit mentally and physically to be able to enjoy these. I had been crazy about any form of sports from a very young age. Rugby and cricket were very high on my priority list. In my heyday, we didn't have gymnasiums or personal trainers. Rugby practises at school focused mainly on ball skills, and afterwards, it was left up to the individual's own devises and commitment to get fit. We fortunately stayed next to the Greytown Golf Course, so I had a very good exercising field at my disposal with uphill and downhill fairways where I could do speed and stamina exercises. Next to our house was a black wattle plantation where I did sidestep and evasive exercises by running as fast as I could in between two rows of wattle trees, trying to dodge all the branches growing into the clearing. These exercises especially favoured rugby, cricket, and athletics. I was very proud of my rugby achievements. I represented Pietermarizburg Schools U13 team as a lock forward. My biggest accolade was when I scored a try, in the south-western corner of the rugby field at Kings Park Stadium in Durban, against Durban Schools U13 team. Eight of my teammates went to school at Pietermaritzburg College. When I was 14 years of age, I represented Maritzburg Schools U15 team for the first time, this time as eighth man. During my second year playing for the U15 team, almost all the members of the old U13 team were re-elected for Maritzburg Schools, including the eight members from Maritzburg College.

By the time I had reached standard nine (grade eleven), I had already been concussed six times while playing rugby. My parents then deemed it wise to take me to a brain specialist in Durban for a professional opinion regarding my injuries. Two weeks prior to the Natal Schools rugby trials, the brain specialist advised us that continued concussion could lead to epileptic seizures and therefore advised me not to continue playing rugby. To add insult to injury, all eight the Maritzburg College guys plus three others who had played in the Maritzburg Schools team with me were all selected to represent Natal Schools. Could/would I have made it? Who will ever know? I quickly came to terms with this disappointment and turned my attention to different sporting activities. In later years, at Stellenbosch University, I again secretly (without my parents' knowledge) played rugby for the Helderberg Hostel's third and fourth teams until I again landed up in hospital with a concussion. That was the end of my rugby-playing days.

During my stay in the KNP as Game Capturer and later as Section and Regional Ranger and even later as Head of Nature Conservation at Skukuza, I continued jogging and took part in sporting activities. I am sharing this with you as it is my intention to get around to telling you about the most exhilarating and enjoyable times I spent in the KNP bush. Many people might be shocked by me unveiling these deep and dark secrets. It is their choice.

About 500 m from the caravan, at Tshokwane, an elephant footpath started/ended at a waterhole in the Munywini Spruit. From this waterhole, the elephant path weaved its way through the bush in a south-westerly direction. This was my favourite jogging route while staying at Tshokwane. From the caravan, I would jog to the waterhole and then follow the elephant path for another 4 km into the bush, turn around, and go back to the waterhole and caravan, a distance of approximately 9 km. Initially, when I went jogging, I took the .38 Smith & Wesson revolver along for my personal protection, which I wrapped in a small towel to protect it against perspiration. The solitude and remoteness of this chosen jogging route made a big impression on me.

On a specific beautiful early spring afternoon, again challenging the elephant path from the Munywini spruit, I impulsively stopped near the waterhole and took off my T-shirt and jogging shorts and hid the wrapped revolver in a bush and jogged further in my birthday suit (not completely though as I did keep my socks and jogging shoes on). What an exhilarating and carefree feeling, something to experience! I was so touched by the complete feeling of freedom and oneness with nature that I took a conscious decision that whenever and wherever I could, I would enjoy nature in this way. To my knowledge nobody, ever knew about these birthday-suit escapades of mine. This made my enjoyment of these escapades even more special. Every time I relived these joyous, satisfying moments, I knew that these were more than skin-deep.

On one of my jogging sessions, I took Bakkies, my boxer dog, along. Very near to the normal turnaround point, Bakkies decided to chase a lone Blue wildebeest bull. No amount of whistling and shouting deterred him from his mission. Approximately 200 m from where I stood, the Blue wildebeest bull summed up the situation and decided that the threat was not as bad as a lion or leopard. It tuned on its heels, and before Bakkies could realise it, the pursuer was now the pursuant, and Bakkies fled rather than face the sharp end of the bull. Unfortunately for me, the dog ran straight back to its owner, with the bull breathing down its backside with the occasional gaff at the dog with its horns. I could see trouble coming and looked for a weapon to defend myself. The only immediate available one was a piece of termite-eaten Knob-thorn branch. By the time I had armed myself with the branch, Bakkies was about 50 m away, and the wildebeest focused and honed in on him. It didn't even notice me. Fortunately, Bakkies didn't stop where I was standing and rushed past. I stood next to the elephant footpath with every muscle tensed and ready for the pursuer. My double-handed forearm came into good use when the wildebeest was about 2 m from me. The site of impact was right in front of me, and the point of impact with the termite branch was between the bull's eyes and the horn boss. On impact, the branch splintered into pieces of bark, soil, and termites, and the bull lost its focus on Bakkies and veered off the path into the veldt. Just after impact, I got the impression that the bull had looked me straight in the eye and had taken my number for future reference.

*   *   *

My first couple of years in the KNP were very special and made a very big impression on me. I had found my niche in life! As part of their leave allocation, KNP staff were entitled to one day of 'occasional' leave per month to go to town to do shopping, cut their hair, service their private vehicles, visit the dentist, etc., etc. Normal things that city dwellers normally do on their way to or from work, during normal working hours. The closest town from Tshokwane was Nelspruit, just 200 km around the corner one way. During my first 2 years at Tshokwane, I didn't even go to town once.

I also very quickly realised that if I wanted to make progress in the KNP structure and climb the corporate ladder, I would need to acquire some sort of formal qualification. I started putting out feelers to academic institutions. I was not interested in part-time studies as I was convinced that one would not be able to give 100 per cent of oneself in the work environment while studying part-time. My best option was to return to the University of Stellenbosch that was prepared to give me exemption for the Engineering subjects that I had already acquired, namely: Mathematics, Applied Mathematics, Physics, and Chemistry. In reality, I would only have to pass Zoology and Botany for 3 years to satisfy the academic requirements for a BSc degree.

This all sounds easy, doesn't it? However, for someone who had not studied Biology at school to be thrown into the deep end with Zoology and Botany at University level was no mean feat. Once back at Stellenbosch, I also attended Geography, Geology, and Statistics lectures for good measure. I eventually obtained a BSc degree, majoring in Zoology and Geology. I enjoyed Geology and found it very interesting. The natural geological environment was the practical proof of the contents of the textbook. Zoology and Botany, on the other hand, were a pain in the neck. At Stellenbosch, these two study directions were focused on an understanding of the evolutionary theory, and there was no reference to ecological studies. I just had to grin and bear it.

At one stage, during a third-year Botany class, we were being exposed to the chemical processes that take place during photosynthesis in plants. Even students who studied Chemistry III found difficulty in grasping what the professor was trying to convey to us. I got up from my desk, closed my books, walked up to the professor, and informed him that if what he was trying to teach us was Botany, he could keep it, and I walked out of the lecture room, never to return. Fortunately, I only required Botany at second-year level to obtain my degree.

I was not designed to sit on my backside for 80 per cent of the day in lecture halls or behind my desk at residence. To be able to cope with student life (they were most definitely not the happiest days of my life), I kept myself fit both physically and mentally by jogging along the mountain route at Stellenbosch on Mondays and Wednesdays (8 km), attending rugby practice on Tuesday and Thursday, and playing rugby for the third team on Friday and the fourth team on Saturday. If it had not been for this fitness routine, I would most probably have thrown in the towel and discontinued my studies.

One Tuesday afternoon, we were kept very late at a Botany practical, to the extent that it was encroaching on our rugby practice time. After the practical, I jumped onto my bicycle, intent on winning back some lost time. At the end of the main street in Stellenbosch, there was a traffic circle to smooth traffic flow. On this specific day, there were about eight vehicles queued up before the circle, awaiting their turn to enter the circle. Between these waiting cars and the cars parked parallel along the road, there was a gap just big enough to accommodate my bicycle. I negotiated this gap at speed so as to waste no time. Halfway into the circle, a plump, elderly Coloured lady stepped out in front of me without looking. There was no space to manoeuvre, and I rode straight into the old lady, at speed, sending her flying through the air. The impact sent my bicycle into the rear end of an Austin 1100. I flew over the handlebars, holding my left hand over my face for protection. On impact, the rear window of the vehicle shattered, and I had a slight cut on the palm of my left hand. I dragged the bicycle with its buckled front wheel to the side of the pavement and ran back to attend to the old lady. I saw a young Coloured man trying to revive the old lady. She came to and was helped to her feet. 'What happened to Auntie?' inquired the concerned young man. 'I don't quite know, but I think a vehicle hit me and raced away!' This was my queue to make myself scarce. I pushed my bicycle back to the residence along the pavement as inconspicuously as the buckled front wheel would allow. Not another word was heard about the hit-and-run accident.

On another occasion, something similar happened. I was on my way back to the residence again on my bike at great speed. There was a slight drizzle, and the road surface was wet. Everybody who knows Stellenbosch will also know of the deep water furrows between the driving surface and the pavement on either side of the roads, supplying irrigation water to the various yards. In front of the entrance to each building, there was a small concrete bridge across the furrow to allow easy excess to the building. The well-known Dorp Street in Stellenbosch was to be the battlefield on this occasion. From the lecture halls, Dorp Street was mainly downhill towards the residence. On this specific day, I was on my way to the residence down Dorp Street as fast as a bicycle could carry me. Nearing one of the T-junctions into Dorp Street, I saw the driver of a vehicle stopped at the junction. He looked up and down Dorp Street for any approaching vehicles. I saw a vehicle coming up Dorp Street towards us. I don't know whether the T-junction vehicle saw me approaching or not. This vehicle decided to turn into Dorp Street before the other vehicle could get to the T-junction. He was most probably in a hurry. He had obviously misjudged the speed of the oncoming vehicle. This vehicle was also in a hurry. Now there were three people in a hurry on a collision course. The one on the bicycle would most definitely come off second best. The T-junction vehicle's wheels started spinning on the wet surface. Turning into Dorp Street, the rear end of the vehicle slid to my side and blocked my passage. The two vehicles fortunately missed one another, and my only option, to avoid the T-junction vehicle was to veer off into the irrigation furrow next to the road. When I looked up, I saw a concrete bridge across the furrow about 15 m ahead. Braking on the slimy surface of the furrow was out of the question. Emergency situations require fast and decisive decisions. Within a split second, my plan was formulated and applied. I immediately jumped off the bicycle at that speed and with long strides kept pace with it until it struck the bridge. It somersaulted over the bridge and landed on the pavement. I carried on for another 10 m or so before stopping. I didn't stop immediately as I had no intention of tearing a muscle or something. At this stage, the two vehicles were too far away to curse. It wouldn't have served any purpose anyway.

This was the second buckled front-wheel rim that I had to replace in less than a year. My risk status was too high, and they didn't want to extend the insurance policy on my bicycle.

*   *   *

That is enough about my student days. I graduated at the beginning of December 1972. With great joy and excitement, I headed back north and more specifically back to the KNP. Before leaving for Stellenbosch, the following conditions for the next 3 years were agreed to by Skukuza Management and me. I would spend all my university vocational leave in the KNP where I would work wherever I was required. Oom Don Louw, the Chief Ranger at the time, was going on pension as from 31 December 1972, and I would be reappointed to the KNP staff as from

January 1973 on the condition that I graduated during December 1972. I had kept my side of the bargain, and KNP Management reciprocated, and they appointed me as Section Ranger at Shangoni as from January 1973. (My personnel number for the rest of my SANParks career was 73003, indicating that I was the third appointee into SANParks during 1973.)

Mike English, the incumbent Section Ranger at Shangoni, was being transferred to the newly created post of Section Ranger at Pafuri. The Pafuri Section came into being after long negotiations with the Makuleke community that had occupied the land between the Limpopo and Luvuvhu Rivers. The Makuleke community was compensated with bigger and better agricultural land to the west of the Shangoni Section which comprised approximately 2,500 hectares of the KNP plus some adjoining state land.

All our personal belongings could fit into one room of the massive Section Ranger's house. The garden in the front of the house had a typical English garden layout with many well-defined flowerbeds with quite a few exotic plants. Whenever time allowed, all the exotics were removed, the flowerbeds were systematically removed, soil was imported, and lawn was planted. I preferred a natural landscaped garden with lawn from the house extending down to the indigenous trees at the bottom of the garden with some flowerbeds along the border which were demarcated with weathered leadwood stumps.

We had a very enjoyable stay at Shangoni, and my mentor during this time was Sergeant Manuel Kubai. With Manuel at my side, I got to know and discover the Shangoni Section. My first priority as Section Ranger was to get to know the whole section. The names of all the drainage lines, springs, natural pans, pickets, and windmill locations had to be memorised. Fortunately, the KNP had very detailed maps available that greatly helped with this learning process. Manuel was one of the old guards, a true gentleman of Mozambiquen descent with knowledge of the veldt second to none. The other well-known/notorious Field Ranger was 'Two-boy' Maluleke. 'Two-boy' was the nickname that he had earned as a very crafty poacher in these areas. He always bragged that 'one boy' could never catch him and that it would take at least 'two boys' to catch him. Mike English and his Field Rangers did, however, catch Two-boy red-handed when he was removing an Impala from a snare he had set. Two-boy was found guilty and sentenced to imprisonment. After having served his jail sentence, he came to Mike English and begged him for a job as Field Ranger. Mike was very sceptical at first but decided to give him a chance. After all, the saying goes, it takes a thief to catch a thief, and maybe Two-boy would be a very good poacher catcher.

It was an eye opener to go on patrol with Two-boy in search of snares. He moved through the veldt like a phantom and never left a spoor behind. On several occasions, we would leave Shangoni at about 03.00 to take up ambush positions at fresh snares that had been discovered along the Shingwedzi River the previous afternoon by the Field Rangers. More often than not, we made successful arrests, and on occasion, the poachers would come in with dogs that would warn the poachers of our presence. This necessitated us shooting as many dogs as possible, thereby putting the poachers out of commission for a while. To try and catch poachers on foot was a futile exercise. They would scatter in all directions, covering the ground like well-trained athletes.

*   *   *

While at Shangoni, I made acquaintance with Oom Jim Meiring, a drill contractor who was contracted by the KNP Management to drill for water for game boreholes at strategic locations. What Oom Jim didn't know about air compression drills wasn't worth knowing. He was a true master of his trade. With my newfound Geological knowledge, I spent hours and hours with Oom Jim at his drilling sites. He had to explain ad nauseam what he was doing and why. What kind of rock chips came out of the borehole? Rock/chip samples were taken at every meter and were analysed and discussed at length – knowledge that later on was of great value to me. He did not believe/use any of the more popular controversial water-divining methods like divining sticks, bottles, wires, etc. He believed that the natural environment would indicate the sighting of the borehole. Oom Jim was very competent, and his divining method was very successful. My learning/apprenticeship with Oom Jim with all his fountain of knowledge and experience stood me in very good stead later on. Oom Jim suffered from very low blood pressure, and his wife Tant (Aunt) Ellie believed in grated raw potatoes, which Oom Jim had to eat spoonfuls of on a daily basis. It must have worked because Oom Jim spent many healthy years drilling in the KNP.

*　　*　　*

On one occasion, I received an instruction from Oom Johan, who was still the District Ranger at Punda Maria, to build a release facility for sable antelopes at the windmill at 'Awie se Dam'. We chopped down 5-m Mopani poles and cut reeds along the Shingwedzi River. The release facility was approximately 70 m long and 40 m wide and narrowed in an egg shape towards the one end where the loading and release facility was placed. The poles were planted 5 m apart and were connected with four strands of steel wire, 1 m apart. Four rows of reeds were tied to these wires to provide a non-transparent shield. The Sable antelopes were darted at the N'waxitshumbe camp and transported to the Awie se Dam release facility one at a time. The capture and translocation operation went without any hitches. Fifteen animals were relocated in this manner and held in the release facility for a week. At one stage, lions tried to cause problems but were quickly chased away. After the bonding period of a week, the Sable antelopes were successfully released.

The only incident worth mentioning was the paranoia of the time. A couple of incidents had occurred in the Eastern Transvaal (now Mpumalanga province) and on the Limpopo border of Northern Transvaal (now Limpopo province) where vehicles had detonated landmines. In the KNP, we were also well aware of the possibility that something similar could happen in the KNP. During the dusky period just after sunset, two of our colleagues were on their way from N'waxitshumbe to Awie se Dam. Somewhere between nowhere and somewhere, the rear tyre of the vehicle burst, and both colleagues were convinced that their time had come. Later on when the story was retold, we could not really determine who had spoken in tongues the most and who had begged for forgiveness the most. Whenever one spoke to them individually, it was always the other one who was guilty.

*　　*　　*

On an occasion, I had the opportunity to canoe in the Shingwedzi River on a borrowed rubber canoe without encountering any crocodile or hippo in any of the waterholes along the way. During the same time, I also canoed on the Wik-en-Weeg Dam in the Phugwane River. A big Leadwood tree, half submerged, stood to one side in the dam. In the lower branches of the tree, about 2 m above the water level, there was a very large Hamerkop's nest with the opening protruding at an angle towards the water from the bottom of the nest. Being inquisitive, I, of course, had to go and investigate. Rowing closer to the nest, I kept reminding myself of stories I'd heard, that some snakes – especially Black mamba – often took refuge in these nests. I had already come too far to turn around now because of some old wives' tale. The closer I got, the more nervous I became and began to believe that there might be some truth in the old folktale and began expecting a big snake to come out and attack me. When the tension was at its maximum, and I was close to the opening of the nest, a Hamerkop flew out of the opening, brushing my face as it flew by. My reaction was so extreme and uncontrolled that I managed to capsize the canoe in an effort to escape. Realising my new predicament of possibly being taken by a crocodile from below did not help matters. I quickly turned the canoe over and clambered on board.

During this time, our parents came to visit us at Shangoni to check if we had settled in properly. The recently completed Maxokwe Dam in the spruit with the same name became full and overflowed. My dad was very apprehensive and sceptical about large expanses of water, and I had my hands full convincing him to join me on a canoe trip on the dam. The dam was safe as it had only been full for just under a week, and there was no way that either crocodiles or hippos could have discovered it and moved in. I very carefully launched the canoe with my nervous dad on board into the shallow water of the dam and then also climbed on board. The deeper we moved into the dam, the whiter my dad's knuckles became as his grip on the canoe intensified. All my encouragement came to naught. Then we heard and felt a scraping sound at the bottom of the canoe. Did I mention that it was an inflatable canoe? Dad lifted himself off the bottom of the canoe in unison with the scraping sound. I was still busy explaining to Dad that the scraping sound was probably made by submerged branches of a tree when a hippo raised its head approximately 30 m from us and with a snort announced that it had taken up residence in the dam.

'You rascal, you lied to me!' Dad shouted at me. If we were on dry land, he most probably would have physically attacked me. For the present, however, I was safe as he would not let go of the side of the canoe for anything in the world.

'Row, row!' he instructed with big eyes and with his head pointing towards the side of the dam. All my explanations were of no avail to convince him that I had not especially ordered the hippo to give him a fright. After the stress levels had improved, I volunteered to take my mom for a spin or rather row. Dad, however, was having none of that.

*   *   *

I was on a foot patrol along the Shingwedzi River one day, visiting all the waterholes, checking on the game activities at them. It was a very hot summer's day, so the game was seeking refuge in the shade of the riverside bush. Even the birdsong was dampened. I encountered quite a number of crocodiles and hippos sunning themselves on available sandbanks. Fortunately, I did not encounter any large predators. Whenever I went on foot patrols by myself, it was my custom not to carry a firearm for protection. I was firmly of the belief that if one wanted to experience the bush intensely, one needed to use all one's senses in order to avoid dangerous confrontations with game. Most of my colleagues, however, carried rifles and inadvertently found themselves in situations where they had to fire warning shots to get them out of trouble. I very seldom, if ever, got into these situations as my safety depended on reading the natural environmental conditions and a well-developed observation ability that I developed over time. During the above-mentioned foot patrol, I was again at peace with the bush. At a fair distance, I became aware of a deep rumbling sound made by a very restful and contend elephant. I very stealthily moved forward and came upon the most magnificent elephant bull that I had ever had the privilege of meeting. The bull itself was not very big, but the two tusks were special. The bull was seeking comfort from the intense midday heat. The mud-and-water bath was just what the bull ordered. I watched the bull for a time and enjoyed its magnificence. Whenever the bull took a breather, the two symmetrical tusks would be planted on the ground to support the weight of the head. I got the impression that it was an effort for the bull to raise the tusks off the ground in order to walk. When the elephant had finished bathing, it walked to the closest bank of the river but could not exit the riverbed as the embankment was too steep to negotiate with the long tusks digging into the embankment. The bull then moved further down the riverbed, looking for an embankment that was less steep. It finally arrived at a rift in the river that protected the riverbanks against natural erosion. At this point, the gradient of the riverbank was approximately 10°, and with difficulty, it managed to negotiate the riverbank until it got onto the level ground next to the river. I enjoyed this magnificent natural phenomenon to the utmost.

In later years, one of the elephant researchers involved with the annual helicopter elephant census decided to photograph the big tuskers in the KNP to identify the so-called Magnificent Seven and to make them world-famous. The wonderful specimen that I had encountered along the Shingwedzi River was one of the seven. This bull was named 'Mafunyane', named after a windmill at a drinking hole in the Bububu Spruit which was a tributary of the Shingwedzi River. This is where the elephant was photographed for the first time from the air. The name Mafunyane was derived from the nickname of one of the old Park Managers, Mr L. B. Steyn, who had worked in the KNP from 1954 to 1961. When he had been the Section Ranger at Shangoni, he had built a little drinking dam in the Bububu Spruit near the present windmill. The borehole and windmill only later came into being. The original literal meaning of his name was derived from 'he who is a glutinous eater' or in Tsonga to funyafunya (the Tsonga language) (From: *Place Names in the Kruger National Park* by J. J. Kloppers).

*   *   *

As Section Ranger, the word *routine* did not exist in my vocabulary. One day was never the same as the other . . . wonderful. The only little bit of routine that there was consisted of a end-of-the-month visit to Punda Maria to submit monthly reports, to receive the monthly salaries of the workers from Skukuza, and to collect dry rations for the month. This was normally a social outing for the workers. They did their private purchases and met with colleagues from other Ranger Stations.

We also socialised with Oom Johan and his wife Pat to catch up on the latest news that had reached Punda Maria by road from Shingwedzi, Letaba, and Skukuza. During the hot and rainy season, from September to April, the northern half of the KNP, from the Letaba River northwards, was closed to tourism for fear of malaria. It was during one of these visits that Oom Johan and I discussed the possibility of me furthering my studies. 'You must not wait too long before tackling your Honours degree,' Oom

Johan warned. 'One can become very complacent and lazy as time goes by and lose one's aptitude for such things.' He instructed me to submit a request to further my studies to him as the District Ranger of the area. He would then add his own motivation and forward it to Skukuza.

The whole issue slipped my mind until September 1974 when we were again at Punda Maria for the routine end-of-the-month visitation. Oom Johan summoned me to his office and handed me a sealed letter. The letter was from Head Office Pretoria and more specifically from the Office of the Chief Executive Director of the National Parks Board. One always notices these things before reading the contents of the letter. My first thought was, 'Oh no, what have I done?' While reading the letter, I could feel the blood draining from my face. 'What is wrong? You look as if you have seen a ghost,' Oom Johan commented.

'Oom Johan, the Board has approved my request to study for my Honours degree in Wildlife Management in Pretoria next year (1975), and I don't have to resign. The Board has granted me fully paid study leave!' I was short of breath and gulping for air after Oom Johan slapped me on the back to congratulate me.

There were now a thousand and one things to do and organise before January 1975. The Wildlife Honours lectures were to commence at the beginning of February 1975 at the Zoology Faculty of the University of Pretoria. During the whole of December 1974 and January 1975, I was preparing for an admission exam that one had to successfully pass for admission. Four of us came from conservation jobs with at least 4 years' experience. The other two students came straight from university. I personally spent a very pleasant year at the University of Pretoria. We learnt a lot from one another and gained a better perspective of Conservation Management as to what we had been exposed to in our working environment. The head of the Faculty of Wildlife Management had recently returned from completing his PhD studies in the United States of America, and even though I have to say so, us 'old hands' managed to teach the Professor a few things as well. The practical excursions, accompanied by the Botany honours students to the KNP and the Natal Parks were very pleasant and educational. At the end of November 1975, we put the graduation ceremony behind us, and I was transferred directly to Tshokwane as District Ranger.

*   *   *

Before going to Pretoria, I was the first Section Ranger, since Jock of the Bushveld era, to acquire a Staffordshire Bullterrier (or staffie for short); I named mine Bieta (according to the Shangaans, the name is derived from the brindle colour of the dog). Bieta was approximately 6 months old when he accompanied us to Pretoria. Staffies have a very docile nature and are usually very forgiving towards children. Pulling their ears or tail or even sitting on them did not make them agitated. On the other hand, they could become very aggressive when antagonised. Every afternoon after lectures, Bieta and I would relax on the lawn under the big pine trees surrounding the complex where we lived. On one occasion, while playing on the lawn, a fully grown Alsatian trotted onto the lawn area from one side and sniffed or lifted its leg against every tree as dogs do to mark their territory. At first, Bieta did not notice the visitor. However, when he saw the visitor, he went over to greet the dog with a friendly wagging tail as a good host should. The uneducated city slicker, however, grabbed hold of Bieta and bowled him over. Bieta was a young dog and did not want to confront the guest and so ran back to where I was sitting, with tail between the legs. When Bieta arrived back, I turned his sharp end towards the intruder and with a slap on the buttocks said, 'Vat hom!' (Get him). Bieta shot forward like an arrow that had just been released from a bow, straight to the Alsatian, and bowled it over, with the Alsatian's fur flying in all directions. In two ticks, the Alsatian departed from the scene as fast as its legs could carry it to where it had initially come from uninvited. I wish you could have seen the look of satisfaction and achievement and Bieta's body language when he came back to me. 'Well done,' I praised Bieta and rubbed his head. It looked as if Bieta had two tails to wag.

*   *   *

Seeing that we lived in relative solitude in the bush at Shangoni and that we were now temporarily staying in Pretoria, I took the opportunity to go and watch the Blue Bulls playing rugby against the Western Province at Loftus Versveld. I wasn't very popular at home when I scrounged together all the money that I could lay my hands on to buy a ticket for the match. There was not enough money to buy milk or bread for the flat, let alone cool drinks or ice cream. I want to re-emphasise that I was not very popular, especially because I wasn't a Western Province or Bull supporter but an ardent Banana Boy. (Or as they are known today, a Shark supporter.) I parked the 'ge-Morrissie' where it didn't cost anything and walked further to Loftus Versveld. I proceeded through a gate that allowed me to walk over the C-field and B-field to the actual entrance gate into the stadium. Suddenly, I saw a R20-note lying on the grass in front of me. I peeped around from under the brim of my hat to see if someone was watching me. I bent down and picked up the money. Ten meters further, I saw another R20 note. 'I can get rich here,' I mumbled to myself as I picked up this R20 note as well. Another 10 m further, I saw a R10 note. How lucky can one be? After picking up the R10 note, I stopped to see if there wasn't anyone backtracking, looking for lost money. No one! Now if I were to announce my findings on the public address system, I would most probably be surrounded by fortune seekers! My decision was made. I would take the findings back to the flat untouched. Back at the flat, after the rugby match, long faces became friendly ones when I handed over the funds. That evening, we treated ourselves to a takeaway meal; we also bought milk and bread for the flat and even had money for collection in church. It was surely predestined to attend the Western Province/Blue Bull match.

*   *   *

During the July vacation, I did 2 weeks' relief work in the Malelane Section in the absence of the incumbent Section Ranger. Here, I was exposed to an aspect of a Section Ranger's work that I, up until now, had not experienced before. What was at stake was the proximity of the permanently flowing Crocodile River forming the southern boundary of the KNP as well as intensive agricultural activities south of the river and also all the people associated with the agricultural activities.

There was one aspect of the management of the river that was very confusing and had already resulted in big court cases. According to the National Parks Act, the description of the KNP boundary was as follows: The description started at the south-westerly corner of the KNP where the Crocodile River started forming the southern boundary of the KNP. From this point, the boundary was described in a clockwise direction along the Western boundary of the KNP up to the Luvuvhu River, then eastwards to the confluence of the Luvuvhu and Limpopo Rivers, and then further southwards along the eastern boundary beacons up to where the Komati River, before flowing into Mozambique, formed the southern boundary for a kilometer or two up to the confluence with the Crocodile River and then along the Crocodile River up to the starting point at the south-westerly corner of the KNP. The confusing description about the Crocodile River was as follows: The southern boundary was the high-water mark on the right-hand bank of the Crocodile River. How stupid or clever could that be? This description led to speculation and one's own interpretation of it, i.e.:

- Which is the right-hand bank of the river? The one when one follows the clockwise description or the one on the right-hand side if one looked downstream in the direction which the river flowed. According to these interpretations, the boundary could be on either the banks.
- Where was the high-water mark of the river? Was it described according to a 5-year flood line, or a 10-year one or a 50-year one, or was it the highest flood line ever attained, etc.?

I share the above confusing legal issues with you as this dictated the working relationship between the Section Ranger and the neighbouring farmers south of the river. Joint operations in the disputed area were the only acceptable solution.

I have included the above information so you have a better understanding of the following story:

Early one morning, Dirk Ackerman phoned me at Malelane. He was then the District Ranger stationed at Crocodile Bridge. The use of a telephone at that stage was quite foreign to me as our normal mode of communication was by radio. Dirk informed me that Mr Klaas Prinsloo had shot at a group of lions that were hunting his cattle. He had killed two and had wounded a lioness. The wounded lioness had run through the so-called Snyman fence or Veterinary fence on the southern embankment of the river into the disputed area. Dirk asked me to come and support him and to please meet him at Klaas Prinsloo's homestead to track the wounded lioness. On arrival at Klaas Prinsloo's farm, he showed us the blood spoor of the wounded lioness to where she had entered the reed bed in the river.

Oom Klaas also introduced us to his Bulldog/Boxer mongrel. It was an overweight bitch that was already huffing and puffing for air like a steam locomotive begging for more coal. According to Oom Klaas, this was the best lion dog in the area, and her name was Queen. When Oom Klaas was out of earshot, I whispered to Dirk: 'Should the Queen meet her king today, she is going to see her backside.'

We very stealthily entered the reeds and moved forward gently step by step. After about 10 minutes of nervous tracking along the hippo footpath, Queen disturbed something and with tail between the legs, barged past us to higher ground. We were ready for action, waiting for the lioness to charge. After another tense minute, we went forward and found the spot where Queen had disturbed a Bushbuck. The adrenaline levels were high, and the relentless sun was beating down on us. Dirk and I exited the reeds simultaneously onto a sandbank that allowed us a clear vision over the river. A movement in the water attracted my attention. I shouted to Dirk and pointed to where the wounded lioness was negotiating the shallows of the river upstream from where we were, towards the KNP. This we had to prevent at all costs. Dirk and I immediately took aim with our .375 rifles. These rifles were not designed and built to be used over long distances. I purposefully waited for Dirk to shoot first. I had previously done a considerable amount of shooting with Dirk and instinctively knew how much he was going to compensate for the distance. He fired, and I could see where his bullet hit the water. I made a further adjustment allowing for the moving target and squeezed the trigger. Waiting for the bullet to complete its trajectory, I enjoyed the recoil of the .375 against my shoulder. The bullet hit home, and it appeared as if the lioness's back was broken.

Dirk fired again. This time, the bullet hit much closer but was still short of the target. I reloaded and fired my second shot and hit the animal in the head, and it disappeared under the water.

Dirk looked at me and questioningly asked: 'Where do you come from?' and then added, 'Well done.' At this stage, a breathless Oom Klaas joined us on the sandbank and fired a .458 round into the water. How could we shoot without him contributing as well? Queen was nowhere to be seen. We indicated to Oom Klaas where we had killed the wounded lioness. 'Impossible!' he exclaimed. 'That is almost 450 m.' Dirk and I had estimated the distance to be approximately 400 m.

'How did you know where to aim?' Dirk inquired. 'I will tell you later,' I answered.

While talking, we could see the lioness's carcass floating downstream, leaving behind a blood spoor in the water that was already attracting fish. After we had said our farewells to Oom Klaas and Queen, Dirk and I returned to our respective sections. I had just arrived home when Dirk phoned to find out how I had known where to aim. I told him it had just been a lucky shot.

'But you hit the lioness with two consecutive shots!'

'Dirk, a guy just needs to have one accurate *'sighter'*, and then you can aim at the same spot.'

'I can see that I am not going to get any sense out of you today!' replied Dirk. 'Well done and goodbye,' were his parting words on the phone.

To this day, Dirk still does not know how I outfoxed him.

* * *

Back at Tshokwane, I felt as if I had arrived. I had now obtained enough papers of the right kind (degrees) to be able to discuss matters with the so-called intelligentsia at Skukuza. I promised myself that I had finished swotting and that I would focus only on getting practical experience and learning from my colleagues. I utilised every opportunity to go into the veldt and looked at the natural environment through different eyes, focusing on the interaction between geology, soil, plant, animal, and climatic conditions. The bush had a story of its own to tell, and we as human beings should refrain from interpreting the natural environment by human comprehension and value systems. I was often almost stoned by outsiders when I explained to them that seeing something die in the natural environment was something of beauty to me as it was part and parcel of the bigger ecological processes and part of Creation. Enough of these philosophical contemplations . . .

*　　*　　*

During the year at Tshokwane, we built a holding facility for Roan antelopes near a natural pan called Rietpan. Six Roan antelopes were brought from the N'waxitshumbe breeding camp between Punda Maria and Shingwetzi to the holding facility and later released onto the Rietpan/ Mlondozi flats. Previously, a group of Roans had roamed this area. The assumption was that this group had crossed the border into Mozambique and had been fenced out into Mozambique when the KNP eastern boundary fence had been erected. It was during this time that the border between the RSA and Mozambique was fenced as a safety precaution, and the fence was 'strengthened' by planting thirteen rows of sisal, 1 m apart, on the KNP side of the fence. This was a project of the Department of Defence, and the funds were channelled through the South African Defence Force (SADF). The actual planting of the sisal was, however, under the supervision of the KNP Management. The KNP Management advised the SADF that the project would not be successful as elephants and other animals would eat and destroy the sisal. The project, however, continued regardless.

Every morning at 06.00, there was a radio session between Skukuza and all the supervisors on the KNP eastern boundary to coordinate this project, to resolve any problems, etc. One of the supervisors was a Portuguese guy by the name of Jose Gonzales (or 'Gonzalvs' as we called him). He was actually a Building Foreman at Skukuza. The project supervisor at Skukuza was Oom Carel Grobler or 'Oom Grobbie'. Oom Grobbie radioed all the supervisors on the sisal project one by one to monitor their progress and to discuss any problems they might have encountered. 'Gonzalvs' was not very fluent in either English or Afrikaans. Working in the KNP, one had to communicate in Afrikaans or Shangane with a bit of French thrown in if one wanted to emphasise a certain point. On a specific morning, when Oom Grobbie called Gonzalvs's radio call, his frustration could clearly be heard.

'Good morning, Gonzalvs. How are things this morning?'

Gonzalvs's answer was loaded with anger and frustration. 'Grobbie me fucking cross. Me put-put sisal and elephant take-take sisal.'

With these few words, Gonzalvs had summed up the frustration of the KNP Management and all sisal-planting teams. Two years after the project was completed (approximately 360 km by thirteen rows of sisal plants 1 m apart), there were only twenty-eight sisal plants to be seen along the entire eastern boundary. Twelve just north of the Komati River and sixteen plants just north of the Olifants River on very steep inclines where elephants couldn't get at them.

*   *   *

When I started working in the KNP as a Game Capturer, one of my goals was to be able to identify and get to know as many of the trees and shrubs of the KNP as possible by their botanical and Afrikaans and English common names as well as their Shangaan/Tsonga names. I initially bought the book *Trees and Shrubs of the Kruger National Parks* by L. E. W. Codd for R7.50. I very quickly discovered that I would make very little progress identifying these trees and shrubs on my own. Plan B was to seek assistance from one of the old Field Rangers whom I took along on these 'get to know the tree' excursions. He would give me the Shangaan name of the specific tree, and I would page through the Codd Index trying to find the tree name that sounded phonetically correct. The tree was then found in the textbook, and the leaf samples in my hand were compared with the sketches or photographs in the book. It was a very slow and frustrating process at first, but slowly, progress was made. When I walked past a tree I had positively identified, I used to greet the tree by all its names, e.g. 'Morning Leadwood, Hardekool, *(Combretum imberbe)*, Mondzo'. This method helped me remember their names.

On one of my foot patrols, I 'discovered' a tree that I could not identify along the Munywini Spruit, west of Tshokwane. Since I had to be in Skukuza the following day, I took a comprehensive sample from the tree to show the botanist at Skukuza. After a thorough investigation of Herbarium samples, we still could not identify the plant. The 'unknown' sample with additional information on soil type etc. was included in a professional sample and sent to the Herbarium of the National Botanical Gardens in

Pretoria for identification. After about 3 weeks, Oom Johan congratulated me during a radio session on the new plant species I had 'discovered' in the KNP in the Tshokwane Section. The name was (*Suregada africana)* or Canary Berry (Afrikaans: Gewone Kanariebessie). This was both very satisfying and rewarding for my efforts to identify the trees and shrubs.

*   *   *

There was one other incident that occurred during my year at Tshokwane that I will always remember. During the rainy summer months, all the Section Rangers and Roads Foreman were continually closing and opening gravel roads for tourists, firstly for fear of them getting bogged down in muddy conditions and having to spend a harrowing night in the bush and secondly to minimise maintenance on these roads.

During one of these rainy periods, we had to close both the lower and upper Vutome loops on the Tshokwane Section to tourists. Sergeant Simeon Mujovu was the head of the Field Rangers Corps at that stage. During our early morning planning session, I requested Simeon and one of the junior Field Rangers to patrol the lower Vutome loop by bicycle to evaluate the condition of the road for possible reopening for tourist vehicles on the following day. I continued with a backlog of office administration. At about 10.30 on that Friday morning, I heard the dogs barking. I did not pay much attention to them as I wasn't expecting any visitors. Suddenly, the office door was unceremoniously kicked open by the junior Field Ranger entering the office. I was at the point of admonishing him for not knocking first when I noticed that he was frightened out of his wits and gulping for air from exhaustion. 'What is wrong?' I queried. All that he could muster was: 'Ngosi, Simeon Ngosi nkulu!' (Simeon has a big problem). I immediately realised that Simeon was in trouble of some sort. I told him to remain in the office while I fetched a strong sugar solution from home. When he had taken two large gulps, and his breathing was almost back to normal, he blurted out that Simeon had been attacked by a lioness and that he had raced back to report the incident. 'How seriously was Simeon bitten?' I wanted to know. 'Simeon was bitten on the fore- and upper arm and on the upper leg.' 'Did he bleed a lot?' was the next question. 'Yes!' was the answer. 'Where did it happen?' He fortunately could give me a distinct landmark. I immediately radioed Skukuza to request a helicopter on standby. Fortunately, the helicopter pilot was at the Conservation Offices, and I could personally give him the exact coordinates of the accident scene. I grabbed my .375 rifle, jumped into the bakkie, accompanied by the young Field Ranger, and rushed to where he had left Simeon. I first of all saw Simeon's bicycle lying in the road, and then only did I see Simeon lying in the shade of an Umbrella thorn. Disciplined as always, Simeon wanted to get up to greet me. I indicated to him to stay put. I quickly inspected Simeon's wounds. Both his fore- and upper arms were severely mauled, fortunately without bone damage. Then there was a substantial wound on his left upper leg, but mercifully, no big arteries had been damaged. Unfortunately, he had lost quite a lot of blood. I told Simeon about the helicopter that was on its way to airlift him to the Nelspruit Hospital. The hospital had also been notified.

The signs of the struggle between Simeon and the lioness were clearly visible in the road. When I questioned Simeon as to what had happened, he related the following: While they had still been merrily patrolling down the road, the lioness had appeared from nowhere and had charged directly at him. He had then jumped off the bicycle and tried to fend off the lioness by keeping the bicycle between the lioness and himself. He had shouted to his colleague to make himself scarce. The lioness had gotten hold of the bicycle and jerked both the bicycle and him to the ground. The lioness had then let go of the bicycle and came at him. He had fended off the lioness as best he had been able to. The wounds sustained on the lower and upper arms had been the result of this attack. At this stage, his colleague had shouted at the lioness and charged at it. For a brief moment, the lioness had let go of her 'prey' and charged at his colleague who had been about 40 m away. Fortunately for him, he had stood his ground, and the lioness had stopped about 5 m short of him. During the shift in the lioness's attention from Simeon to his colleague, Simeon had been able to get hold of his hatchet that had fallen to the ground during the wrestling match with the bicycle. The lioness, on losing interest in his colleague, had again turned to her original 'prey', Simeon, and grabbed hold of his upper left leg. Simeon had then hit the lioness with the blunt end of the hatchet on the head. The lioness had been temporarily dazed and let go of Simeon's leg and retreated a meter or two. She had again rushed in to finish off the 'prey'. Simeon, however, had been waiting for the charge, and this time, he had hit her with the blunt end of the hatchet between the eyes. Again, the lioness had stumbled backwards and looked at Simeon with dazed eyes. Simeon's colleague had now taken the initiative and with raised waving arms, had charged at the dazed lioness. The lioness had immediately retreated and run off into the bush. When I questioned Simeon as to why he had hit the lioness with the blunt end of the hatchet, his answer to my question was: 'Mbazo, we are here to protect animals and not to hurt or kill them.'

What can I say? Where does one still get such commitment to a cause?

'What do you think? Why did the lioness attack you, Simeon?' 'I really can't say! The lioness was in good physical condition and not lactating' – protection of cubs was, therefore, not the reason. 'It just shows – one can never be certain of the behaviour of wild animals!' continued Simeon. The behaviour of wild animals can be 99 per cent predictable, but beware of the 1 per cent that proves our man-made judgement wrong. While waiting for the helicopter, we made Simeon more comfortable and looked around for possible causes for the aggressive behaviour of the lioness. We, however, could not find any clues. Just goes to show – never trust a wild animal.

I could hear the approaching helicopter before I could see it. I ran to the bakkie to grab a small mirror to attract the pilot's attention. This was, however, not necessary as the pilot had spotted the bakkie from a distance and was flying directly towards us. The local medical doctor at Skukuza was also in the helicopter. After he had administered the necessary injections and professionally attended to the wounds, we made Simeon comfortable in the back of the helicopter. We waved goodbye as the helicopter took off for Nelspruit Hospital.

After they had left, the junior Field Ranger and I tracked the lioness to try and fathom the cause of the aggressive behaviour. Being summer, the grass was very long, and in some places, we had to crawl on hands and knees under thorn trees. These were not ideal conditions to be charged at by an ill-tempered lioness. After about 1 hour's harrowing tracking, we gave up and went home.

Two days later, we paid Simeon a courtesy visit at the hospital. We took along a small transistor radio and a bowl of fruit. We first of all had to show him how to operate the radio so that he could listen to the Tsonga programmes. Simeon looked much better and excitedly told us of all the things that he had seen from the helicopter. Needless to say, this had been a first for him. Simeon spent another 2 weeks in hospital, and we visited him twice more during that time. Everyone at the hospital was surprised by Simeon's speedy recovery and attributed it to his fitness and healthy lifestyle. When Simeon was dismissed from the hospital, we went to fetch him. We only arrived back at Tshokwane late on Friday afternoon. The staff had organised a homecoming function for him. Early the next morning, I heard a faint knock on the back door and found Simeon standing with the transistor radio and a brown paper bag in his hand. He handed over the two items in his hand, saying, 'Mbazo, thank you very much for everything you did for me.'

My eyes filled with tears, and I could not utter a word. In the paper bag, there were two cokes and a packet of Lemon Cream biscuits. I gave Simeon a hug but could feel that he was not comfortable with my show of affection as he pulled back immediately from me. While writing about this experience, my eyes again fill with tears. This was the first and last time in the KNP that I experienced a gift of gratitude from one cultural group to another for a kind deed done for a fellow man.

* * *

Jackson (I have forgotten his surname) was the Manager of the Tshokwane Tea Room/Picnic Spot. He was a stately old man and took his responsibilities very seriously. He managed his staff with an iron rod. His 3-year-old son and our son Morné often visited each other and either played in the dust or, if it had rained, in the mud and especially in the water. Morné actually got his name 'Tandamanzi' (isiZulu for he who loves water) from these escapades. Jackson's son's name was 'Appearance'. We often wondered what the origin of the name was. One morning, Jackson came and visited me in my office to inform me of his leave arrangements and to inform me about the arrangements he had made for someone to relieve him. He also requested that I keep an eye on the Tea Room/Picnic Spot during his absence. We continued the discussion about his work and his pending leave. I eventually mustered up the courage and asked him about the name Appearance. 'Oh, that is easy,' he responded. 'My wife experienced a very difficult birth with him, so the doctor eventually decided to do a caesarean. My son was, therefore, not born – he appeared, and hence, the name Appearance.' 'Very apt,' I said, shaking his hand and wishing him a very peaceful holiday.

*   *   *

Our next transfer was from Tshokwane to the Great North and more specifically to Punda Maria as District Ranger with the Sections Shangoni, Shingwedzi, and Pafuri reporting to me. The Vlakteplaas Section came into being during this tenure from April 1977 to April 1980. Moving into the big, old, unpractical house at Punda Maria was a great honour for me. Quite a few important people had stayed there before us. The most outstanding features of the yard were the massive stone terraces behind the house, the massive Sycamore fig tree at the one corner of the veranda, and the Angola fig that dominated the right-hand side of the garden. Then there was the controversial Baobab tree with the nameplate announcing the name of the planter and 1937 being the date it was planted. This specific tree generated a lot of speculation regarding the growth rate and age of Baobab trees. Punda Maria was also my first exposure to a tourist rest camp with an incumbent Rest Camp Manager and his wife as neighbours. They stayed in the original old Police Station that had been renovated to become a residence. To fill you in on a bit of KNP history: The area around the Ranger's house, old Police Station, and rest camp featured these massive stone terraces filled up with soil to create level ground against the southern slope of the Dimbo Mountain. During the early history of the KNP, migrant labour from Mozambique came through the KNP to go and work on the gold mines on the Reef (present-day Gauteng). To be able to complete the necessary documentation for this, a certain amount of money was required. The Mozambiquens had no money to speak of, and the KNP Management formulated a clever plan to smooth over the problem. The money that was due was equal to the salary for 14 days' labour in the KNP. The following arrangement was, therefore, negotiated with the potential mine labourers: they would work in the KNP for free for 14 days, and the KNP Management would then complete the necessary documentation for 'free'. These labourers quickly became known as the 'Mafourteens'. The stone terraces at Punda Maria and other labour-intensive projects in the KNP were completed by these Mafourteens.

Due to its location, Punda has a very moderate temperature and, with Pretoriuskop in the south of the KNP, receives the highest rainfall in the

KNP. The surrounding terrain is very hilly with the dominant geological formation being Waterberg sandstone. More to the east and northeast, the geological formation was mostly from the Karoo geological system. These circumstances were ideal for unique plant communities, and I indulged myself in the large variety of plants, many of which occurred only in the Punda Maria area in the KNP. Our neighbour on the Pafuri Section was Flip Nel. He previously had been a technician for the botanists at Skukuza and was a master at plant identification. He also had a B.Com degree that he had attained extramurally while working at Skukuza. Our neighbours to the south at Shangoni, were Piet and Assie van Staden; both of them were ex-teachers. Piet could recite all the names of the trees and the specific page number of these in the book *Trees of the Kruger National Park* by Piet van Wyk; although, he had only encountered a couple of these in the 'flesh'. The three of us got together on a regular basis for plant-identification excursions.

We did a couple of 'discovery patrols' along the Luvuvhu River from Dongadzivha, where the Luvuvhu River begins forming the Northern boundary of the KNP up to Pafuri. Another patrol was from the upper reaches of the Madzaringwe Spruit to the confluence with the Luvuvhu and through the interior to Pafuri. We also did a couple of patrols along the Nkovakulu Spruit to the Baobab Forest area. These areas had a particular natural beauty and with the Cave sandstone formations, formed a unique destination that one wanted to visit over and over again. During all of these 'discovery' patrols, plant identification was paramount. Every so often, we would stop with Piet being the scribe and Flip and I identifying plants and calling out the names while Piet struggled to keep up. There were a couple of events during these patrols that will always be remembered.

One cold early morning, with heavy dew still on the grass, we started with a plant plot at the Tshipudza Spring. Piet sat himself down on a relatively bare piece of vlei grass and started jotting down plant names as Flip and I identified and called out the names. After about a half an hour, Flip called a halt and asked whether it wasn't coffee time yet. Flip and I approached Piet from different directions to come and make coffee. Suddenly, Flip said, 'Piet, sit very still, and don't move!' Fortunately, Piet listened and did what he had been instructed to do. 'What's wrong?' he wanted to know, his eyes big. 'Piet, turn your head slowly to your right, and tell me what you see between yourself and your rucksack.' Piet slowly turned. First, he didn't see anything; then suddenly: 'Oh shit! SNAKE!' he shouted, departing the scene like greased lightning, scattering pencils, clipboards, and plant samples all over. For the past half an hour, he had been sitting next to an almighty Puff adder. Fortunately for Piet, these snakes are not very active when it is cold. Piet jumped around like a cat on a hot tin roof for a while before calming down with a nice cup of coffee.

The Punda area is well known for the Lebombo ironwood forest that occurs in the area. Often, when I wanted solitude, I would go and sit in one of these forests and listen to what the wind was saying and thoroughly enjoyed the atmosphere. We were on our way from the Madzaringwa mouth to Pafuri on one of our plant identification excursions. We were walking along a well-used elephant footpath. At this stage, I was leading the expedition, followed by Flip and Piet, with the two Field Rangers forming the rear guard. On these excursions, neither Flip, Piet, or I carried any rifles as it would have made all the paraphernalia we were carrying too heavy and cumbersome. The Field Rangers, however, each carried their .303 rifles. As was my habit, I carried a throw-able rock in each hand when I was walking in the bush. It gave me a measure of security.

The elephant footpath threaded its way through the Cave sandstone 'koppies' and Lebombo ironwood trees that covered the area amongst the koppies. A picture perfect scene. At one stage, there was a flat piece of Cave sandstone clearing, the size of a tennis court, in the Ironwood forest. The footpath bisected the clearing. As was the norm for these sandstone outcrops, there was a weathered depression that collected all the rainwater that fell on the flat, rocky surface. This was the ideal drinking spot for animals that used the elephant footpath.

As it was almost coffee time, I walked straight to the waterhole and was in the process of unbuckling my rucksack when a young elephant bull walked through the Ironwood trees and into the clearing with the same thirst-quenching intention as we had. When the elephant saw us, he immediately showed his discontent with competition at the waterhole. He made himself as large as possible by maximally spreading his ears, lifting his head with trunk erect, and giving a mock charge with trumpet sounding. We outnumbered the elephant by five to one, and I told him in no uncertain terms that he needed to 'voertsek', and I let him have it with the two stones I was carrying. The one stone hit him on the ear and the other high up on the trunk. The elephant's body language indicated to me that we had the upper hand in the initial confrontation. I searched around and fortunately found two more projectiles, and before the elephant could regain its wits, the second round of barrage followed. I charged forward and again told the elephant in no uncertain terms to 'voertsek'. The elephant spun around. Now was my chance; I grabbed hold of a piece of wood and a rock, and I let him have it on the backside. The elephant disappeared into the Lebombo ironwood thicket with great protestation. Turning around, I saw that what I had thought was 'us' confronting the elephant was actually only 'me'. Flip and Piet had found refuge high up against the Cave sandstone koppie. The two Field Rangers with the rifles sheepishly appeared from the thick Ironwood trees where they had found refuge. One of the most important lessons that one was taught as a young Ranger/Field Ranger was never to run when confronted by one of the big five. Easier said than done. One's instinctive reaction is to run and to find refuge in a safe haven. We gathered around the waterhole, drinking coffee and discussing the recent elephant episode. I must say, I detected a measure of embarrassment when my colleagues tried to justify their actions . . .

The most important planning that went into these plant-identification excursions was to make sure that the route went past potable water sources i.e. springs, flowing spruits, or rivers etc. to fill up on depleted water resources as one could only carry approximately 5 l per individual. Walking in the very high temperatures of the KNP required continuous water supplementation. We did not have those fancy water purification tablets, and all our water was boiled before consumption, mainly in the form of coffee or Rooibos tea.

On one of these excursions, we decided on a route that was not very familiar to any of us. We were hoping to find unusual plant species, and our expectation was high that in the relatively unknown area, where no or very few people on the KNP staff had ever been to, we would find such plant species. We assumed that somewhere along the route, we would find water to replenish empty canisters. We departed into the 'unknown' very early one morning and everywhere along drainage lines or spruitjies did plant sampling and surveys. At midday, the ambient temperature was in the vicinity of 35°C. Nowhere along the route did we find any water; although, the aerial photographs that we had studied to determine the route indicated features that we thought could be associated with a spring of some sort. We did stumble onto a dried up spring, but that was of no use to us. Later on, when again studying the aerial photos, we realised that these had been taken during high summer and during an above-average rainfall cycle. Under these conditions, the spring would definitely have been active. Our water was depleted, and plant surveys became a very low priority. We were still confident that the elephant footpath we were following would lead us to water, seeing that there were relatively fresh signs of elephant activity along and on the footpath. Around 14.00, with an estimated ambient temperature of 38°C, we were beginning to suffer. The elephant path led us straight into a Tamboti thicket. We could sense from Piet's body language (he was walking up front at that stage) that he had made a big discovery. 'Water!' he yelled. In the shadows of the Tamboti clump, there was a crystal-clear pool of water, almost 30 m long and 5 m wide. Hidden amongst the Tamboti's, the water wouldn't have been visible on the aerial photos.

'You must not drink this water,' warned the most senior Field Ranger. 'The 'Ndzopfori' (Tamboti) put 'poison' in the water.' The waterhole was surrounded by Tamboti's, and through the crystal-clear water, we could see Tamboti roots in the soil surrounding the pool. Piet, Flip, and I debated our predicament. The warning vs. our need for water! We unanimously decided that if we boiled the water twice for at least 5 minutes, all the 'poison' would be out of the water. At this stage, we were very eager to top up as we were starting to suffer from dehydration. Our Field Ranger colleagues refused point blank to drink anything made with this water. Satisfied and refreshed, we continued on our expedition to Pafuri. That evening, we had planned to stay overnight at the Nkovakulu confluence with the Luvuvhu River. This was one of the most idyllic overnight areas imaginable. The Nkovakulu is a seasonal spruit (drainage line) that has eroded a ravine approximately 30-40 m wide and approximately 100 m deep through the Cave sandstone formation, leaving behind a breathtaking water-eroded rock formation. The Luvuvhu River, on the other hand, is a perennial river that has left behind a ravine between 150 and 200 m wide and also approximately 100 m deep. The colours of the eroded Cave sandstone varied from almost white through pink and all the shades of orange to black, and it was wonderful to observe the changing colours as the rays of the setting sun illuminated them. At the Nkovakulu mouth, there was a sandbank that extended approximately 10 m into the Luvuvhu River. We were going to spend the evening on this sandbank. What a wonderful experience to lie on the sandbank observing the closing of the day. The 'silence' was ear-splitting. The Luvuvhu River formed rapids downstream. The baboon troop came to rest in the krantz with their usual moaning and groaning and occasional bark and lamenting of a small baboon bidding the day farewell. Various birds entertained us with their sunset chorus, and upstream, a herd of hippos made themselves known by snorting and guffawing in the water as they prepared to go grazing. Later on, we heard the leopards sawing in the distance with the baboons moaning nervously in response. Giant Eagle owls, Fish owls, and various nightjars and lesser owls completed the silent symphony . . . beautiful!

Early the next morning, at about four o'clock, I was awakened by a strange twisting and turning in my stomach. A sound downstream attracted my attention, and I could see Piet in a crouched position at the edge of the sandbank with his bare backside facing towards the water. I quickly had to unzip the sleeping bag and scrambled out of it before it was too late, to take up the same position as Piet. Then we heard Flip getting rid of his sleeping bag and also rushing to assume the same position. Excuse the French, but we 'shat like storks'. I could swear I saw a smile on a Field Ranger's face that peeked at us from under his blanket and saw the three bare bottoms facing the river. Flip's first words were: 'Those guys didn't lie, did they?'

After the most severe stomach cramps had subsided, we decided to rekindle the campfire to boil river water for coffee. We were still about 15 km from Pafuri, and we could not afford to dehydrate further. We broke camp earlier than planned and left for Pafuri. Identifying plants and admiring the natural beauty were now things of the past, and our only objective was to get to Pafuri and medication as soon as possible. We achieved this but not without another two pit stops each. On reaching Pafuri at approximately 11.00, we were physically exhausted (kaput). All three of us took a gulp of Flip's muti, and Piet and I departed for Punda Maria where Piet and I again took medication. After 2 days, we had recovered, and we resumed normal activities. The three of us unanimously decided that in future, we would not ignore good advice from people who had more superior knowledge than ourselves.

*   *   *

One of my favourite haunts was Xantangalani, and I always made time to do foot patrols through this area. The surrounding area comprised of a series of Cave sandstone koppies. Actually, these were not koppies as koppies were made up of loose rocks piled onto one another. These structures at Xantangalani were comprised of one single outcrop of Cave sandstone that varied in size between 10 and 12 m in height. The Xantangalani area covered approximately 100 hectares comprising of approximately 300 individual rocks/koppies. Two big elephant footpaths wound their way between the 'koppies' in a north/south direction. Other than that, there was very little indication of game movement in the area. Now and again, I observed leopard spoor on the elephant paths, and occasionally, Klipspringers were seen on the 'koppies'. Between the koppies, there was thick sand covered with typical sand veldt vegetation. The erosion patterns and colours of every 'koppie' were unique and very beautiful. Each time I visited Xantangalani, I would approach it from a different direction. When one was amongst the koppies, one's vision was limited to the two or three koppies in the immediate vicinity. I purposefully tried to get 'lost' in order to see and investigate as many of the 'koppies' as possible. After having finished a discovery expedition, I would climb to the top of the nearest koppie to view the horizons and to determine a direction to 'escape' from Xantangalani. At the Nkovakulu mouth, the 'silence' was comprised of many natural sounds. Here at Xantangalani, however, there was a deathly silence that made Xantangalani a mystical experience.

*   *   *

During one of these visits, a dark blaze behind a big Shakama Plum (*Hexalobus monopetalus*) up against the koppie attracted my attention, and I went closer and started clambering through the dense branches. The dark blaze, at closer investigation, was the opening of a cave approximately 1.8 m high by 3 m wide. I froze and listened very intensely. If there was a leopard inside, I would have to move away very stealthily. I could not determine the depth of the cave. The roof of the cave went down at an angle to the back of the cave with a very dark area about 1 m high where anything could be hiding. I, however, could not detect any spoor in the very soft, dusty floor of the opening to the cave. On the right-hand side of the cave opening, there was a slab of rock that stretched from outside the cave opening into the cave itself. Anything could enter or exit the cave on this rock slab without leaving any visible spoor. I observed all these details in the blink of an eye, and it only added to the unease of the situation. I picked up a dry branch and threw it to the back of the cave and stood ready for any eventuality. My heartbeat was picking up, I had butterflies in my stomach, and the adrenaline levels were on the rise. Nothing came rushing out of the cave. Round number one was done and dusted. I repeated the branch-throwing exercise to make doubly sure. Again, nothing happened. My self-confidence increased, and I very slowly entered the cave. It seemed as if one had to obtain permission from somewhere to enter the cave. Inch by inch, I moved deeper into the cave with my whole being focused on the dark spot at the back of the cave. All my muscles tensed for the fright-and-flight action. Suddenly, I heard this very strange sound coming from within the innards of the cave directly ahead of me, and I couldn't see a thing. The hairs on my arms stood on end between the goosebumps. I became aware of something honing in on me. I sidestepped to the left to the best of my ability and fell flat on the cave floor in order for the 'thing' to jump over me. I became aware of the first group of large fruit bats flying over me. I burst out laughing in a nervous laugh like a hyena that had choked on something. I stayed put on the cave floor to pull myself together.

Fortunately, there was sufficient light in the front of the cave to be able to see. 'Bushman paintings,' flashed through my mind when I saw the human and animal caricatures on the cave wall. This was the first time that I had seen Bushman rock art in the KNP. I felt very insignificant while inspecting the age-old art form. I could distinguish a giraffe, an eland, a Sable antelope, an elephant; I mumbled to myself looking at a distinct elephant painting. I wasn't a Bushman rock art expert, but to my knowledge, no elephant paintings had been seen in the KNP up until now. I started rummaging through the soft soil and ash covering the floor and 'discovered' signs of archaeological artefacts. I again experienced the mystical Xantangalani atmosphere while beholding the remnants of these primeval beings. At radio session the next morning, I reported my 'discoveries' at Xantangalani to Skukuza and was especially proud of the elephant painting. After the radio session, one of my colleagues, Mike English, called me on the radio. Mike was the fundi on Bushman rock art in the KNP, and he confirmed that the elephant painting was a first for the KNP.

*   *   *

During the late 70s, the Arab world held the rest of the world to ransom by cutting down on oil production and artificially pushing up and keeping oil prices high. The consequences of this were even felt deep in the bush. Section Rangers were dependant on vehicles and power generators and diesoline and petrol to be able to function effectively in terms of patrols, water provisions, fire control, etc. For SANParks, on the whole, it was a big setback. SANPark's income was dependant on vehicular tourism that came from all over and once in a park to be able to be mobile to experience the different parks. The KNP Management's counteraction was to scale down from big one-and-a-half-ton American bakkies to three-quarter-ton Japanese bakkies, with a suitable trailer when load space was required. On top of this, a motorbike was issued to each Section Ranger. This was my first exposure to a motorbike. A group of us went to Malamulele to complete the necessary documentation and tests to be issued with code 2 motorbike licences. We were now ready for action in a changing environment. I approached the motorbike thing cautiously and analytically and decided that there were a few motorbike skills that I would need to master to be able to cope with the many unpredictable situations that could come my way in the bush. Emergency braking was one of these skills on various surfaces, i.e. tar roads, gravel roads, ordinary two-track roads, and loose sand surfaces. Emergency stops were practised to perfection on all these surfaces, each with its own methodology and problems. Just as one thought that a specific skill was mastered, the motorbike would come up with an angle that wasn't anticipated. Fortunately, I didn't fall off while practising these skills. Seeing that a motorbike did not have a reverse gear, other techniques had to be mastered to make provisions for this deficiency. The technique was to make a 180° u-turn/skid under emergency braking situations on all the above mentioned surfaces. This was the most important emergency skill and was practised until perfected.

To me, personally, the motorbike was the most important piece of equipment that was ever issued to a Section Ranger. I spent many kilometers on the motorbike, patrolling the in-veldt on elephant and hippo

101

footpaths. Area coverage by motorbike combined with foot patrols was the most effective method to get to know the in-veldt intimately.

*   *   *

Amongst other things, the KNP's far north is known for its big cobras and Black mambas. My practised emergency-stopping ability on many occasions saved the day and prevented me from running over one of these monsters. On one occasion, I could not avoid driving over a big Black mamba with my bakkie. The mamba had struck back at the bakkie but fortunately missed the cabin. This was one of the nightmares I did not want to experience on a motorbike. Every time that I had encountered cobras on the motorbike, I had fortunately managed to stop 4-5 m from them in a big cloud of dust. The snake would then very slowly slither off the road and without fail lift its head about 1 m above the ground, looking back at the motorbike with a typical cobra-hooded head, as if saying: 'You escaped me this time, but watch out next time!' and then disappear into the long grass on the side of the road. Black mambas, on the other hand, would leave the scene of the encounter very quickly. The one thing that I realised very early was that one should never become overly confident and feel that one was in control of the motorbike under all situations. The Workshop Manager at Shingwedzi radioed one day and asked me to check on the battery system at the radio repeater station on top of Dzundwini Hill as he was of the opinion that the radio problems we were experiencing during the heat of the day were due to the batteries not being fully charged. I never let an opportunity to enjoy the freedom of the bush on a motorbike go a begging. The road leading up Dzundwini to the repeater wasn't an engineering masterpiece, and the last 200 m of the road to the top ran perpendicular up the slope of the hill. The driving surface was, thus, very rough and irregular due to the erosion furrows coming down the hill, and to add to that, the surface was overgrown with grass, and consequently, progress up the hill was very slow and a low-gear affair on the motorbike. I also had to stand on the footrests to be able to negotiate the best route. Then I suddenly noticed that the front wheel had ridden over a snake that was now directly beneath me and between the front and rear wheels of the bike. Due to the long grass, I could not identify the snake immediately. However, as the snake started lifting its head, the hooded shape became apparent. 'Cobra!' it flashed through my mind, and I was immediately covered with goosebumps. Even before the adrenaline levels could kick in, I had already reacted. I threw the motorbike down on the rising sharp end of the snake and jumped a 'mile'. Fortunately, the motorbike fell on top of the snake. Then I saw the snake emerging from between the stalled engine and the frame and sailing away into the grass. The high adrenaline level now kicked in. I started shaking like a leaf. When I was certain that the snake was long gone, I tried unsuccessfully to right the motorbike, due to me shaking and the steep slope. I decided to catch my breath and calm down and tried again. This time successfully. I straddled the motorbike and reminded myself what had to be done – clutch left front, front brake right front, gearbox in neutral, try to kick-start the bike. The steep slope did not make matters easier. The adrenaline levels were still high and the legs jittery. At the first attempt to pull away, the motorbike stalled. Even though the front brake was pulled tight, the motorbike slid backwards on the slope. The last try before giving up hope was successful. As I tried to pull away against the slope, the bloody thing stalled again. We tried again. I was certain that if the cobra had had a sense of humour, it would have hired me to entertain others. Only after getting over the fright completely was I able to get mobile again and to proceed to the top of Dzundzwini and the repeater station to complete my mission. By the time I got back to Punda, the whole cobra episode was something of the past. All the previous skill and manoeuvring practices would not have made this specific cobra episode any easier . . .

*   *   *

On one occasion, I was travelling in a southerly direction on the Middle firebreak road through the big Mopane tree forest. The road meandered through the forest, and the dense Mopanes made vision ahead very difficult. Every so often, my motor-racing insanity came to the fore, and I could not resist pushing ahead with the motorbike. There is one thing that I could never understand about adrenaline levels. Under certain circumstances, it would render one a shaking, useless wreck, and under other circumstances, it would make one razor sharp with the best observation ability possible, coupled with lightning-quick reactions. With the motorbike taxed to the utmost, speeding southwards on the Middle firebreak road, everything changed in an instant when I rounded a corner to be confronted by a whole herd of elephants slap-bang in the middle of the road. Emergency procedures kicked in instinctively. The hand and brake pedals were applied with the necessary feel to maintain the necessary balance so as not to lock the front brake which would result in a head-over-heel tumble, or if the rear brake locked, the motorbike would skid from under me. The motorbike was skilfully manoeuvred through a 180° u-turn. Glancing back over my shoulder, I could see the dazed and surprised look in the neerest elephant's eyes. The cows lifted their trunks and trumpeted their appreciation while the calves milled around nervously between the legs of the adults. Needless to say, the motorbike was already in the appropriate gear and the engine rpm at the right level for a quick getaway before it came to a standstill. When the Matriarch cow rushed forward to collect my signature for the 2-year-old calf following her, I thought it best to depart from the scene. Fortunately, the motorbike now had five forward gears, and I could flee the attention of the admirers.

*　　*　　*

Late one afternoon, during a full-moon period, I decided to sleep out somewhere on the Middle firebreak road, to listen for possible poaching rifle shots along the western boundary and to enjoy nature. I loaded my stretcher and sleeping utensils and departed at 17.00 from Punda to a site just south of the Marithenga firebreak road crossing with the Middle firebreak road. I stopped the bakkie in the middle of the road and pitched the stretcher 10 m in front of the bakkie. The sun was just disappearing behind the horizon and displayed a setting that one could only experience in the Lowveld. I opened the camp stool next to the stretcher and enjoyed the coffee and sandwiches that I had brought along from home. The 'coming to rest' period of the day was my favourite time in the bush. Everything surrounding one was saying goodnight, and gradually, a serene silence settled in the bush. This silence was, however, of short duration as the night-loving things became active. Seeing that the night-loving things were far less in number than the day-loving things, their activity sounded far less intense, and the relative silence made their sounds more audible. I enjoyed the various night sounds, the distant yelping of the Black-backed jackal, and the barking of the White-tailed jackal. I heard lions roaring and the faraway sawing of a leopard. The Spotted hyenas were particularly quiet, and I did not even hear one call. At sleep time, the moon was so bright that only the brightest stars in the heaven were visible. I lay flat on my back on the stretcher, contemplating the wonder of creation until sweet sleep overcame me.

Just after midnight, I was awakened by a sixth sense. I lay very still but couldn't identify the awakening. I lifted myself onto my elbow and looked straight down the firebreak road. I saw an almighty big elephant bull sauntering down the firebreak road straight towards me. The bull was still almost 80 m away. The bull was at ease and coming up the road; it would pick a branch to the left of it and then one to the right and stuff it into its mouth with its trunk. I still had sufficient time to seek the safety of the vehicle. I, however, decided against it and thoroughly enjoyed the advancing bull. If the elephant didn't stop to pick a morsel, it would slowly saunter down the road. The ears were flapping from side to side with the head bobbing rhythmically up and down with every forward step. The whole demeanour was of restfulness. I was at the point of wakening the bull out of its slumber sleep walk by clapping my hands, when it suddenly stopped, at 15 m away, lifted its head, and spread its ears as wide as possible in astonishment at the strange thing in the road. The bull lifted its trunk and tested the air to try and determine what was blocking the road. The bull shook its head with ears flapping and advanced 2-3 m to try and intimidate the thing in the road. The bull repeated the intimidation routine several times, moving closer and closer. The distance between the stretcher and the bull was now approximately 10 m. I was seriously contemplating dashing for the safety of the vehicle when the bull slowly started retreating up to 30 m away and turned right into the veldt. The bull probably realised that the thing in the road was not able to be intimidated and decided to circumvent it at a safe distance, still focusing on the thing. After completing the half-moon deviation, the elephant bull again came back to the road, looked at the thing, and continued with its rudely interrupted slumber sleep walk, plucking branches alongside the road. The elephant bull was a real old gentleman. During this whole episode, the bull did not trumpet once, probably not wanting to awaken the 'thing' unnecessarily.

*   *   *

One Sunday, we as a family arranged to meet Piet and Assie from Shangoni for a picnic at the Mooigesig Dam that was built in the Maswitakale Spruit. The Field Ranger of both sections would join forces to do in-veldt patrols to check if there were any poaching activities deep inside the KNP. Normally anti-poaching patrols are concentrated close to the boundaries where most poaching activities take place. We all took our fishing rods and gear along and promised the Field Rangers that they would get a bag full of fish on their return. Morné and Magnus did not have real fishing rods but fishing rods made from straight, Russet bush-willow shoots with a fixed length of fishing line tied to the tips. We used porridge and earthworms as bait, and it was quite evident that the fish in the Mooigesig Dam had never tasted these delicacies before. The rule was that all catfish smaller than 60 cm in length were returned to the water. At one stage, we had caught twenty catfish of which only five went to the Field Rangers' bag. We then decided that these small catfish had to be returned to the dam opposite to where we were fishing. The ratio of big to small catfish now improved. Magnus was struggling to get his porridge-baited hook deep enough into the water. We believed our sons had to battle on their own as part of their learning process and to make the time go by faster. Magnus eventually succeeded in getting the bait in deep enough. It wasn't long before I saw a fish pulling the line tight when it took the bait. I walked towards him to see if I could assist as it was evident that it was a big one. I had explained to them that they had to play the fish first, until it was tired, before pulling it out. I could see that this fish was getting the better of Magnus.

'Run!' I shouted at Magnus with the intention that he should hold the fishing rod and run up the embankment to pull the fish out. Magnus looked at me with big, confused eyes, threw down the rod, and ran for dear life up the embankment, thinking that I was warning him against a monster on the line that wanted to cause him harm. I saw Magnus's rod being pulled to the water's edge. Fortunately, I was close enough to prevent this just before it disappeared into the water. I then called Magnus back to come and complete his half-caught 'fish'. He looked at me as if I had lost all my marbles. First, I had instructed him to flee the danger, and now, I was calling him back to the danger zone. I could see that he was confused and explained my plan of action to him. He reluctantly came back to take hold of the rod and slowly proceeded up the embankment. The fish was fighting back for all it was worth. Eventually, Magnus was the victor, and when the fish was pulled out of the water, it was identified as an eel. Magnus was now more apprehensive. He had never heard of or seen a snake that lived in water. After diligently explaining to him what an eel was and that it was not poisonous, he came and helped to take the hook out the eel's mouth. This eel was not destined for the Field Rangers' bag and was returned to the water by a very proud Magnus after everyone had congratulated him on his spectacular catch.

* * *

Although our stay at Punda Maria was very eventful and enjoyable, two incidents took place that firstly disappointed me immensely and secondly frustrated me no end. Morné and Magnus, due to circumstances, found playmates amongst the kids of the junior staff that stayed in separate living quarters. Patric, the son of one of the Field Rangers, and Morné were of the same age and played happily together. Late one afternoon, Morné arrived back home and came to ask me, 'Dad, what is a bloody fucking Boer?' I was totally flabbergasted. 'Morné, where did you hear that?' 'Patric told me so!' 'What happened? Why did he call you that?' Morné told me that they had been busy playing with their toy cars in the empty swimming pool. They had been comparing the speed of their individual toy cars going down the slope from the shallow end to the deep end of the swimming pool. Because Morné's yellow car was always winning, Patric had grabbed Morné's car and claimed ownership. One thing had led to another, and just before they had gotten physical, Patric had jumped out of the pool and yelled the above phrase at Morné. What was very disconcerting in the above context was that Morné at that stage was fluent in Shangaan, Patric's mother tongue. This whole episode saddened me and made me realise again that children were indoctrinated by older people to sow hatred among different ethnic groups at a very early age.

* * *

I also battled through the most frustrating and traumatic time in the KNP, while at Punda Maria. During radio session one morning, I was informed that a team of geologists from the Department of Geological Surveys would be at Punda from such and such a date for a month to update the geological maps of the area or, similarly, to map the geology of the area on a large scale. I would have to support them during their visit. I was very excited about the prospect as it gave me an opportunity to expand my academic geological knowledge with practical veldt experience and because the geological formation of an area was the foundation of all ecological processes from rock, to soil, to plants, to plant-eating species, to meat eaters. This sequence of ecological procedure wasn't just applicable to the larger species, but to all living things. The geologists arrived at Punda on the given date, and we had an introductory meet at the rest camp reception. What surprised me somewhat was the fact that there was not a single South African amongst them. There were two Czechoslovakians, one Polish citizen, and one Serbian. We could only communicate, with difficulty, in very Basic English. They opened up their neatly rolled-up maps and indicated to me the focus area of their visit. I immediately got wind of something fishy going on. Their focus area was limited to the Karoo rock formations, and they had no interest in the Waterberg rock formations that covered more than half of the area. When I questioned this, I was quickly informed that that was the instruction received from their Head Office, whoever that might have been.

I quite regularly accompanied them on their mapping expeditions. Something that I immediately realised was that a geologist without any botanical training had a severe handicap identifying geological change. Geologists without a botanical background could only determine a geological change from rock outcrops. On many occasions, I could detect a geological change 30-40 m before they could, by just looking for a change in vegetation or soil. The group of foreigners were very surprised when I showed them this ecological method of mapping. They would, however, not adapt their mapping method and stuck to their outcrop method. What did they know about Lebombo ironwoods, Baobabs, Bush willows, Mopane, etc. anyway? So they continued mapping the Karoo formations, from the purple Beaufort mudstone, through the desert (aeolian) deposited Cave sandstones, to the volcanic deposited Basalts and Rhyoliths.

About a month after the mapping was completed, the big shock came. Again, during a radio session, I was informed that on such and such a day, a ground team would be arriving to prepare a camp terrain for a drilling team that would arrive later to sink a number of test boreholes. This team also had to prepare access roads to predetermined drilling sites. Deep in the bush, we did not have access to regular wireless broadcasts or to the printed media. Gradually, the news spread from Skukuza to Punda Maria by means of officials doing their rounds, who paid us a visit. Eventually, the Chief Ranger paid us a visit while on an official visit to the north of the KNP. He informed me that the National Parks Board had made an announcement through the Chief Director Mr Rocco Knobel that they had agreed to the implementation of a scientific research project under the leadership of the Department of Geological Survey to determine what exactly was going on under the Earth's surface. Human interpretations from the updated geological maps were speculative and had to be grounded on scientific knowledge obtained from samples obtained by drilling.

Somewhere far away in Cape Town, a United Party Member of Parliament Mr Rupert Lorimer voiced his discontent at the National Parks Board transgressing its own National Parks Act by allowing prospecting to be done in a National Park (KNP). The KNP Officials submitted all kinds of scientific reports pointing out the potential negative ecological impact that mining would have on a very sensitive and unique ecological system. The public started getting involved, objecting very strongly to the potential desecration of their beloved KNP. 'Why the fuss?' the National Parks Board mouthpiece Mr Rocco Knobel wanted to know. This was only a geological scientific research project like any other research projects on plant ecology, animal ecology, soils, etc. that were accommodated within the National Parks Act.

Very few or no outsiders were aware of the official visit of the then Head of ISCOR to Punda Maria. ISCOR was a parastatal and the biggest steel producer in the Republic of South Africa (RSA). To have a better understanding of my frustrations, you need to understand that the RSA at that stage was involved in military activities against 'malevolent' forces (the so-called Total-onslaught period in the history of the RSA) The Head of ISCOR specifically came to Punda Maria to be updated on the preliminary results of the geological research project. During his visit, I followed him like his own shadow. At one stage, while having coffee on the restaurant veranda, I started questioning him about his specific interest in the Coking-coal samples, specifically in the depth at which the Coking coal occurred, and the thickness of the Coking coal layer. He started giving me a detailed lecture on the strategic value of Coking coal in the iron industry to rid the molten iron ore from impurities. Gradually, two plus two started adding up to four. Somewhere down the line, someone had convinced someone that there was 'cheap' Coking coal to be had on State land – the KNP – that could be mined to produce cheap iron and/or steel for the State's war initiatives. He continued explaining to me how many millions upon millions of rand the Coking-coal deposits in the Punda area could save the Government in the present political climate.

'Mr ISCOR, I have listened to your motivation. Please grant me the opportunity to state my case. If the KNP were to be the only place where South Africans could see an elephant in its natural environment – in the present political environment of isolation, this was not an unrealistic question – what would be the value in rand and cents for that person? We could continue and do this monetary evaluation for every animal, insect, and plant species. How much would it be worth to this South African if he could climb onto a koppie and have a 360° view of natural landscape without any man-made infringement? Once we had completed this financial evaluation, we could again draw up a balance sheet to compare relative values. Even more so as mining had a limited life span as opposed to what we were trying to achieve in the KNP. Mr ISCOR, you see, we are in the FOREVER BUSINESS'. Leaning back in his chair, Mr ISCOR said, 'But, Mr van Rooyen, you can't put these nebulas ideas on the table. You have to be realistic!' How does one go about convincing such a person that there are other core value systems apart from his 'hard cash' concept?

The experimental drilling programme, however, continued, and it felt as if I was fighting a lonely battle at Punda. There was no communication with the outside world. No newspapers or radios, and discussions with colleagues about this, had the same frustrating end. One late afternoon, I received a message that I had to go and see the Rest Camp Manager. He informed me that he had seen two high-ranking South African Police (SAP) officers and that they wanted to see me at hut no. 12 at 19.00 that very evening. 'Who are they, and what do they want?' I queried. He shrugged his shoulders and indicated that my curiosity would be satisfied that evening. As usual, I was early for my appointment, and I found the two gentlemen outside hut no. 12, enjoying the Punda atmosphere. One was a brigadier and the other a colonel. I must have committed a hideous crime for two high-ranking police officials to want to see me. After completing the normal formalities, the serious part of the discussion followed. They had been instructed to investigate the case opened by Mr Rupert Lorimer against the National Parks Board for allowing prospecting in a National Park in contravention of the National Parks Act. I now faced a big dilemma. Should I defend the point of view of the National Parks Board, or should I give my honest opinion? I decided on the latter even though it could have huge repercussions on my personal future in the SANParks organisation.

I explained to them that I was also a qualified geologist, even though I had never practised. My understanding of prospecting was as follows: If a geologist was merely walking in the veldt picking up or sampling rocks and from these actions, he could deduce or make an informed decision of what lay below the surface he was prospecting. A further improvement of the concept would be to draw accurate geological maps of an area and to make deductions from these. The ultimate would be the method employed at Punda where the core sampling drill only drilled to a depth where the depth and thickness of a Coking-coal layer could be accurately determined. If the present drilling programme at Punda was to be a scientific research project, a predetermined depth criterion would have been decided on, and all boreholes would have been drilled to that specific predetermined depth. The present borehole depths varied from 20 to 800 m, a very clear indication that they were 'searching' for something. According to my understanding, the so-called ISCOR-driven scientific research project in the Punda Maria area of the KNP was a prospecting exercise for Coking coal.

The two high-ranking police officers looked at one another and asked me what my recommendation would be. I remained silent for a while, contemplating my options. I would charge the Chief Director of National Parks, Mr Rocco Knobel, for contravention of the National Parks Act for allowing prospecting in the Kruger National Park. I was simultaneously relieved and anxious after giving my verdict. Relieved that it was off my back and anxious regarding the consequences it may have for my career in the KNP. The Brigadier wanted to know if my statement should be 'anon'. 'No!' I said 'I will stand good for my statement.' He thanked me for my cooperation and undertook to keep me informed regarding procedures. After a week or three, I was informed that the court had rejected Mr Rupert Lorimer's accusation against the Board on technical grounds. According to law, one cannot accuse a Board (number of individuals) but only an individual. Mr Lorimer should either have laid a charge against the Chairperson of the National Parks Board or the Chief Director of National Parks.

A while later, it was announced that the potential mining of Coking coal would not go ahead due to the tectonic nature of the area. There were too many geological faults causing the Coking-coal layers to be situated at varying depths that would make mining operations very costly. We at the KNP rejoiced at the news. Being the ultimate pessimist when it came to mining issues, I warned that geological reports that are filed in archives have the tendency to resurface after many years to be dusted off and implemented. The general public's (KNP's clients) very strong opposition to the mining in the KNP was the turning point in my opinion. We had won the battle but not necessarily the war.

*   *   *

I was never one of the best passengers in an aircraft, be it a fixed-wing or helicopter. I cannot recall a single flight of more than an hour's duration that did not leave me with flight sickness of the worst degree. However, if the opportunity presented itself, especially with the helicopter, I would jump at the opportunity to fly. The overview of the KNP from a helicopter was special. When one spoke to helicopter pilots, they were all in agreement that the flying done during buffalo and/or elephant culling was most probably the most dangerous helicopter flying imaginable. We at the KNP were very fortunate in having the most gifted helicopter and fixed-wing pilots. I had two flying predilections. One was the annual elephant and buffalo census, and the other was the annual Roan antelope and anthrax immunisation project in the north of the KNP.

While I was stationed at Punda Maria, Oom Johan (then at Skukuza) would be the one marksman. He was left-handed and occupied the left rear seat in the helicopter, and I was the right-handed marksman from the rear right seat. The immunisation project was a big affair. It was combined with the fixed-wing ecological census conducted for all other species excluding elephants and buffaloes. Everybody involved converged on the Xingomeni picket to camp there for the duration of the project. Twelve to fifteen officials were involved, some of whom brought their spouses and kids along. The campsite resembled a circus town. The purpose of the anthrax immunisation project was to find as many of the Roan antelopes on the eastern flats between Punda and the Shingwedzi River and to immunise them with darts. The far north area of the KNP was an anthrax endemic area with regular anthrax outbreaks when environmental conditions were favourable. Roan antelopes are very susceptible to anthrax, and their numbers on the eastern flats were low.

The modus operandi was as follows: the fixed-wing census team had to be airborne by sunrise, and they would continue with their ecological census, flying in parallel strips at a fixed height and counting the game species encountered. Whenever they spotted a herd of Roan antelopes, the helicopter team would be activated. For the duration of the immunisation of the herd, the fixed-wing would operate as a 'spotter' plane. It would circle above the herd until the helicopter arrived. The helicopter team then took over and started immunising the Roan. Any animals breaking away from the herd would be followed by the 'spotter' plane to call in the helicopter at a later stage. It wasn't child's play getting a shot at a Roan antelope running through the Mopane shrub veldt. When one culled elephants, they would normally follow a relatively straight path, not dodging small trees and shrubs or fallen tree trunks. The correction factor for relative movement was very small. During buffalo culling, the correction factor for relative movement would be bigger. Darting Roan antelopes, however, was a different story. They were continually changing direction, dodging between shrubs, small trees, and fallen tree trunks and also weaving from left to right, always keeping an eye on the big helicopter bird up above. During Roan immunisation, one would very rarely have a straightforward shot where the speed and direction of the animal would be similar to that of the helicopter. Most of the shots were angled to the front or perpendicularly down or even to the back. On many occasions, one would have to predetermine a route for the animal; would it go left around an obstacle or to the right? One would then have to aim and fire into the gap before the animal had reached the gap. If one's choice was correct, the dart and animal would meet in the gap. One hardly ever used the sights on the immunisation rifle, and more often than not, it was a feel for relative movement and anticipation that determined when the trigger would be squeezed.

The helicopter team consisted of four individuals, the most important being the pilot. We had to place all our trust in his flying ability. At left front was the scribe who had to keep record of all important aspects such as herd size, number of adult animals, number of calves, how many animals were immunised, time of day, locality, etc. Then there were the most sought-after positions in the chopper: the two marksmen. Radio communication between everyone in the chopper and between the helicopter and 'spotter' plane was crucial. While Oom Johan was focusing on one animal, he would pass another on to me. 'One is passing underneath the chopper.' And I would be ready for it, and as it immerged, I would dart it on the rump. Initially, we had difficulty in keeping track of darted and non-darted animals, especially if they stayed in formation in the herd. Or even when an animal broke away from the herd, the spotter plane did not know whether it had been darted or not and later guided the helicopter to it unnecessarily. Our ingenious dad again came up with a solution. He used the rubber suction sections found at the back of eye – or ear-drop dispensers and drilled small holes on the rounded ends. This rubber section was then placed over the needle and secured onto the dart head. The rubber was then filled with a purple-coloured liquid. On impact with an animal, the rubber section would be compressed, and the purple liquid would squirt out through the small holes and leave a purple blob where the animal had been darted. Double immunisation of Roan was now something of the past. On one occasion, even this ingenious plan did not live up to expectations. We were busy honing in on an individual animal when it tripped over a fallen trunk and fell down head over heels. I could not resist the open-belly shot. How does one identify an animal with a purple blob on its belly button from the helicopter?

It very often was very hectic in the back of the helicopter, what with loading darts, keeping track of animals, passing on information, etc. One was often forced to lean far out of the chopper with one's foot on the landing skid to be able to get a good shot. On one occasion, I felt something hit against my right boot secured against the landing skid of the chopper while we were busy with a group of Roans. Once back on terra firma, I noticed that there was a clear cut over the toe section of the boot. It had just cut through the leather section. On closer inspection, we found evidence that the cut was caused by the branch of a Leadwood tree. One safety mechanism that the marksman had was a so-called monkey chain that was tied around the waist of the marksman and secured onto the chopper. If one were to fall out of the chopper, one was assured of not reaching the ground. A 'monkey chain' – gets one thinking, doesn't it? Fortunately, the monkey chain was never tested operationally. It was a big honour for me to have been part of this well-oiled helicopter team that did everything so fast and effectively and as accurately as possible.

*   *   *

After I completed my degree in Geology at Stellenbosch University, Oom Johan involved me in all kinds of water-drilling programmes varying from water for game, for household purposes, (new rest camps, wilderness trail camps, and new entrance gates), support boreholes, and so on. As I mentioned previously, I had an intense interest in groundwater, and Oom Johan and I had had many discussions regarding this. The time spent with Oom Jim Meiring at Shangoni also stood me in good stead. I had also tested all the different water-divining 'sticks' from a large variety of tree species, water bottles or a brick balanced on one's hand, chains that swing, carrying a rifle by the trigger guard, etc. None of these 'foefies' worked for me. I could, however, deduce from geological information and natural indicators such as trees and anthills, etc. that there was a possibility of groundwater in a specific area. I, however, could not put my heel to ground and proclaim: 'Drill here!' This frustrated me no end and resulted in two or three boreholes having to be wasted before a successful one was sited, making use of deductions from drill chips that came out of the unsuccessful boreholes. This was a waste of time and money, and a 30 per cent success rate was not acceptable to me (usually three holes per site to produce water). I enjoyed all the drilling projects that Oom Johan involved me in. After approval of every annual KNP budget, Oom Johan would summons me to his office, and he would walk to the KNP map on the wall and say: 'I want water here and here. A budget of x amount has been approved. The drill will be arriving at such and such a gate on a given date. Arrange your things so you can accompany it.' I necessarily had to make a recce to every site to determine whether it was necessary to grade an access road for the drilling machine to travel on.

During one of my first drilling projects I had to divine water for the development of a new Wilderness Trail base camp. The correct planning procedure to follow was to first get water and then do the necessary infrastructure planning. More often than not, however a beautiful site for a camp was decided on, and then water had to be found in the vicinity placing a huge stress on the search for water. The Wolhuter Wilderness Trail camp was one such project. Two days before the drill was to arrive, I went to recce the area and decided on two potential drilling areas – with emphasis on the area and not the drilling pegs. I was quite excited about the two potential spots. As arranged, I met the drill at Malelane Gate and escorted the drill equipment to the Wolhuter camp terrain. On his arrival, I indicated to the owner of the drill where to drill. 'What made you decided on that specific spot?' he queried. I indicated to him the geological formation and supportive big trees and anthills. 'Would you mind if I checked it out?' 'Go ahead,' I said. He produced two L-shaped brass rods that were used for Oxy/Acetylene gas welding. He held the short ends of the L's in his hands with the long ends swinging freely above his fists. He walked around in the area and also criss-crossed the drilling peg. 'Yes,' he said, 'we can drill on this peg.' I had previously used similar galvanised wires without any success.

'Would you mind if I walked around with your wires?' 'Go ahead,' he responded and continued organising the drilling equipment. I walked with his divining wires and almost did a double take when the wires turned in my hands of their own accord. I held the L-shaped wire in my fists almost 30 cm apart, with the two long sections parallel to the ground, and whenever I walked over a specific spot, the tips actually moved inwards towards one another. A dark uncertain world suddenly became clear. Now I just had to learn to interpret what the divining wires were trying to convey to me. I walked around in a big area, making marks on the ground whenever the divining rods 'indicated' something, and tried to make sense of the confusion. The drill operator continued drilling, throwing out drill samples after every meter as I had requested. I, however, had discovered a new 'toy' and didn't even bother to look at the drill samples. I was about 400 m from the drill when I heard jubilation above the sound of the drill and someone calling me. When I arrived at the drill site out of breath, I could see water splashing all over. The first aquifer was encountered at 58 m, and over the next 3 m, the formation was very soft and weathered and the volume of water had steadily increased. There was another weathered section 1 m thick at 79 m. The estimated yield, by means of a blow test, was estimated at approximately 6,000 l per hour.

This yield was sufficient for the purposes of a Wilderness Trail base camp. Beg as I might, the drill operator did not want to part with his brass divining rods. I went back home early that afternoon and, at radio session the following morning, informed Oom Johan of the successful borehole. I did not say anything about the divining rods, apprehensive that it might just have been mind over matter. Early the next morning, I was at my father's workshop and begged him for two similar brass welding rods. Now there was no stopping me. I now had the 'ability' to dig in my heel and proclaim 'Drill here!' It, however, wasn't that easy. I first of all had to learn what the divining rods were conveying to me and what it was that made them turn in my hand. At long last, I convinced myself that there was 'something' associated with groundwater that radiated electromagnetic rays through the Earth's crust. When I then walked over these electromagnetic radiation areas with a conductor in my hands, it would induce motoric action (the movement of the divining rods). This deduction of mine was based on one of the rules of Physics that governs the functioning of an electrical motor. Let's, however, forget about the technical explanation and focus on what the divining rods were indicating. The areas/lines where the rods moved, I called 'activity lines'. I very soon realised that these activity lines could be a single movement of the rods (or a single line on the Earth's surface) or 1 m, or up to 20 m wide and everything in between. I had to plot out these activity lines on the surface and even had to make sketch plans of these for fear of becoming confused with activity lines crossing one another or changing direction. From these sketch plans, I decided where to drill, taking into consideration the geological formations, if visible, as well as making use of other natural indicators such as trees and anthills. It was also evident that there were specific tree species that somehow were connected with these activity lines. Leadwood, Baobab, Sheppard's tree, Apple leaf, Ana tree, etc. were typical examples of these.

*   *   *

Oom Johan called me in and asked me to go to the Pioneer Dam area to look for water. The KNP Management was contemplating building a 120-bed rest camp (the so-called Mopane Rest Camp) on the shores of the dam. The dam was not perennial, and it would have been too expensive to pump water from the Letaba River. Large quantities of water would be required to warrant the building of such a large rest camp with its entire support staff. I packed the caravan and pitched camp in the general area. On the first day, I did a 360° recce around the proposed rest camp terrain, studying the geological formations and checking out the natural indicators. To the north, south, and west, I did not see anything that excited me too much. But to the east lay the Basalt flats and the Xipandani Spruit with big Leadwood trees, and they excited me. I criss-crossed the whole area and put the activity lines on paper. This kept me busy for almost the whole week. On Saturday, I studied all the sketch plans of the activity lines and decided where I would place the drilling pegs.

Early on Monday morning, I met up with the drilling contractor at Letaba and escorted him to the potential rest camp terrain and the drilling pegs. At approximately 14.00, the drill was positioned over the first drilling peg and the drilling commenced. At a depth of 15 m, the dust that came out the top of the borehole disappeared. 'That was too soon,' I mumbled to myself. Between 20 and 30 m, a muddy muck came out of the hole. Then suddenly, from 40 m, there was water and plenty of it. The water yield gradually increased to a depth of 50 m. From 55 m, the geological formation became very hard. The drill contractor and I conferred and decided to stop at 55 m. To be able to make a reasonable estimation of the yield, a big dam was built around the borehole with the material that had come out of the hole. In the wall of the dam, a piece of casing was placed to drain the water spouting out the borehole and into the dam. We then measured the time required to fill a 20-l container with the water flowing through the casing. In this specific case, it took mere seconds, and the yield was calculated to be in the vicinity of 60,000 l per hour. Wow! Although I was very surprised and delighted with the yield, I was quite worried about the depth at which the water was found. Would the borehole be perennial enough, especially during a long-drawn-out draught? I immediately made radio contact with Oom Johan at Skukuza to share the information. Although, he was very delighted with the yield, he also expressed concern about the depth at which the water had been found at. The second borehole was drilled, and the estimated yield was in the vicinity of 48,000 l per hour. Between these two boreholes, with a sufficiently large reservoir, a rest camp of 120 beds could be operated. The third borehole only produced water at a depth of 60 m. The estimated yield was 8,000 l per hour. The fourth one yielded 10,000 l per hour. I wanted to drill borehole number five approximately half a kilometer further to the east in case boreholes one to four were interconnected and on the same water source. Number 5, however, yielded only 1,200 l per hour and was not suitable for rest camp purposes. Borehole number six was drilled 1 km to the west of the rest camp site and yielded 12,000 l per hour. The engineers at Skukuza were very satisfied with the potential yield of the boreholes. They rightfully insisted that the boreholes be professionally evaluated. They would not commission a R60 million rest camp without being 100 per cent sure of the status of the most important commodity: water. They were advised to make use of a firm 'Boegman Boordienste' from Pretoria. For this purpose, I had to meet Mr Boegman and entourage at Letaba on Monday, 2 weeks later, and escorted them to the boreholes, for the potential Mopane rest camp, to test the boreholes.

On the prearranged date, I met Eric Boegman and his wife Henna at Letaba. On our way to the boreholes, the conversation turned to water divining. I explained the method that I had used. Eric confirmed that he also used divining wires/rods but that he also had the ability to 'see' ground water. Who was I to be sceptical about this, I who believed/trusted brass rods to divine water? Both these methods would be questionable to the majority of people, not to mention the academic world. I decided to test Eric's *seeing* ability. After having arrived at the first borehole, I asked Eric: 'On what grounds did I decide on this specific spot?' Eric looked me straight in the eye, and I could see that he was saying to himself, 'Oh, this youngster is trying to test me!' He went and stood next to the borehole and took in a 360° vision of the area. 'I can *see* a big aquifer, almost 2 m wide, running parallel to the tar road and crossing underneath the tar road about 40 m from here. The borehole is sited very well on this aquifer. From the right-hand side, there is a very small aquifer making a strange kink before crossing the big one. The borehole was sited on this crossing point.' I opened my sketch plan of the activity lines, and what Eric had just described and my sketch plan were images of each other. I had to bite my lip to prevent my mouth from hanging open. What did Eric *see* that I couldn't and that the divining rods could 'see'? 'What is the yield going to be?' I tested Eric some more. He looked intently at the borehole and said: 'You can expect a good yield probably in the vicinity of 48,000-60,000 l per hour. I am just a bit concerned about the depth.' I was still not totally convinced about Eric's seeing ability. We proceeded to the next borehole, and again, I queried Eric as to why I had divined the borehole at that spot. He again went and stood at the borehole and studied the area. 'There is something very strange going on at this site,' he said. 'There is a big aquifer from the top, and it is then suddenly displaced by about 2 m and then keeps on continuing in the same direction. There is a definite line on the displacement, and you put your peg halfway between the two big lines on this displacement line.' At this stage, my mouth did hang open. Eric noticed it and said that I had better close my mouth before something flew in. I showed Eric the sketch plan of the activity lines and explained to him that the big aquifers were displaced by a geological fault zone that was younger than the formation of the big aquifer. 'How much water, Eric?' 'This yield is not as good as the first one but will most probably deliver between 40,000 and 48,000 l per hour.' I showed him boreholes three and four, and again, what Eric saw was identical to my activity line sketch plans. For Eric's final test, I explained to him that I wanted to site the fifth hole away from the rest of the holes along the Xipandani Spruit for fear that they were all on the same water source. 'Where are you going now?' he questioned on our way. 'There is no water in this area.' 'Just you wait,' I said and drove further. Eric most probably again expected a strong borehole similar to the previous ones without seeing one. Getting closer to the fifth borehole, I pointed in the general direction. 'Why did you drill here? There is only a small aquifer. If that borehole delivers more than 1,200 l per hour, I will eat my hat!' When we arrived at the borehole, I showed him my sketch plan and the estimated yield. Eric had 'seen' and confirmed everything.

Our paths crossed often after this, and we were involved in many drill-and-borehole evaluation projects in the KNP and elsewhere together. I learnt a great deal from him, and he admitted that I had also contributed somewhat to his knowledge of water divining. What bothered me the most, however, was that I had toiled for a whole week in the hot sun and in a tick-infested area to decide where to drill, and along comes Eric and confirms my sightings at a glance and within minutes.

The following morning, Eric fitted his biggest test pump to the testing rig and lowered it into borehole number one to start the 8-hour pump test. After the test had been completed, he gave the following borehole utilisation management plan: This borehole could be pumped for 24 hours a day and for 7 days a week at a yield of 60,000 l per hour without damaging the water source in any way. The engineers and architects were already sharpening their pencils. The management prescripts for hole number two were: This hole could be pumped at a yield of 40,000 l per hour for 16 hours with a rest period of 8 hours before pumping again. The engineers and architects now proceeded with full-scale planning and design. Borehole three and four delivered yields of 8,000 and 10,000 l per hour respectively and would be utilised as water sources for staff accommodation facilities.

I was flabbergasted by the fact that a R60 million project was the result of two L-shaped brass welding rods. Henceforth, I would not refer to these as 'wires' but as 'instruments'.

During the next couple of years, Eric and I periodically worked together on drilling-and-borehole evaluation projects. We had long arguments about the 'workings' of the instruments, depth determination, shadow activity lines, the fact that certain tree species only occurred on these activity lines, and why these only occurred on the activity lines. We were, however, convinced that with the newfound 'scientific' knowledge at our disposal, we could defend or argue in the highest academic circles. These high academic circles were, however, convinced that we were busy with witchery. The fact of the matter was that the success rate of geologists was in the vicinity of 40 per cent, while Eric and my methods had a success rate of between 90 per cent and 100 per cent. Our experience indicated that geologists more often than not drilled next to a ground water source and not on it.

I am very proud to say that in later years, I divined twelve boreholes in the Kalahari Gemsbuck National Park – all of them successful. In the very dry mountain desert of the Richtersveld National Park, I divined three out of four holes successfully. In later years, while doing rehabilitation of old irrigation lands in the Mapangubwe National Park, I managed to convince a student from Potchefstroom University to register a research project on the rehabilitation project. I plotted out the activity lines on the bare irrigation land, and his research project consisted of monitoring the well-being and growth rate of trees planted on and away from these activity lines. I am not going to bore you with all the scientific details but only reveal to you that for one or the other reason, the trees planted on the activity lines, morphologically and anatomically, outperformed all those planted away from the activity lines.

*   *   *

To conclude the water divining section: A few points to ponder. A colleague, Ted Whitfield, wore a copper bangle for rheumatism. He explained to me that the old people maintained that the copper bangle would not work for rheumatism unless it had a gap, the width of one's

121

forefinger, in it. As I had a very high regard for Ted, I also had to wear a copper bangle just for the show, but it had nothing to do with rheumatism. Through the course of time, the copper band wore away, and the end points of the gap became sharp. Often, when I played squash, tennis, or cricket, and I had to bend my wrist in a certain way, these sharp ends penetrated the skin and hurt me. During one of the game-handling projects, the bangle got hooked on to something and severely damaged my wrist. When I got home, I took the worn copper bangle off and placed it in the drawer next to the bed. The copper bangle lay forgotten for almost 9 months. After the approval of the annual KNP budget, Oom Johan called me into his office one morning and disclosed the amount that had been approved for a 'water for game' drilling project. He again went to the big KNP map on his office wall and indicated where he wanted boreholes to be drilled. 'Make the necessary arrangements to go and divine these holes and to accompany the drill'. The drill contractor would be coming through the Phalaborwa Gate on such and such a date. Seeing that it was almost a year since I had last used the 'instruments', I dusted off the instruments when I got home, got onto the motorbike, and travelled to the closest windmill where I had successfully divined a borehole. I had to do a few practise runs at a known site! I parked the motorbike and went to the known activity lines with the instruments. Nothing happened. There was no movement of the wires (not instruments anymore). I was dumbstruck! The borehole was divined on the cross point of two activity lines, and it made no difference how I walked over the activity lines – fast, slow, at an angle, or even backwards; no movement was discernable. I was a very worried man to say the least. I had to go and divine for water, and the divining wires did not want to cooperate. Back home, I went and lay on the bed, trying to figure out the cause of the problem. What was different? Suddenly, it struck me like a thunderbolt – I wasn't wearing the copper bangle anymore! I was grabbing at straws. I rushed to the curio shop at the rest camp and selected a grand copper bangle. After having learnt my lesson with the previous bangle, I did not leave the forefinger-width gap in the new bangle but had the two ends against one another. I would not get hurt if the ends of the bangle were to wear down. I again jumped onto the motorbike and raced off to the windmill. I had great expectations when I neared the first known activity line. Nothing happened! I again tried walking from all angles, then even wet my hands to get better conductivity, took off my boots, and walked barefoot. Nothing! Back home, I again went and lay on the bed, waiting for inspiration. What now? Eventually, I convinced myself that the only difference between then and now was the fact that the forefinger width gap was not there. I went to the workshop and as accurately as possible made the forefinger gap; on this occasion, the motorbike only touched ground here and there. It was already late afternoon when I neared the activity line with great apprehension. I almost made a summersault when the instruments (not wires anymore) functioned as of old and indicated the activity lines as I remembered them. I returned home in a jovial mood. The question, however, remained. How can a forefinger-width gap intended for rheumatism have an influence on water divining? Maybe it was witchcraft after all!

*   *   *

During the 1980s, the KNP Nature Conservation Section was comprised of three Regions: the Northern Region with the Regional Post situated at Shingwedzi, the Central Region with the Regional Post at Phalaborwa, and the Southern Region comprising half of the KNP, with the Regional Post situated at Lower Sabie. The Southern Region stretched from the Crocodile River in the south to the Olifants River as the northern boundary. It was my privilege to be transferred from Punda Maria to Lower Sabie during April 1980 with the following sections in the Southern Region: Houtboschrandt, Kingfisherspruit, Satara, N'wanetsi, Tshokwane, Skukuza, Pretoriuskop, Stolznek, Malelane, Crocodile Bridge, and Lower Sabie as well. The size, ecological diversity, and particular nature management challenges was a big challenge for me and one that I relished, but unfortunately, it necessitated my being away from home often for extended periods to the detriment of my family. This resulted in tension in the home which contributed to Mela and me slowly drifting apart and eventually in each of us going our own way. I would very much like to give all young people, especially those in the conservation field, the following advice: when one starts out in an organisation, the tendency is to spend 90 per cent of one's time focusing on the new work and its challenges to the detriment of your family. As one grows older, and children appear on the scene, approximately 80 per cent of your time is taken up by official duties. As the kids grow up, the official time percentage drops to 70 per cent. The older one gets and the older the children get, the official time may drop to 60 per cent, with 40 per cent devoted to the family. I would like to warn that in the long term, the above is not acceptable to a healthy family relationship. Spend more time with your house folk! Amen!

*   *   *

While at Lower Sabie, I was compelled to attend various meetings, workshops, etc., and I had the opportunity to rub shoulders with the staff of the Technical Services or Engineering Section. Our biggest arguments naturally centred around the engineering philosophy of the time that the shortest and most cost effective route between point A and B was a straight line. This philosophy was not necessarily reconcilable with nature conservation and ecological principles and the aesthetical values that we wanted to expose tourist to. They often argued that most tourists couldn't care two hoots about aesthetics and that they were only ever happy when they had encountered the big five on a visit to the KNP. I conceded this was generally true to the technical guys but also used it as a counter argument as to why we should educate the general public and tourists to the KNP: so that they could also have an aesthetical experience in the KNP through our architectural design and road construction methods. One day, I got involved in a heated argument with the Roads Dept. Foreman, or 'Piet Pad' as we called him, regarding the removal of woody vegetation (shrubs and young trees) along the tar roads. These were growing in an artificial environment where they benefited from runoff water from the road surface and in some places created a very dense fringe along the road. I wanted to convince 'Piet Pad' that he should thin the trees out in a selective manner in order to create shaded areas where tourists could stop and relax under these big trees. The thinning out of the trees should be done randomly. The distance between trees should vary, and the distance of the tree from the road surface should vary so as not to create an avenue effect, but it should reflect a natural random effect. 'Piet Pad', on the other hand, believed in the total eradication of this woody vegetation. He was taught at Technicon that the root systems of these trees would/could undermine the foundation of the tar road and eventually cause the tarred surface to crack and crumble. The argument got very heated until 'Piet Pad' finally declared: 'I am in charge of the road servitudes in the KNP. You should rather focus your attention on the areas other than the road servitudes.' Somehow and very slowly, I must have made an impression on my engineering colleagues as they gradually involved me more and more in the road planning and the alignment of tourist roads.

During the planning phase of the Lower Sabie/Tshokwane tarred road, I was involved right from the beginning. For more than half of this distance, the road would have to traverse over heavy Basalt clay soil. Even if a Roads Construction Engineer wasn't scared of a Game Ranger, he had a lot of respect for road construction on clay or turf substrates. The road foundation had to be a very thick neutral gravel material to be able to absorb the movement inherent in clay soils. This caused the road surface to be raised up to 1½ m above the surrounding area, causing an ecological barrier and extremely deep gravel pits.

'Why can't we remove the clay material from the road alignment itself and stockpile it next to the gravel pit for filling in the gravel pit during rehabilitation?' I asked.

'No! The cost is going to be too high!' was their first reaction.

'I think you owe it to Mother Nature!' was my reply. After a lot of arguing, my recommendation was accepted, and although we couldn't build the road as fast as originally planned, the overall construction costs were equal to the budgeted amount. One of my other recommendations also contributed to achieving this. The alignment of the route as planned by the traditional road construction method shied away from the Nkumbe Hill. My recommendation entailed rerouting the road along the crest of the hill to give tourists an unobstructed westward and eastward view over the KNP from well-sited viewpoints. 'No! That won't work! Vehicles will be visible from far.' Now they were using aesthetical arguments against me! To add to that, clearing the alignment over the very rocky environment would leave big scars, and drainage of the road would be very problematic. Fortunately, I had done my homework thoroughly beforehand and had workable solutions for all their technical problems. At one stage, the Chief Roads Engineer was summoned to act as arbitrator. He listened and evaluated the recommendations of my road construction colleagues and turned to me and said: 'Can you improve on that?' 'If you are prepared to come with me, I will show you a better and aesthetically more pleasing alternative,' I responded. 'Will it be cheaper?' he questioned. 'Let's go and see,' I responded.

I first of all had to convince him that it would not be necessary to clear the road alignment with all the resultant damage to the environment but that the road foundation material could be dumped onto the undisturbed *in situ* soil and grass material. The other woody vegetation could be removed by hand instead of by a D8 caterpillar. During normal road construction, the total length of the road alignment is cleared and divided into sectors that reach completion simultaneously. At Nkumbe, that wouldn't be the case. The road construction would start at one end and would progress up and over the hill like a python coming out of its aardvark-hole dwelling. My recommended alignment used natural features to provide the necessary obstruction to conceal vehicles at or near the natural horizon. There would be very little lengthwise or perpendicular draining from the road surface and water that would fall on the road surface, would run off into the natural surroundings without any drainage pipes. When we came to one of my intended viewpoints with an unobstructed view, without any man-made impingements, up to the Drakensberg of Mariepskop, my recommendation triumphed.

'This time, I will give the devil his due!' was his only response.

Anyone of you who isn't convinced – do yourself a favour and travel on the tar road from Lower Sabie to Tshokwane.

I was involved with the alignment of various new tourist roads. The first one was the Mahogany loop around the Dimbo Hill at Punda Maria where I left two big Rhodesian Mahogany trees slap-bang in the middle of the driving surface. Then there was the Gomondwane loop between Lower Sabie and Crocodile Bridge. Then followed the road from the Berg en Dal rest camp to the Skukuza/Malelane tar road and from there along the Byamiti River to the Malelane/Crocodile Bridge road and another one from the N'watimhiri tourist road to the Randspruit road. It was during the clearing of the alignment of the last one that 'Piet Pad' and I again crossed swords. At one stage, the two of us were quite a distance in front of the D6 caterpillar that was opening up the alignment on my pegs, when we came upon a Knob-thorn tree that had been pushed over by an elephant. The elephant spoor was visible all over. 'Yes!' Piet Pad snorted; 'If the D6 had pushed the tree over, all hell would have broken loose, but because it was an elephant, not a single word of condemnation would be uttered.' While rubbing shoulders like this, Piet and I became good friends with mutual respect for each other's work.

*　　*　　*

During a helicopter census of elephants and buffaloes during the early eighties, we became aware of large-scale elephant poaching on the eastern flats north of the Letaba River. A number of elephant carcasses were spotted from the air, with tusks removed. The KNP Management was shocked and tried everything to get to the bottom of this. The elephant-poaching activity took place from across the Mozambiquen border. The Mozambiquen people had recently been involved in a civil war between Renamo and Frelimo forces. Both these war factions were armed with AK-47 automatic rifles. These were the rifles of choice during elephant-poaching raids. Most of the Field Rangers manning the eastern boundary pickets were Mozambiquens, and it very soon became evident that these colleagues were being threatened and intimidated by the Mozambiquen poachers with death threats and execution of their families who were still living in Mozambique. A small minority of these Field Rangers were actively cooperating with the poachers, whereas the others turned a blind eye to anti-poaching patrols. Both these actions were totally unacceptable to the Wildlife Management Section throughout the KNP, and approximately half of these Field Rangers were dismissed, and the others who still showed any loyalty were transferred to western boundary pickets.

Wildlife Management decided that the deployment of Field Rangers had to change drastically away from the picket system to one where all the Field Rangers were centralised at the Section Ranger's station from where they were randomly deployed. After lengthy negotiations with the South African National Defence Force (SANDF), all Section Rangers and Field Rangers of RSA descent were incorporated into the Commando system and issued with R1 semi-automatic rifles and underwent intensive military training. The whole Ranger's Corps (Section and Field Rangers) now did a week-long rotational stint on the eastern flats between the Letaba and Shingwedzi Rivers. Initially, the anti-poaching activity focussed on manning the observation/listening posts high up against the Lebombo Mountain range from where one had an uninterrupted view westwards of the flats below, where the elephant bulls normally grazed.

I very soon became bored sitting in one place, observing elephant bulls through binoculars, and being on the lookout for untoward human activity.

I convinced my colleagues that if untoward human activity were to be observed from the lookout post, an elephant might have been killed by poachers during the time it would take us to descend from the mountain to launch an offensive attack. I recommended that if an elephant were to be observed, one should spend the whole day in its immediate vicinity, guarding it. One now had to take cognisance of wind-direction changes, wind lulls, etc. in order for the elephant not to become aware of human presence. The one danger associated with this method was that the poachers would be just as or even more veldt-wise than me, and there was the possibility that the poacher and I could unexpectedly bump into one another on the same side of the elephant. I, therefore, had to focus on environmental conditions, the elephant, and be on the lookout for a potential poacher. The poacher would not have to worry about my presence as he would not have been expecting me. The chess game obviously intensified if more than one elephant were in close proximity to the other. Although one was exposed to high levels of stress for the whole day, I found it very educational to move along with an elephant for the whole day, observing their mannerisms and feeding habits. During the normal course of a Section Ranger's work, one very rarely had time to spend quality time with an elephant bull to be able to make similar observations. Fortunately, it never transpired that a poacher and I met next to an elephant bull.

*   *   *

During one of these 'watch the elephant' projects, I came upon a drama that played itself out along the Makhadzi Spruit. The storyline of the drama was to be found in clearly visible signs on the ground and utensils that I picked up along the way. The drama must have played out during a slight drizzle as the signs were very clearly visible on the ground as if they were transcribed in mud. On my way to walk with an elephant I had observed on the flats, I approached a shrub Mopani thicket along the Makhadzi Spruit. Just before entering the thicket, I saw a very clear elephant spoor that had been imprinted in muddy conditions. As elephants usually follow the easiest route, I followed the spoor. After a while, I noticed a spot where the elephant had suddenly stopped. The brake marks were easily discernable in the then muddy conditions. In my mind's eye, I could picture the elephant bull with widespread ears, head held high, trunk raised, kicking forward with one leg, and with big eyes looking down at whatever gave it a fright, the whole demeanour of the elephant saying: 'What the hell is going on here?' I could not yet determine what that had been, seeing as I had not reached that muddy page. On the next muddy page, the elephant bull had made a mock charge, the start and stop spoor clearly visible. I noticed something lying amongst the shrub Mopani. I investigated and found a water calabash with a braided leather carrying loop lying under a shrub. Now I knew what had happened here. I walked forward and saw where a person had stood. He had been wearing 'ramphashans' (sandals made from motorcar tyres). In my mind's eye, I again saw the person throwing his water calabash at the charging elephant in a desperate effort to frighten it away. The elephant obviously hadn't been scared off and made a second charge. The person had made an about-turn and fled for his life, with the elephant following. At one stage, the person had had to make a sharp turn around a Mlala palm bush. Here, he had lost one of his ramphashans. The elephant, naturally, had taken a shortcut over the Mlala bush. In my mind's eye, I saw the person fleeing and every so often glancing over his shoulder at the pursuing elephant, seeing the distance between them shrinking. Suddenly, I saw the brake marks of the elephant stopping for some reason, ears spread out, head and trunk held high. Here, I found the other ramphashan. What had caused the elephant to stop? I looked around and found a small home-made hatchet on the ground. Now I knew! The person had played his last trump card. He had turned around, facing the charging elephant, and with arms waving and with a loud yell, had called the elephant to a halt. When the elephant had stopped, the person had ten to one charged at the elephant and had thrown his hatchet at the elephant. I don't know where the hatchet had struck the elephant, but it had to have made an impression on the elephant. The elephant must have observed the shouting, gesticulating, and desperate figure in front of him for a while longer. Unfortunately, we were now out of the muddy area and on to a hard gravel substrate, and the storyline disappeared. I criss-crossed the area, looking for further clues. However, I did not find or smell anything. I made the reasonable deduction that the person had escaped the elephant ordeal unscathed. It was a wonderful experience to be able to follow the storyline of this drama that was especially written for me under those muddy conditions.

This person, whoever he was, was extremely fortunate. Was he an elephant- or ordinary poacher? I did not think so! If he were an elephant poacher, the elephant most probably would have come second. There was no evidence that the person had been carrying snares as these would also have been discarded during the chase. The person was most likely a Mozambiquen fugitive. Someone who found it so impossible to make a living where he stayed and was prepared to face a charging elephant en route to find a better future in a strange country. I often wondered how many similar dramas had played out in the KNP that we were not even aware of and that had a similar format as the above drama. We periodically came upon pieces of torn clothing lying in the veldt while on patrol – evidence of less successful attempts of fugitives.

*　*　*

On another occasion, four Field Rangers accompanied me to the Hlamvu Dam area to do foot patrols. We were travelling by vehicle to this destination. At about 14.00, I noticed human spoor crossing the road diagonally. On closer inspection, it was evident that these spoors had been made by four adults and a child. The spoors were following an elephant footpath, and we decided to follow them. The ambient temperature was far above 30°C. Approximately 3 km from where we had left the bakkie, we suddenly came upon them. There was an old man and three females of varying ages. We found them all huddled underneath a Mopani shrub, seeking shade from the harsh sun. They were very dehydrated and in a weak condition. We gave them water, and after a while, the old man (the grandfather) started telling their story. They were refugees from deep within Mozambique. They had decided to leave the perilous conditions back home and tackle the long and unknown route to the RSA to seek a better life. 'Did you know that you could have been confronted and killed by wild animals crossing through the KNP?' I asked. 'We were prepared to take the chance. Our future in Mozambique was very bleak, and death would most likely have been our fate had we stayed,' was his thoughtful answer. The womenfolk were his children. 'Where is the young kid that accompanied you?' I wanted to know. According to the spoor, a young kid had been part of the fugitive party. 'He is my grandson,' was his answer. 'Where is he now?' I wanted to know. 'At sunrise this morning, we came upon a small spring where we could fill a 1-1 water container with difficulty.' This was about 10 km into Mozambique. 'The day quickly became hot, and between the five of us, the water lasted only until midday.'

(As mentioned, the ambient temperature was in the vicinity of 37°C.) They had then had an emergency meeting and decided that the grandson of approximately 5 years old would go back to the spring to get water. At this stage, they had been approximately 10 km into the KNP. One litre of water between five people with ambient temperatures hovering around 37°C could not have lasted very long. I instructed two of the Field Rangers to escort the four people back to the bakkie. The other Field Rangers and I followed the spoor of the grandson as fast as we could. The sun was already low on the horizon, and we had a maximum of 3 hours' daylight-tracking available to us. About 2 km to the east of where we had left the bakkie, we lost the spoor of the grandson. At this stage, we spread out on either side of the elephant footpath and progressed up to the Mozambique/RSA border when it became too dark to search further. On the way back to the bakkie, we shouted and whistled as hard as we could, hoping for a counter reaction. Nothing! Arriving back at the bakkie, our news was greeted with trepidation and sorrow. We promised to continue with the search at first light the next morning.

That evening at our base camp, I reflected on what had transpired during the day, and I tried to rationalise it. The distress in the group must have been huge for them to decide to send a 5-year-old kid back into the wilderness with all its dangers to go and collect life-giving water almost 20 km away. The grandson must have realised the predicament that they were in and accepted the instruction because it was their only chance of survival. I wondered if any Westerners would have made the same decision under similar conditions. I could not think of any Western child of 5 years who would have been prepared to adhere to the same instruction irrespective of the magnitude of the emergency. I did not have a peaceful sleep at all with all the possible things that could have happened to the grandson on his heroic rescue mulling through my head. At first light the following morning, we were on the spoor again. We only saw lion, hyena, and elephant spoors that had used the path during the previous evening. During this search expedition, we were two Field Rangers stronger and could, therefore, cover a larger area. We again searched up to the Mozambique/ RSA border without any success. We even illegally continued the search into Mozambique. After a 2-hour search in Mozambique, we decided to return to the KNP. Back in the KNP, we extended our search wider than in the morning. During late afternoon, we returned to the bakkie none the wiser. We went back to base camp very depressed to convey the bad news to the disconcerted refugees. They resignedly accepted the news as if they had already made peace with the fate of the grandson. What upset me the most was that we were legally obliged to hand over these refugees to the powers that be for deportation back to Mozambique. After all the hardship experienced during their flight from their homeland where they had no future and no hope of survival, they were again back where they had started. According to my perception of what a hero should epitomise, this 5-year-old grandson qualified in all respects. This 5-year-old kid will forever live in my heart as a true hero who was prepared, against all odds, to give up his life for his folks. We will never know how his fragile little life came to an end . . .

*   *   *

The members of the KNP Commando were comprised mostly of KNP Officials (male and female) supplemented by staff from neighbouring private nature reserves and farms. Once a year, we had a big Commando camp. During the elephant-poaching era, the Commando camps were especially planned to be done in the poaching heartland to show military presence. All the military procedures, for example, ambush drills, temporary bases, different patrol formations, etc., were practiced and executed. The most basic operational structure of a soldier was a Section comprising of seven individuals. The leader of the Section was a two-stripe corporal. During one of these Commando camps, I was privileged enough to be a commanding Corporal. The Section members were mostly 'Office Johnnies' as we field staff referred to them. In my section, two worked in the Financial Department, one was from the Administrative Section, one was a computer boffin in the Research Section, one was the Warehouse Foreman at the Lisbon Estate just outside the KNP, and the last one was a Research Official with good veldt knowledge but had never before had to carry a weapon under these circumstances. We were all issued with the necessary kit, rations, and equipment, and I had to attend a briefing session to receive more specific instructions.

The general objective of the exercise was to give maximum area coverage, from the Olifants River northwards to the Xilowa Hill, focusing mainly on the Lebombo Mountains. We would be away from the base camp for 4 days and three nights. Our section's task was to set up a temporary base at or near the Ramiti Pan and do foot patrols in the area, lay ambushes, etc. depending on our observations and findings. We were dropped off by a military vehicle along the Makhadzi Spruit, from where we had to scale the western slope of the Lebombo Mountain range to get to the top plateau. The Lebombo range is very rocky, and it took quite a while to get the 'Office Johnnies' not to sound like a buffalo stampede over a rocky terrain while we patrolled. A potential elephant poacher would have had at least a half a kilometer's early warning of something approaching. On top of the plateau, there was a considerable improvement as there were less loose rocks, and we could practise tracking. We did not come across anything untoward during the course of the day. The 'Office Johnnies' became blasé and relaxed. We arrived at Ramiti Pan during the late afternoon and set up the temporary base with 360° vision and defence. I wasn't a good military man, and I deviated from the stipulated military procedures required to set up a temporary base, lead a patrol, etc. and made my own adaptations according to my own experience and the terrain and the need at the time. I was most definitely not the military role model of corporal or section leader. After we had eaten our meal of dry rations, we finalised the guard duties. A very slight half moon provided a semblance of light. The star-studded heaven was very beautiful. The first Black-backed jackal gave a 'bark-yelp', and the nightjars were in full song. Since there was still a fair amount of water in Ramiti Pan, the frog choir also added to the symphony. Later, a hyena also lamented in the distance. One by one, the 'Office Johnnies' came to find out what they needed to do if a lion or elephant pitched up. 'Enjoy the privilege and experience of sleeping out in the bush,' was my sympathetic answer. 'Should any of these threats present themselves, come and wake me up so we can all be scared together!' During my guard duty, the frog choir stopped. The little moon that there was had set, and I could not see anything. 'Human or animal?' I wondered when I heard a sound. Then I heard the deep rumbling sound, coming from an elephant's stomach; it was on its way to drink water at the pan. 'Relax and enjoy the moment,' I reminded myself. Before sunrise, we were all on the go again, and I could detect a certain amount of relief from most of the 'Office Johnnies' that the dark night had eventually come and gone. The rest of the day went very uneventfully, and we spent a lot of time discussing geology, soils, plants, birds, and 'goggas' (all creepy-crawlies). No foot soldier can survive without this necessary survival information, and you can ask any veldt man for confirmation of this. Everyone was very tired by the end of the day after having covered several square kilometers on foot and was looking forward to a good night's rest. The evening was very calm and restful. A beautiful Lowveld evening on top of the Lebombo Mountains under a star-studded sky. Wonderful!

At first light the next morning, we were rudely awakened by two rapid rifle shots. We looked wide-eyed at one another. 'What direction?' I asked. I got four different wind directions as answers. 'Break camp,' I instructed. One of the 'Office Johnnies' was instructed to stand on the side to determine the direction if another shot was fired. We had just finished packing when two more shots were heard. By this time, everyone was wide awake and in agreement on the direction of the shot: to the south-east of us, in the direction of the Mozambique/RSA border. The shots were from a big-calibre rifle and not from an automatic rifle. I took the lead in the direction of the shots. After a quarter of an hour, I indicated stop (hand signs). I wanted the adrenaline levels to subside after the initial excitement following the shots. I could see the expectation on every scared face. Being exposed for the first time to the knowledge that one could be fatally shot at or that one might be exposed to the reality of having to shoot to kill in the execution of one's duty was not easy. I tried to be calm when I explained the plan of action if we were to be exposed to a fire-fight confrontation. I was still busy explaining when another shot was heard. We were still in the right direction, and I guessed the distance away to be in the vicinity of half a kilometer. 'Stay calm, guys,' I indicated to them, moving forward slowly, with every sense and sinew alert and tensed to the utmost. The seven pairs of clumsy feet of earlier now glided over stones and branches. I had seldom 'heard' seven people move through the bush as silently as this group. I was scared of looking around at the group of foxterriers behind me. I could instinctively 'feel' how they expected a poacher to jump out from every bush. Another shot, approximately 200 m ahead. I indicated to the group that they had to go down on their haunches and listen for any telltale sounds. Nothing! We again moved forward very stealthily. After a further 100 m, I suddenly saw the eastern-boundary fence line. I again went down on my haunches, and the rest of the group followed. The guys at the back didn't know the reason and were expecting bullets to fly. I indicated to everyone to gather around for a discussion. I showed them the eastern-boundary fence and indicated that we were not allowed to cross the fence and that the shots we had heard originated from across the border. What do we do now? The team was divided 50-50. Half the team wanted to go and show the poachers a thing or two, and the other half said: 'Stop right here!' To me, it was very interesting who voted for what.

My character analysis was only 40 per cent correct. I also knew that the decisions were taken in a 'team' environment and that if the decisions were to have been made individually, it would have been different. My casting vote determined that we remain within the KNP. We stayed where we were and drank water. Our mouths were dry from all the tension. No further shots were heard. We thereafter patrolled up and down the fence line, looking for possible border-breaching. Nothing! At about midday, we returned to Ramiti Pan for a debriefing session. I was surprised by everyone's feedback on how they had experienced the past couple of hours. I was of the firm opinion that if one wanted to bring out the true character of an individual, one had to take him or her into the bush and expose him or her to some sort of stressful experience. A human being is a wonderful thing . . .

* * *

One of my Section Ranger colleagues, Johan Steyn (behind his back, we called him 'halfmens' – half human), sometimes came forward with the weirdest behaviour patterns, often to his own detriment. On one occasion, the two of us with our teams were combating a fire that had spread into the KNP from Mozambique. One of our colleagues, Wilkie Wilkens, from the Engineering Department, who was responsible for the maintenance of the eastern-boundary fence, and his labour team came and gave much appreciated assistance. We eventually were able to stop the head of the fire against the Molondozi firebreak road. At one stage, the three of us were together walking down the firebreak road, making the fire safe by dragging logs deeper into the burnt area and scattering smouldering elephant and buffalo dung. At this stage, we were approximately 2 km away from the vehicles. The fire was under control, and the three of us walked back, chatting, to the vehicles. After the necessary cordialities, we thanked Wilkie for his help as he and his team drove off. Wilkie was about 200 m down the road when Johan sat down on the ground and took off one shoe. 'What's wrong?' I queried. 'I just want to remove the stone in my shoe!'

I could see that the stone had made a hole in the sock and that there was a big blister on the side of Johan's foot. 'Johan, how long has that stone been in your shoe?' I wanted to know. 'From when we left the vehicles,' he answered. 'Are you daft? Why are you only taking the stone out now? We have been fighting the fire and making it safe for close to 2 hours and have walked about 4 km!' His agitated answer was, 'I refuse to take off my shoes in front of an engineering guy! I also have my honour!' I threw my hands up in despair and shook my head in disbelief.

'Well, if you want to be hard-arsed, then you must suffer,' was the only sympathy he got from me.

*   *   *

Wilkie was one of those rough diamonds – more rough than diamond. While doing fence maintenance on the Lower Sabie eastern boundary, he would sleep over in the Lower Sabie Rest Camp. He had the habit of having a few before going to bed. While in the camp, there was a late-evening thunderstorm that caused an Eskom power failure. There was a standby generator a distance from the camp, specifically for these kinds of emergencies. The Rest Camp Manager at that stage was Oom Eddie Bonnin (he was from Polish descent if I remember correctly). Oom Eddie had difficulty in expressing himself in Afrikaans. He was a dear old man, almost 2 m high, with a wild salt-and-pepper beard that came to his chest. Oom Eddie was not mechanically inclined, and he knew that Wilkie from the Engineering Department was booked into the rest camp, and he decided to ask for assistance to start the standby generator. There were a lot of perishables in the various fridges and freezers in the rest camp that could not be allowed to perish. Oom Eddie had another peculiarity, in that he slept in a long white robe, and he wore a strange tussled cap, probably something to do with his Polish ancestry. Because the lights were off, and he did not possess a torch, he took one of the old paraffin lamps called a 'sketekete', or 'lamps hurricane' as it was registered on the Asset Register, to light his way to Wilkie's rondavel. He knocked on the door but was only greeted by loud snoring. He knocked again, but still there was no response. Fortunately, the door was not locked when he tested it, and he went in. 'Vilikie, Vilikie,' he called in his Polish-Afrikaans accent to wake Wilkie. At this stage, Wilkie half awoke from an intoxicated deep sleep and heard someone calling. I don't know whether Wilkie was dreaming before he awoke. In front of him, he saw this white apparition with a tussled cap on his head and a long beard. The beard seemed to move when the flickering light of the 'sketekete' fell on it. To add to all this, the apparition called his name! Wilkie decided the day of reckoning had come and that it was time to pay for all his sins. He decided that under these circumstances, he had to be very humble and respectful. He crawled up to the headboard of the bed and rolled himself into as small a bundle as possible.

'Please, Oom Devil, I promise, I will never do it again! Please, Oom Devil, never again,' he whispered with his hands in front of his eyes. He could not look the Devil in the eye.

'Vilikie, it's me, Oom Bonnin.' In due course, Wilkie came to and realised what was actually happening. He accompanied Oom Eddie to start the standby generator, and with electrical lights shining everywhere, he then went back to bed. To this day, I still wonder what it was that Wilkie promised never to do again.

*   *   *

I must also tell you about Awie de Qlerq, the Section Ranger at Crocodile Bridge. He was a thinly built guy of medium length. He had unruly hair, and with his type of haircut, his hair was permanently standing on end. Being a Section Ranger at Crocodile Bridge was not an easy task. One sometimes had to have hair on one's teeth to be able to work with the hostile and very difficult neighbours on the southern side of the Crocodile River. At one stage, Awie and one of the farmers, a sturdy well-built man, had altercations about accusations that 'our' hippos had taken a liking to his tomato fields and had caused considerable damage.

'Hippos don't eat tomatoes, especially not if these were in such a bad condition as yours were in.' One thing led to another, and the two of them became hot under the collar. I must quickly clarify that one could fit two Awies into the size of this disgruntled farmer. When the farmer was close to becoming physical, Awie realised that he would now have to tread carefully, or he would come off second best by a large margin.

'Yes!' snarled the very cross farmer. 'What are you intending to do about the matter?'

'I am going to spit on your shadow and run away!' was Awie's quick answer. For a while, the farmer gasped for air, but then he saw the funny side and started laughing.

The very same Awie was summoned to give expert evidence at a Circuit Court at Komatipoort. Officials from the Provincial Department of Nature Conservation, or Fauna and Flora as they were commonly known, had apprehended a man for killing and being in possession of 'Rooibok' meat (Afrikaans for Impala). During the investigation, this person said that he had not killed a 'Rooibok' but an Impala. In defence, he said that he had made a thorough study of the Provincial Ordinance (the Afrikaans version), and nowhere did he find that one could not shoot an Impala. According to his understanding, a 'Rooibok' and an Impala were not of the same species. 'Rooibok', on the other hand, was listed, but he had not shot a 'Rooibok' but an Impala. On the designated day, Awie pitched for the Circuit Court dressed in his best KNP uniform, especially for the court procedures. When it was his turn, he was requested to take the stand.

'Mr de Qlerq, do you have any problems taking the oath?' asked the judge.

'Not at all,' said Awie and was taken through the normal formalities to promise to tell the truth and nothing but the truth.

'Mr de Qlerq, do you understand that you have been called as an expert witness?'

'Yes, Your Honour,' he replied.

'Where do you work?' was the next question. 'Can the man not see that I am dressed in my best cleanest KNP uniform?' he thought to himself.

'In the Kruger National Park, Your Honour,' he answered with a smile.

'How long have you been working in the Kruger National Park?'

'Almost 10 years, Your Honour,' was the answer.

'Would you say that the 10 years' service would qualify you to be called an expert witness?' 'Is this guy looking for trouble?' wondered Awie.

'I would reckon so, Your Honour,' was the friendly answer.

'Mr de Qlerq, the accused is of the opinion that he shot an Impala, not a "Rooibok",' as stipulated by the Provincial Ordinance, (goeverning the hunting of animals). 'Would you please, in your expert opinion, describe to the court what the difference is between an Impala and a "Rooibok"?' 'This guy wants to catch me out,' thought Awie. Why had he asked the question in such a roundabout way? Awie could see the judge's furrow wrinkle when he hesitated to answer. Awie cleared his throat and answered: 'The same difference as there is between your anus and your asshole, Your Honour!' Needles to say, pandemonium broke loose in the courtroom, and the court had to be adjourned until order was restored. Fortunately for Awie, the judge saw the funny side of things and found the person guilty on the grounds of Awie's expert evidence.

*   *   *

I had always wanted to build a tree house, preferably next to a natural pan where one could overnight in relative safety. Approximately 4 km on the Lubyelubye firebreak road, from where it branches off from the Skukuza/Lower Sabie tarred road, there was a natural pan with a Leadwood tree growing right next to the water's edge when the pan was full. During the rainy season and into early autumn, there was water to be found in the pan. During one of the drilling projects, I convinced the drilling contractor to donate a borehole near the pan to the staff of the KNP. Fortunately, the peg that I had divined was successful as I only had one chance. The yield of the borehole was estimated to be in the vicinity of 4,000 l per hour. Now I could continue with the construction of the tree house. The Leadwood tree would form one of the four pillars of the tree house and could also serve as the entrance route up to and into the tree house. I first of all had to tell Oom Johan of my intentions, and I motivated it as a place where we could expose the staff of the KNP to the wonder of sleeping out and experiencing the bush in relative safety. It was not very difficult to convince him, and his only prescript was that there should be order and control at all times.

Very few of the Skukuza staff did not spend an evening or two in the tree house, and stories of exceptional experiences were told: a herd of elephants that came to drink at the pan; two lions that roared in the vicinity during the whole evening; a White rhino cow and calf that came to drink; a leopard that came to drink and entertained the tree-house occupants, sawing at close quarters (a sound that very few people have experienced). One guy told the story of a hyena that came rummaging around and found an interesting smell on the left front tyre of his car and bit a hole in it. When the tyre started deflating, the hyena got a big fright and ran away with a *yelp-laugh*. Others said that they had seen nothing but that the 'utter silence' was a magical experience. My most cherished moment at the tree house was when Morné, Magnus, and I spent a while at the tree house from just before sunset on a dark-moon evening. This was my favourite time of the day, when all day-living things came to rest; the francolins bid the sun farewell for the evening, with the Pearl-spotted owls, Scops owls, various nightjars, and the Giant eagle owl welcoming the night.

The tree house faced westwards. It was early winter, and the western horizon slowly changed from light orange, to all its shades, to almost red as the sun disappeared further behind the horizon. These beautiful colours were reflected on the mirror-smooth water surface. Between the water reflection and the tops of the surrounding Delagoa thorn trees, it was pitch-black, and we could not make out any detail. 'Please keep very quiet,' I said to Morné and Magnus. I thought I could hear something approaching. I couldn't see anything but had the feeling that there was something. Suddenly, I saw movement in the red water. The movement, however, was not in the water, but it was an upside down reflection of an elephant bull nearing the pan to come and drink. The scene was indescribably beautiful: a perfect upside down reflection of a big tusker drinking water at the edge of the pan. The small water ripples caused by the elephant's trunk sipping water created a mystical atmosphere to the reflected colours and the reflection of the elephant. I could sense that the two boys were also enjoying the scene. 'Wow, Dad, but that is beautiful,' they almost simultaneously whispered. We enjoyed the scene until the elephant had finished drinking and had silently moved into the darkness. We lingered on at the tree house until it was pitch-dark and then returned home to go and tell the story.

*　　*　　*

During my tenure at Lower Sabie, SANParks imported a number of Black rhinos from Kwa-Zulu Natal Parks to the KNP and more specifically to the Lower Sabie Section. I was instructed to prepare offloading ramps along the Lubyelubye firebreak road. This was ideal Black-rhino habitat, and furthermore, there were several evenly spaced natural pans, including the one at the tree house, along the Lubyelubye Spruit. None of the KNP Officials, at that stage, had any practical experience of Black rhinos. The last known information on Black rhinos dated back to 1937, when the last of the Black rhinos was destroyed along the N'watimhiri Spruit. The N'watimhiri and Lubyelubye Spruits were situated in the same plant community and were approximately 15 km apart. Natal Park's staff did the transport of the Black rhinos and pitched up at Lower Sabie on the predetermined date. Every time the big transport lorry came to a stop, one could hear the whistle-grunt of the Black rhinos fighting with 'something'. As soon as the transporter started moving, no fighting sound was audible as the Black rhinos now had to concentrate on not losing their balance inside the moving lorry.

Needles to say, the media was present in their hordes to report on the historical occasion. Photographers and reporters in general were not party to being told where to stand or sit or hide. Especially not hide. They always knew better. The one photographer from the *Scope Magazine* was adamant about where he would stand to get the best shots and would not be dictated to. I am jumping ahead with the story. After having arrived at the offloading site, the big transporter had to reverse up to the offloading ramp as the exit door was located at the rear of the lorry. These doors would be opened at the appropriate time to allow the Black rhinos to walk down the ramp to freedom in the Lubyelubye bush – in your dreams!

A Land Rover station wagon with a sturdy roof rack was parked approximately 20 m from the transporter, and all the cautious media representatives who were prepared to listen took up a vantage point on the roof rack: some sitting down, some kneeling, and some standing upright. The *Scope* photographer, however, parked himself behind a Delagoa thorn tree and strung his second camera up on a broken branch in front of him. I again tried to explain to him the folly of his position, but: 'I know what I am doing,' was his answer. My chosen safe place was between the two rear wheels of the transporter's double axle. I could quickly dive in there if required, and no Black rhino could reach me there. The Natal officials wanted to know if we were all ready. They opened the rear doors. No Black rhino made its appearance. We could hear the animals fighting with the sides of the transporter. One of the Natal officials threw me a mealy meal sack and indicated to me to wave the sack in front of the open doors. Just one wave of the sack was sufficient. The first Black rhino charged through the door and down the offloading ramp: very agile for such a big animal. At the bottom of the ramp, it turned around and with its small beady eyes searched for the guy who had been waving the sack and took in the lay of the land. Naturally, I was already safely under the vehicle. Then I heard 'CLICK' as the *Scope* photographer immortalised the scene. The Black rhino also heard the sound and took exception to it. The animal did not see the man behind the tree, but it did not like the bright thing that hung from the broken branch. The Black rhino charged forward and hit the camera with its horn, shattering the camera and distributing bits and pieces of it over the whole area. The *Scope* photographer stood frozen with shock behind the tree. The rhino spun around when it heard other cameras '*click*' and '*clack*'. I shouted at the poor *Scope* guy to seek refuge underneath the Land Rover. He listened for once in his life and made a dive for the relative safety underneath the Land Rover. As he dived under the vehicle, the Black rhino spotted him and charged. As his feet disappeared under the Land Rover, the rhino struck the vehicle with a loud thud. The rhino hooked its horn under the body of the Land Rover and tried to pick it up. The media people on top of the vehicle's carrier lost their balance and grabbed onto one another and anything they could find to prevent falling off. The rhino let go of the vehicle, which fell back to the earth with a thud. 'Ouch!' shouted the guy under the Land Rover, and this enraged the rhino more. The vehicle was again lifted and dropped with another 'Ouch!' coming from below the vehicle. The Black rhino did not fancy the 'ouching!' and repeated the action. I realised that I would have to intervene. I left the safe haven under the transporter and, with waving arms, the mealie meal sack still in my hand, shouted and charged at the enraged animal. The rhino then focused on me and charged. I allowed the rhino enough space and dived back under the transporter. When I looked around, I saw the enraged face of the rhino some 2 m away. The Black rhino glared at me for almost 5 seconds and with a snort, ran off into the surrounding bush. After I had helped the *Scope* photographer out from under the Land Rover, the first thing we saw was his bloodied face, and he was shaking like a reed in a strong current.

'Why didn't I listen to you . . . ?' were his first words. 'Regret always comes too late. I had to risk my life to save you!' I rebuked him in Afrikaans and hoped that the other bilingual media people would not tell him what I thought of him. Where the *Scope* guy lay under the Land Rover, he had been directly under the shackles of the rear leaf spring, and every time the rhino had lifted and let go of the vehicle, the shackles had gashed holes into his head. We 'patched' him up as best we could, and one of the other vehicles rushed him off to the local medical doctor at Skukuza. We were later informed that he had received fifteen stitches and lots of sedatives before he looked human again. Photographers normally take many photos and then select the best. On this day, however, they only had one chance! The other journalists, however, after having calmed down, had lots to report.

After all the commotion had normalised, we had the opportunity to open the second compartment of the transporter to release the second Black rhino into its new environment. What a contrast! This animal calmly walked down the ramp, liked what it saw, knew that it was going to enjoy staying in the KNP, and ran off into the bush.

During the next week, I visited the veldt pans along the Lubyelubye firebreak road every day – on the motorbike – to see if I could find any Black-rhino spoor. I travelled slowly on the motorbike on the water's edge to see if I could spot any spoor. It was very hot on the third day after release, and midmorning, I again went looking for black-rhino spoor. The tree house pan was the first one to be visited. I turned off from the firebreak road to the closest edge of the pan and with the motorbike in low gear, travelled along the water's edge. When I got opposite the tree house, my eye caught something amongst the rushes askance of me. It, however, was already too late.

If one is suddenly pumped full of adrenaline, one registers and reacts very fast, but one remembers slowly. I remember seeing the Black rhino getting up out of the water and charging. To the left of me, all the leadwood poles of the tree house blocked my potential escape route. To the right of me was the water and mud of the pan. That would be a foolhardy choice of escape. The motorbike didn't have a reverse gear, so that route was also out of the question. It was already too late to jump off the motorbike and escape on foot. The Natal guys had warned us that Black rhinos had the habit of charging through or over an obstacle and only stopping on the other side of the perceived danger. I could picture my destiny. I remained seated, straddling the motorbike, clutch depressed; I remembered being in first gear. I played with the throttle, opening and closing it to make as much of a racket as possible, adding to my screaming and shouting. All the above flashed through my head as I decided on a plan of action, while the Black rhino was charging from approximately 7 m away. The racket of the motorbike revving, my shouting, and a silent prayer – it was a very short one – caused the Black rhino to stop about 1 m in front of the motorbike, and it glared at me with those small, watery, beady eyes. The Black rhino swayed its head very slightly from left to right, then looked at me with its left eye and then with its right eye. There was no false note in the revving motorbike and my shouting. This was a little too much for the Black rhino. It took a slight step backwards and turned its backside towards me. 'Now,' I thought to myself and took the gap. As I rushed past, the rhino took a swipe at the motorbike with its horn. It missed, and I picked up speed, with the Black rhino in hot pursuit. I had to navigate an escape route through the Umbrella thorn and Sickle bush. I got badly scratched but remained in front. When I hit the firebreak road, I had a 5-m lead. The motorbike now had five forward gears, and I could kick dust in the eyes of the charging Black rhino. A kilometer further on, I stopped to get over my fright. Now the flipside of an adrenaline overload kicked in. I trembled like a reed in a strong flowing current. I could hardly stand up straight and tried to say a prayer. No sound was audible, just the movement of trembling lips.

*   *   *

A week after the first two rhinos were offloaded, the next group of two arrived from Natal. Without the presence of the media and with only officials being present, the offloading went more smoothly; although, the

Black rhinos were still short-tempered. After the successful offloading along the Lubyelubye firebreak road, I was on my way back to Lower Sabie. As I turned onto the tar road from the Lubyelubye firebreak road, I saw a vehicle standing on the Skukuza side of the Lubyelubye Bridge. Steam was coming from the front of the vehicle. I decided to go and investigate. Most probably, it was a tourist who had forgotten to check the water level in the radiator, and with the slow driving in the park, the vehicle had most probably overheated. Getting closer, I could see that there was something big amiss.

The front of the Datsun Laurel appeared a bit modified and quite recently as well. On nearing the vehicle, I could see a man and a woman in the vehicle. Their faces were as white as sheets, and they were frightened out of their wits. I got out of my vehicle to find out what the matter was. They simultaneously began talking gibberish. I held up my hands. 'Whoa, calm down first, and then you can tell me what happened,' I said, looking at the man behind the steering wheel. After a few deep breaths, he started: 'We were parked along the road, looking at the bee-eaters catching flying insects. They were operating from that dead tree over there.' For your information, that was between the tar road and the river. Their attention, therefore, had been focused away from the in-veldt. He continued, 'Suddenly, we heard and felt a hard thump at the front of our vehicle. We saw a large rhino standing in front of the vehicle. The monster charged again, and fortunately, the horn penetrated the radiator, and hot water and steam squirted into its face. With this, the rhino ran off into the bush. Sir, I promise you, we did not make the rhino cross.' 'Yes,' said the woman, 'we were only watching the bee-eaters over there. I hope the rhino wasn't hurt.' 'The woman's heart is in the right place,' I thought. A rhino attacked and damaged their vehicle without provocation, and their first concern was for the safety of the rhino. I recommended that we leave their vehicle on the edge of the tar road and that they accompany me to the Lower Sabie Rest Camp, where they could get some refreshments (on the house of course), and we could contact the local Automobile Association (or AA) at Skukuza for emergency repairs and to assist them to get mobile again. On our way to the rest camp, I explained to them how unpredictable Black rhinos could be. I naturally didn't tell them that we had just offloaded Black rhinos from Natal in the general vicinity that morning. According to my assessment, that could have been the only logical explanation for the Black rhino's strange behaviour.

* * *

With every offload of Black rhinos, there was some sort of drama. The transport vehicle that brought the third group had mechanical problems en route and only arrived at Lower Sabie early in the evening. We decided to only offload these early the next morning. The offloading process wasn't worse than any of the previous offloads. However, when I turned right at the Lubyelubye firebreak T-junction with the tar road, my heart sank into my shoes. I found a Black rhino running in front of me in the middle of the tar road, on its way to Lower Sabie. The tourist gate at Lower Sabie was due to open in about 15 minutes' time, and I could visualise the drama if this ill-tempered Black rhino were to meet up with an unsuspecting tourist head-on.

My brain worked overtime on a possible plan of action. I needed to get in front of the Black rhino so that I could 'lead' it to a destination of my choice. How would I be able to get in front of the Black rhino without it destroying both the vehicle and me? I negotiated the vehicle to just on 5 m from the Black rhino's backside. The animal continued down the middle of the road, glancing at me over its left shoulder, and there was no way that Black rhino could stop suddenly to confront me. I moved to the right-hand side of the road, and the animal moved to the left hand side in order to keep an eye on the vehicle. 'I have got it!' I said to myself. 'I am going to outfox you.' I now moved to the left-hand side of the road, and the animal complied by moving to the right-hand side to watch the vehicle. I now got as close to the left-hand backside of the animal as I could. I changed down to a lower gear and accelerated as hard as I could. The Black rhino was caught off guard. It moved closer to the vehicle, and we touched lightly. The animal shied away a little from the contact. The gap increased sufficiently, and the vehicle was still accelerating. In passing the Black rhino, I glanced in the rear-view mirror and saw the animal looking at the rear of the vehicle. To judge speed and relative movement in a rear-view mirror and at that speed wasn't easy. I tensed my body for the impact with the vehicle. 'How am I going to motivate the damage to the vehicle on an accident report form?' the thought flashed through my mind. I didn't feel anything and glanced in the rear-view mirror and only saw the back of the Black rhino as it tried to hook the rear of the vehicle. 'My plan worked!' I smiled to myself. Now I just had to stay in front of the animal and entice it

146

to try and get hold of the vehicle. I glanced at my watch. Another 2 minutes before the gate opened for tourists. I couldn't have come this far for the plan to fail now. I could see the rest camp gate. It was still closed.

About 100 m in front of the gate, there was a T-junction to the left that gave access to the low water bridge over the Sabie River and Tshokwane. I had planned to get the Black rhino over the low water bridge and as far away from the waiting tourists as possible. I, however, still had to negotiate the 90° turn at the T-junction without rolling the vehicle. I flashed the headlights at the Security Guard at the gate. Fortunately, he was wide awake and did not open the gate. How was I going to negotiate that sharp corner? I accelerated a little and saw that the Black rhino still had eyes only for the rear of the vehicle. I accelerated even more. The distance between the Black rhino and the vehicle was now approximately 20 m. The distance between us had to be just sufficient to keep the attention of the rhino focused on the vehicle. I was approaching the 90° turn and suddenly applied the brakes, caught the Black rhino off guard, and went into a bit of a controlled slide as we negotiated the 90° turn. The Black rhino followed its own route around the turn and went wide into the veldt. The animal's speed into the corner was too fast for the hulking body to stay on the road. Now the Black rhino was extremely agitated and charged at the vehicle with increased speed; now to lead the Black rhino across the low water bridge!

All low water bridges in the KNP have the same construction pattern. On the edge of the bridge at 2-m intervals, there were concrete blocks approximately 30 cm high above the driving surface to make the low water bridges negotiable during relatively small floods that submerged the driving surface. When the vehicle-and-Black-rhino train hit the bridge, the Black rhino component saw a threat in every concrete block and in passing gaffed at every block. On the other side of the bridge, I allowed the Black rhino to catch up again. On the Mlondozi Loop, I led the rhino on for another 2 km and gradually increased the distance between us. When the distance was about 150 m between us, the Black rhino lost interest in its adversary and ran into the veldt. I uttered a sigh of relief and returned to the rest camp, thanked the Security Guard for his prompt action, and smiled at the disgruntled tourists who had been kept in the rest camp for a minute or three longer than the official opening time. It was now 6.05, and I was already tired.

In later years, I frequently met up with Black rhinos on foot during patrols. None of the above violent/outrageous behaviour was experienced. With the warning, of course, that Black rhinos have to be treated with the utmost respect under all kinds of circumstances.

*   *   *

Just as you people, living outside of the KNP, have altercations with your neighbours, so also the Section Rangers who are responsible for law enforcement in the KNP have periodic altercations with tourists. Regardless of very good environmental education programmes, transgressors were plentiful. The most general transgressions were: speeding, feeding of animals, littering, getting out of vehicles, sitting on the vehicle's roof, standing upright through the sunroof, sitting on the windowsill, disturbing animals, and many more. I personally wrote out very few traffic tickets or general tourist transgression summonses. I usually got very good results from verbal reprimands that usually took the following course after the transgressor had been called to order:

'Good day, sir/madam. I saw you (followed by the specific transgression). I would like to accept that you are a law-abiding citizen (more often than not, there were children in the vehicle) and that you strive to be a good example for your children. Please, would you be so kind as to explain to me and your children why you' (followed by the specific transgression). The transgressor at this stage usually turned red in the face from shame, let his head hang, and mumbled something incoherent. The children then usually started to giggle to add to the adult's discomfort. I very seldom encountered someone who became aggressive during or after the verbal reprimand. 'Sir/Madam, would you please do yourself the favour of reading the dos and the don'ts on your entrance permit again, and do enjoy your holiday further! Good day!'

Littering was a major problem. Every year after the big tourist season, from April to September, the KNP Management had all the litter, comprising of bottles, tins, and other disposed items, picked up between Skukuza and

Pretoriuskop Rest Camps. It was very seldom that two tipper trucks were not filled to maximum capacity. The Section Rangers had to do the same on the secondary roads. Something that I could not handle was the habit of tourist mothers who threw soiled nappies out of the windows for someone else to pick up. 'Sis on you!' It was not the babies' fault. That is what babies do! It was, however, bad planning from someone who should have known better.

I also had a grudge against everyone who transgressed the prescribed speed limit. Why do these people visit the KNP? How many beautiful and interesting sightings are missed at that speed! It was tantamount to going into a shop with a shopping list, running down the aisles, and not seeing any of the specials on offer. On top of all this, these speedsters placed animal lives and their own at risk.

I once had a very embarrassing experience on my way from Skukuza to Lower Sabie. The maximum speed limit for officials was 65 km per hour. At this given speed, one would naturally slowly catch up and pass a law-abiding tourist travelling at 50 km per hour. If a tourist vehicle could not be overtaken, it was speeding. I encountered just such a vehicle one day. I had to increases my speed in order to catch up with the vehicle. A francolin put paid to my plan when I passed the vehicle to call the speedster to halt so I could deliver my verbal reprimand or sermon. At the very moment that my vehicle's nose was passing the offending vehicle's nose, a francolin flew across my path, and I struck the unfortunate bird, killing it outright, with feathers scattered in all directions and even over the offending vehicle's bonnet. Now why did I feel guilty? I just travelled past the offending vehicle, moved to the middle of the road, and slowly decreased my speed to the prescribed tourist speed. The tourist got the message, and in the rear-view mirror, I could see a broad smile on the driver's face. He would have had mitigating evidence against me if I had gone ahead with my usual reprimand.

* * *

On another occasion, the whole family was driving back to Lower Sabie in our private vehicle after a school athletic meeting at Skukuza. In the vicinity of the Nkuhlu Picnic Site, a white BMW (tourist vehicle) came past us. The passing speed was due to the fact that we were travelling in our private vehicle, and so the driver had not recognised me as a KNP Official. I fell in behind the white BMW and moved in alongside him. I indicated to the driver through the open window that he must reduce speed and stop. I was not wearing my KNP uniform. I moved to the side of the road to stop. The white BMW, however, just raced past. I could feel the children thinking: 'What are you going to do now, Dad?' My blood pressure went up a notch. I put foot to the accelerator and caught up with the BMW again. Now the BMW tried to prevent me from going past him by swerving left and right across the road. I later took to the verge alongside the tar surface to get past. At this stage, we were travelling at almost 120 km per hour. Now I was ahead and started reducing speed and kept the BMW behind me until we were both stationary. Just as I was about to get out of our vehicle to give the BMW a piece of my mind, he came forward and stopped next to me and shouted through the open window: 'You do that again, and I will squash your throat!' With squealing tyres and gravel flying, he pulled away and raced down the road. Now I was completely calm and rational and drove off at normal speed. At one stage, the BMW was caught up in a string of other vehicles that were travelling at a slow speed. I drove past all of them as if nothing had happened. The BMW most probably thought that he had given me the fright of my life by threatening me. I continued to Lower Sabie Rest Camp, where my wife, Liza took over. She and the kids continued to our house, and I walked to the rest camp. At Reception, I indicated to the Receptionist that I wanted to sit in the Rest Camp Manager's office for a while. From the office window, I could see almost all of the parking area in front of the building and could keep an eye on passing vehicles. The white BMW, however, was not spotted. I was at the point of leaving the office when I heard the following agitated conversation between someone and the Receptionist. He relayed in detail about someone who had forced him off the road and had indicated to him that he was going to cause him bodily harm etc., etc. Furthermore, he wanted the KNP Management to urgently address the matter and to act accordingly. He gave our vehicle registration number to the Receptionist. He indicated that he was a medical doctor and that he would gladly bear witness to the fact that the driver of the above-mentioned registration number was either under the influence of alcohol or drugs or both. I remained in the Rest Camp Manager's office for a while longer and then went to the Reception.

'You probably overheard the accusation and request for action?' asked the Receptionist. 'Yes, thank you,' I replied. 'It was aimed at me!' The Receptionist looked at me with big eyes because she knew that I wasn't inclined to take drugs and/or alcohol. 'Who is the complainant, and where does he stay?' I queried.

After having consulted the accommodation list, she said he was Dr so and so from chalet 38 and 39.

I calmly walked back to the house, put on my official uniform, got into the official vehicle, and drove back to the rest camp to chalets 38 and 39. I saw the BMW parked next to one of the chalets. As the devil would have it, a man came walking from the chalet to the BMW, most probably to collect something from it. He had a long white safari suit on - typical doctor! I had to control myself from not bursting out laughing. The doctor had a slightly deformed lower leg and foot. I wasn't tempted to laugh at the doctor's deformity but at the image in my head of the doctor standing on my throat and choking me with the deformed foot and how I battled to prevent this by pressing my chin onto my chest. I parked behind the white BMW, got out of the official bakkie, walked to the man, and introduced myself. 'Wow, you people certainly attend to a complaint quickly. I am Doctor so and so . . .' I again had to suppress my laughter. 'Please to meet you,' I said. He immediately and incoherently started giving his account of the story as if he had as yet not had time to prepare his speech. 'Slow down, Doctor,' I said to him to calm him down. 'Please start right from the beginning. I need all the details.' The doctor came into a sort of an 'attention' stance. He could, however, not perform a proper military 'attention' due to his slight deformity. He started with his version of what had transpired, how the man had wanted to push him off the road with his vehicle for no apparent reason, the aggression of the man, how he had wanted to climb out of his vehicle to do him bodily harm, and how he (the doctor) was able to, just in time, race away from the lunatic. 'The man attempted to push me off the road on two occasions, but I was able to outfox him!' 'What was the matter with the man?' I queried. I wanted him to repeat what he had said to the Receptionist. 'I am a medical Doctor,' he reiterated. 'According to my professional opinion, the man was either under the influence of alcohol or drugs or both. His behaviour was totally irrational.'

'That is a very serious allegation,' I warned. 'I am prepared to attest to this fact under oath if you so require. Let me give you my business card in case you need me as a witness.' He took one from the BMW and gave it to me. 'Thank you very much,' I responded on receiving it. Now I had him cornered. 'Now, then, Doctor so and so' I said. 'The person you have just described is now standing right in front of you. Would you please be so kind as to repeat your professional diagnosis?' I saw the colour drain from his face. He looked like a chameleon, I thought to myself, when the colour of his face took on the white of the BMW. He did not stand on skew attention anymore but was leaning against the BMW, most probably the cause of the doctor's white colour. I then informed him of how I had experienced the happenings of the past hour or so. 'I am tempted to lay a charge of deformation against you!' I threatened. He nervously stood around and said: 'It will not hold up in court as it is your word against mine,' he retaliated. 'Not so fast,' I interrupted him. 'For your information, I was in the Rest Camp Manager's office when you gave your learned opinion of me to the Receptionist.' He now didn't lean against the BMW anymore; he practically lay on top of it. The more contact with the surface of the white BMW made his face even whiter! I looked him straight in the eye and said in a measured tone, pointing his business card at him, 'Thank you very much for your time. Enjoy your stay in the KNP. You will hear from me again.' I got into the bakkie, and as I drove off, I saw him still leaning/lying against the white BMW. Involuntarily, I pulled my chin against my chest to ward off his little foot from squashing my throat. I burst out laughing. The doctor had made my day. I did not know how the rest of his KNP holiday panned out. It would most probably have been more enjoyable had he known that I wasn't considering pressing charges of deformation. I really hoped the clubfooted doctor had learnt a lesson!

* * *

One Saturday evening just after midnight, during the Easter weekend, the Rest Camp Manager woke me up by banging loudly on the front door. He was very agitated and had white foam at the corners of his mouth like someone who had spoken at length without swallowing. 'What is the matter?' I wanted to know. He told me that a group of drunken students in the rest camp were making life unbearable for him and would not pay heed to his requests or threats. He had had several complaints from tourists about their unruly behaviour and the unacceptable loud noise that was spoiling the other tourists' enjoyment of a quiet night in the bush.

To put things into perspective, it has been my experience having worked in the KNP that you instantly become the most popular friend or family member, often being expected to provide a free holiday in the KNP. Some of the families were so far removed that one had to study the Family Tree to trace the connection. Friends naturally also had friends who also had friends. One of the newly appointed tourism officials (a very young lady) had come to me just before the Easter weekend to request that I pitch one of my tents on the lawn, in front of her flat, due to lack of sufficient accommodation in the flat; a group of her good student friends would be coming to visit over the Easter weekend, and they would be bringing some friends along. 'You are looking for trouble,' I had warned. 'No,' she had replied. 'They are all nature lovers and are coming to the KNP for the right reasons.' 'What about the friends' friends?' I had wanted to know. 'They as well,' she had replied. I had pitied her. She had most probably also wanted to brag about the KNP, and I had agreed to her request. That had been a BIG mistake. As it turned out, it was some of the male friends of the friends who were causing the trouble. When she could not control them any longer, she had gone and sought assistance from the Rest Camp Manager. He, however, had almost burst an artery trying to no avail to restore order. Now it was my turn. With my uniform on and armed with a hippo-hide shambuck, I set off for the rest camp.

I soon realised that I was in for a long night. I very calmly started arguing with the two ringleaders. Inebriation, however, ruled the argument. I argued this way and that way but couldn't make any headway. Both the ringleaders were my physical superiors. I tried my best to get under their skins to make them aggressive, hoping that they would physically attack me. I could not wait to take them out with the hippo-hide shambuck. How I found the patience not to just jump in and take them apart, I don't know.

At one stage, one of the most inebriated ringleaders came and stood in front of me, poking his forefinger into my stomach, asking, 'What do you intend on doing, you fucking bald-headed old ranger?' I calmly looked the guy in the eyes, hoping that he would physically attack me. I wouldn't just have taken him apart; I would have annihilated him. 'I am going to throw you out of the KNP,' I answered. One or two of the other students (less inebriated) saw that my patience was running out. They started packing the ringleaders' belongings into their vehicle. When the ringleaders saw that their two pals had also deserted them, they climbed into their vehicle. I instructed the female official to drive their vehicle and escorted them to the Crocodile Bridge gate. At 03.00, we assisted them out the gate and waved them farewell. On the way back, the female official could not stop begging for forgiveness for the poor behaviour of the friends' friends. 'I hope you learnt your lesson,' I replied when I dropped her off at her flat. She must have as I never got a request for a tent on the lawn again.

*   *   *

On another occasion, I had to sleep over in Skukuza one Saturday evening. Ben, the resident Section Ranger, came and woke me up. Ben's native name was 'Masbambela' (when he gave a hand, things happened). He came to request my assistance to go and quieten down a group of rowdy and drunk tourists. Why he needed my assistance, I did not know. Ben was big and strong enough to sort out five sober tourists single-handedly. He most probably wanted a dependable witness if something went wrong. The altercations, especially with one drunk, became quite heated to the point where Ben and I decided that it would be best for the surrounding tourists, for this guy himself, and for us as well to throw this unsavoury character out of the KNP at Kruger Gate. 'Sir, will you please get onto the back of my bakkie,' Ben requested in a friendly tone. The guy adopted a high-and-mighty attitude and refused. Ben again reiterated his quest for cooperation. 'I haven't lost anything on the back of your bakkie,' was his cheeky answer. Ben stood closer, grabbed hold of the guy's shirt collar with one hand, and, with the other hand, grabbed hold of the seat of his pants, picked him up, and threw him onto the load bed of the bakkie. Fortunately, the lid to the load bed was open. We did not want the guy to get hurt even if he had climbed onto the back of the bakkie of his own accord in his drunken state. The guy skidded across the load bed like a greased commodity. He hit the front of the load bed with a wheeze as the air was knocked out of his lungs. In this crumpled state, he looked at Ben and said, 'You meant what you said, hey?' With the guy's permission, of course, I drove his vehicle to Kruger Gate, with Ben following with his very fragile cargo. We hoped that the cold

154

night air on the back of Ben's bakkie would sober the guy sufficiently so he could find alternative accommodation for himself outside of the KNP.

*   *   *

Fortunately, these kinds of altercations with tourists were few and far between. It is, however, very sad that the majority of law-abiding tourists' KNP holidays have to be spoilt by egocentric individuals who could not care less about fellow tourists. Something that has recently become a great worry to me is the fact that the younger generation especially will do anything to get to a lodge, game farm, conservation area, etc. and on their return can only talk about the awesome party that they had had and will not mention anything about their bush experiences. To me, this is a very sad day if this has become the 'in-thing': to go to the bush to get sloshed and not to revitalise the soul and to charge the overextended batteries. What has happened to: I went to the bush to find spiritual rest and to find myself or to renew contact with my Maker?

Since I started working in the KNP, I have been of the opinion that the conservation 'ethics of the Afrikaner' were similar to the conservation ethics of the 1820 Settlers when they had arrived on our shores. At that stage, the majority of 1820 Settlers had already urbanised and had left the industrialised environment for a better beginning in a more natural environment than the one they had been used to. In contrast, the majority of Afrikaners stayed on farms, and those who had been urbanised still had grandparents, parents, or friends who stayed on farms. During holidays, they went and visited someone on a farm, in my opinion, to satisfy their unaware longing for the natural environment. This situation gradually changed as grandparents, parents, and friends also became urbanised. A greater appreciation for the natural environment, conservation areas, and more specifically National Parks started developing amongst the urbanised 'Afrikaner'. Earlier, when one had asked an 'Afrikaner' boy what the best kudu was that he had seen, his answer generally had been: 'The one that I saw through the sights of my rifle.' This situation gradually changed to one of appreciation of being able to see and observe a kudu in its natural environment. Communication between field staff and tourists was high on the KNP Management's agenda, and Section Rangers were required to attend information sessions on the natural environment given in rest camps to inform tourists. I wasn't very partial to these kinds of gatherings as I preferred going to various lookout points at dams and made myself available to anyone who wanted to communicate on things natural or the KNP in general. I never forced myself onto anyone by initiating a discussion. Initially, I was taken aback by the fact that it was mainly English-speaking tourists who came and introduced themselves and initiated discussions on various wildlife management topics such as the KNP burning policy, the water provision policy, utilisation of natural resources, culling/control of animal population numbers, etc. Now and then, an 'Afrikaner' would also come to chat. 'Hallo, Boet, how much rains have you guys had recently?' When I started explaining to them about long-term climatic cycles of above- and below-average rainfalls, the topic quickly changed to rugby and/or politics. I was pleasantly surprised at how this attitude gradually changed during the 30 years that I was privileged to work in the KNP. Experiencing this change, I am even more saddened by the fact that the modern 'in-thing' (or is it rather an absurdity?) is to go to the bush to have a party or a jollification.

*   *   *

Let's put an end to the pessimism. I previously alluded to the fact that the one 'thing' that attracted me most to Section Rangers work was that there was no routine and that each day was different from all the others. How would you have liked to experience five different modes of 'transport' during the execution of a day's work? The day unfolded as follows: During the early morning debriefing and planning session, the Field Rangers reported that during the previous day's river patrol, they had come upon a hippo carcass next to the Sabie River. This specific place was relatively far from any road system. With two Field Rangers as guides, we took to our bicycles with balloon tyres to get to the carcass. For 90 per cent of the distance, we travelled freely on elephant/hippo paths. For the last kilometer or so, we had to go on foot due to the rocky and very rough terrain. We couldn't find anything untoward with the carcass and took blood smears as a precautionary measure for the veterinarians at Skukuza to make a learned diagnosis. Back home, a Field Ranger came to report that during their early morning patrol, they had seen that the Jacana windmill was not delivering any water. I got onto the motorbike and went to Jacana to try and determine what the problem was in order to get the windmill operational again. Back home, at midday, we awaited the arrival of the helicopter from Skukuza to do a recce to locate the Salitje buffalo herd for culling purposes during the late afternoon. Flying back to Lower Sabie, the helicopter pilot requested that I arrange a vehicle to go back to Lower Sabie after the culling as he had to return to Skukuza directly after the culling operation. Back at Lower Sabie, I made arrangements for my 4 × 4 bakkie to accompany the culling ground crew so that I could return to Lower Sabie after the culling. There you have it — five modes of transport in one day: on foot, a balloon tyre bicycle, a motorbike, a 4 × 4 bakkie, and a helicopter. Not bad, hey?

*   *   *

One morning, I was summoned to Skukuza for one or the other urgent special meeting. Dressed in my uniform shorts and short-sleeve shirt, I jumped onto the motorbike and went to Skukuza. It was a very pleasant, hot morning. The meeting degenerated into longwinded rhetoric by some researchers. To illustrate the point, I noticed my friend and colleague Whytie scribbling something on a piece of paper that he passed over to me under the table. He summed up the nature of the meeting in a few words that contained wisdom that guided my ecological thinking in the future. I still don't know whether he had just wanted to sum up the meeting or whether he just was passing on some insight/wisdom. The note read as follows:

Ecology consists of three components

- The A-biotic component
- The Biotic component
- The Idiotic component

The A-biotic component comprised of geology, soil, climate (temperature, wind barometric pressure, humidity) etc. The Biotic component comprised of all living organisms (plant and animal). Then, of course, the Idiotic component comprised of man's interpretation/misinterpretation and knowledge of ecological processes based on the limited knowledge at that time. I always tried to adhere to the 'Precautionary Principle' that advised that: 'One does not do if one does not know!' in ecology. Circumstances often forced one to do something without the necessary knowledge. During

157

these instances, decision-making was very conservative, and doubtful decisions were reversible.

We finally finished the meeting late that afternoon. A typical Lowveld thunderstorm was brewing and had coloured the eastern sky in a dark hue. My courage left me. That was where I was headed. Lower Sabie lay east of Skukuza. My colleagues looked at me in disbelief when I refused refreshments after the meeting and said that I needed to get home as soon as possible. Seeing that I did not want to be peppered by big ice-cold raindrops while on the motorbike, I stole a couple of kilometers per hour where tourist traffic allowed. Just before the Nkuhlu Picnic Site, there was a long straight stretch of road approximately 1 km long. There were no tourist vehicles in sight, and I pushed on. The black thunderclouds became more threatening as I drew closer, and I could even detect lightning playing in the dark clouds. Approximately three quarters down the straight stretch, I saw a troop of baboons on the tar road. I pressed the motorbike's hooter to attract their attention, and those baboons that could judge relative movement recognised danger when they saw it and moved off the road. I repeated the warning and more moved off. I quickly switched the motorbike off and on with a resultant loud backfire. This had the required effect and the whole troop moved across the road from the Sabie River's side to the in-veldt?

At this specific point, the foundation of the road was raised to accommodate an Armco drainage pipe under the driving surface of the road. As the baboon troop was moving off the road, I again started accelerating. Just before reaching the spot where the baboon troop had sat on the road, my eye caught movement against the embankment. A juvenile baboon (we called them duck tails) that had split off from the troop to do some mischief suddenly realised that it was alone when it heard the roar of the motorbike. Its only mission was to get back to the safety of the troop. It raced up the embankment at full speed. I had to make a very quick decision. The relative movement section of my brain interpreted the situation at hand and advised that at the speed and acceleration at hand, I would pass point x (the accident scene with great pain and misery) before the baboon. The baboon had also made its deductions and had come to the same conclusion. I accelerated and the baboon sped up as well. When I reached the point of no return, about 5 m before point x, the baboon questioned its own calculations and with outstretched front legs slammed on brakes, skidding towards the tar road in that posture. As it skidded onto the driving surface, I drove over its extended fingertips. I looked in the rear-view mirror and could see the baboon screaming in agony and fright and shaking its hands, cursing the motorbike. The loud screaming attracted the female baboon to the road. She threw the youngster onto her back – probably to go and scold and shout at the youngster for straying away from the troop. I drastically reduced speed and played out in my mind's eye what could have happened: the front wheel of the motorbike hitting the baboon at point x and me flying through the air like a rag doll, hitting the tarmac and leaving behind pieces of clothing and flesh and blood while skidding down the road. I drove slowly back to Lower Sabie! The ice-cold raindrops peppered my bare arms and legs as well as the areas on my face not protected by the crash helmet and goggles.

The wet uniform and cold air caused my whole body to be covered with goosebumps. I hoped that it was because of the cold and not because of having escaped a very serious accident.

*   *   *

At about midday one late winter's day, I received a message from Reception that a tourist had reported that a small elephant was stuck in the mud of the remaining water/mud pool in the Mlondozi Dam. Arriving at the lookout point on the motorbike, I found a large crowd of people 'oohing' and 'aahing' at the drama in front of them. My resolve dropped into my shoes. I didn't like crowds. If one were to/had to do something, the crowd would have ringside seats in the amphitheatre, and the drama would be playing off in front of them. The lookout point was approximately 200 m from the mud pool and elevated above the empty basin by about 60 m. My resolve dropped down further when I noticed the elephant breeding herd next to the dam basin. The herd was obviously under stress with raised trunks and periodic trumpeting. Although the crowd's focus was directed on the drama in front of them, they also noticed the KNP Official sitting astride the motorbike.

'Sir, what are you going to do? You cannot leave the baby elephant to die,' begged an old lady, and the kids begged in a chorus. 'Please save the baby!'

Shooting the elephant calf disappeared from my line of thought. Waiting until after gate-closing time was also not an option. This crowd of tourists wanted and expected action. I begged and asked the tourists to leave the lookout in order for me to do 'something' without being scrutinised by thirty pairs of eyes! They just looked at me as if I had lost my marbles. How could I expect them to do that?

'What are you going to do?' they wanted to know. 'I still don't know. I will make a plan,' was my feeble answer. I started the motorbike and drove to the T-junction where the Mlondozi Lookout road turned off from the Mlondozi Loop and closed the entrance with branches. I did not want the crowd to increase. I then followed an elephant path to the side of the empty dam basin.

The elephant breeding herd spotted me and started milling around trunks in the air and kicking up dust. I looked to my right and saw the crowd watching me. I felt the amazement in their attitude. What was he going to achieve alone on a motorbike? I also didn't know! The dried-out dam base provided a good riding surface, and all the potential obstructions in the form of rocks, depressions, and old tree trunks were clearly visible. I was relieved that I had come on the scrambler (motorbike) and not with the 4 × 4 bakkie. I could easily weave through the obstacles if need be, even at speed. I tested the water (figuratively speaking) and slowly drove onto the dam basin. Straight at the elephant herd. The herd milled around uneasily and slowly moved off into the veldt next to the dam. It seemed as if the Matriarch cow had also given up hope on the calf stuck in the mud. I turned towards the mud pool to determine how desperate the situation with the calf really was. From a distance, I could see the calf desperately kicking and trying to free itself from the mud. All in vain! I suddenly felt the hair on my neck rising and looked behind me and found the elephant herd rushing down at me at full speed. I pulled away and accelerated past the mud pool. I glanced over my shoulder and saw the herd also changing direction and coming for the motorbike. The terrain, however, allowed me to leave the herd behind. The herd came to a halt in a cloud of dust as they saw the danger (to them and to the helping hand according to the crowd of onlookers) disappearing in the distance. The herd again moved off the dam basin and into the veldt next to it. Gradually, a plan was formulating in my head. It was very important for the elephant calf to conserve energy and strength and to not waste it on a futile effort to extract itself from the mud. I again did the previous test run with the same results.

I now drove back to the edge of the dam basin and switched off the motorbike. I wanted the elephant calf to rest. The calf was lying flat on its side, and the chance of drowning was practically impossible due to the absence of sufficient water. The breeding herd had also settled down and wasn't milling around anymore. A calm restfulness was observed in the herd. The crowd of tourists was most probably wondering whether I had given up trying to rescue the calf, dejected like a crowd at a rugby match, seeing the time running out and their team going to lose. I waited for approximately 20 minutes for the calf to get a good rest. During this time, the calf didn't once try to extract itself from the mud. I was sure that if I were able to get close enough to the calf to give it an adrenaline shock by revving the motorbike and kicking up my own racket, it would be able to free itself from the mud.

I started to put the plan into action. I switched on the motorbike and slowly approached the breeding herd. The closer I got to the breeding herd, the more I followed a zigzag pattern. I wanted to confuse the herd and try to get them as far away from the mud pool as possible. The Matriarch cow made a couple of mock charges, and I retreated a bit and then gradually applied pressure again. At one stage, I had manoeuvred the breeding herd about 400 m away from the mud pool. I turned the motorbike in the direction of the mud pool, and immediately, the Matriarch, followed by the rest of the herd, charged; it was as if they knew which was the sharp and which was the blunt end of the motorbike. I quickly turned around and slowly gained lost ground. I now kept the sharp end of the motorbike facing the herd. After another 10 minutes, the herd had calmed down completely, and individual animals were actually picking titbits from the surrounding vegetation. The herd was approximately 80 m in front of me. I looked over my shoulder, determining the quickest route to the mud pool through the grass, fallen trees, rocks, and shrubs until I could get to the empty dam basin.

'Now!' I shouted to myself, turning the motorbike in the direction of the mud pool. I had caught the herd unawares, and some of the elephants even turned around in a fleeing direction. Now there was only one route. The quickest one to the mud pool! When I reached the dam basin, I glanced back and saw that the herd had recovered from its initial shock, and the Matriarch was now leading the herd in a counter attack. I, however, had a lead of approximately 150 m that I could increase on the open dam basin. I raced directly to the mud pool, slammed on the brakes a way back, and skidded to a halt in a cloud of dust on the edge of the mud pool. I started kicking up a racket with the engine revving and me shouting at the calf at the top of my voice while waving my arms. The calf strived to lift itself out of the mud and with the rested body and heightened adrenaline shock, half succeeded in doing so. 'Come on,' I shouted and willed the calf to greater efforts. I glanced at the breeding herd. They were almost 100 m away at full charge now, also on the open dam basin. The calf put in a 'super elephant' effort. The front half of the body was halfway out of the mud. I could feel the crowd of onlookers willing the calf on to greater efforts. I glanced back and saw the elephant charge was now 50 m away. It was now or never! I shouted at the calf and revved the engine. The calf again put in maximum effort. Just one back leg was still stuck in the mud. I instinctively felt the proximity of the herd. At the last moment . . . the herd approximately 10 m away. I pulled away, with the rear wheel spinning and kicking up dust. At about 20 m, I dared to look back and saw the Matriarch cow gripping the calf's trunk with her own and pulling the calf out of the mud. I have always believed in teamwork! About 60 m away, I stopped and saw the calf milling around amongst the herd. The Matriarch cow raised her trunk and trumpeted until the earth shook. Was she thanking me or what? I looked up at the Mlondozi 'pavilion'. There was much jubilation with raised, waving hands. I left the scene and went to the T-junction that I had previously closed off with branches. There was a tourist vehicle at the junction. 'Why was the road closed?' asked the driver. 'I don't know,' I replied. 'They sent me to open up the road. The maintenance team have probably been doing maintenance work on the toilet facilities or something.' 'Oh,' said the driver and drove on to the Mlondozi Lookout point. To this day, I still don't know if the driver heard the true story about the dam.

*   *   *

On one bright moonlit evening, I was on my way back to Lower Sabie from a water-drilling programme at Numbi Gate. About 12 km from Skukuza, one passes the Msimuku Spruit and windmill with the same name. The tar road crosses the spruit over a concrete bridge that was raised 1½ m above the level of the spruit. I instinctively reduced speed as I had on previous occasions seen rhinos (Black and White) at the drinking trough. On that night, however, there was nothing to be seen. When the vehicle's lights shone on the bridge, I saw a hyena scurrying off the bridge and disappearing into the bush. As I was crossing over the bridge, I caught sight of movement on the downstream side of the bridge. I stopped and reversed back onto the bridge with the vehicle about 1 m away from the protective wall about 30 cm high, running the length of the bridge. I got out of the vehicle and walked around it to the downstream side of the bridge where the movement in the bright moonlight had caught my eye. I now experienced one of the most dramatic natural productions, performed only once, that I had the privilege to attend. Right in front of me stood a big kudu bull with its backside pushed half way into the gap under the bridge. Directly in front of the kudu bull were two hyenas rushing in and retreating. If the hyenas dared to come too close to the bull, it would gaff at them with its massive horns. The giggling hyenas then retreated a safe distance away. I was so close to the kudu that if I were to kneel down on the bridge and stretch down, I would have been able to touch its back. The kudu couldn't have cared less about the human being on top of the bridge as it was solely focused on the life-threatening hyenas in front of it. This fight for life and death played off right in front of me just 3 m away. The hyenas were rushing in, and the kudu bull was parrying them away.

I could just wonder at the circumstance that led to the kudu bull being trapped with half of its body trapped under the bridge. How long ago had the chase begun? Was the kudu bull injured? Why had the hyenas singled this animal out for the chase and possible kill? The questions mulled through my head as I watched the fight from the bridge. There didn't seem to be a clear-cut winner at that stage. A sudden movement again caught my eye as a third hyena – the one that had previously disappeared into the bush – very slyly moved across the road to the upstream side of the bridge. I temporarily ignored the third hyena as I was totally enthralled by the drama in front of me. Suddenly, I saw the kudu bull go down on its haunches. The two hyenas in front of it now rushed in with new vigour as the bull was now in a more vulnerable position. The kudu bull jumped up to counter the new onslaught with its horns. Then I heard it! The *'grit-grit'* sounds emanating from under the bull. The third hyena had crossed over to the upstream side and had gotten hold of the kudu's stomach from the rear. When the bull now came upright to ward off the frontal attack, the third hyena underneath it would *grit* away at the bull's stomach. When the *'grit-grit'* chewing on the stomach became unbearable, the kudu bull went down on its haunches to squash the third hyena under it. The other two hyenas then rushed in with their frontal attack. The third hyena would then continue chewing on the stomach – *'grit-grit'*. Gradually, the kudu bull was losing the battle. The moonlit drama continued for almost an hour before the three hyenas got the upper hand. It was immaterial whether the conflict was lost due to loss of blood or fatigue. The fact of the matter was that a group of skilled hunters/predators more often than not will get the upper hand over a single prey species.

'Why didn't you intervene to save the kudu?' many people would want to know. Who was I to intervene in the course of natural events? Ten to one, the kudu bull was injured or old or both, and it is the ecological function of hyenas to utilise these kinds of situations to ensure their own survival. I often hear people talking about/longing for the peace, quiet, and serenity of the bush, not thinking/realising that out there in the bush, it is more often than not a question of 'dog eats dog', and bloodshed is a quest for survival.

*   *   *

With the advent of wilderness trails in the KNP, Management insisted that the Trail Rangers get the best possible training to ensure the safety of hikers on a wilderness trail. A Trail Ranger would be in charge of eight hikers accompanied by an Assistant Trail Ranger. Both of the rangers were armed, the Trail Ranger with a big-calibre rifle, usually a .458, and the Assistant Trail Ranger with an R-1 semi-automatic rifle. Proficiency with these specific rifles was a very high priority. Bush-lane firing was regularly practised.

Experienced veldt staff would familiarise them with the big five, with both species of rhinos included. They were taught to respect these animals under all circumstances and, most crucially, where to hit the animal, to kill it with one shot, in the event that they had to safeguard the tourists during an emergency situation. Target images were made or skulls were used, and the Trail Rangers had to indicate where they would aim to kill from all directions and angles. Proficiency with a rifle was the order of the day. However, the most important traits that a Trail Ranger had to prove were steadfastness and calmness during an emergency situation. How could a crisis situation be simulated to evaluate this very important aspect of a Trail Ranger's make-up? One of the veldt staff recommended a brilliant plan of action. We could use the culling of elephant bulls as a trial exercise. The modus operandi would be as follows: The Trail Ranger in training would be positioned at a certain predetermined spot, usually on the perimeter of a sodic area or open piece of veldt. The helicopter pilot would then herd an elephant bull directly at the open area, and on reaching, it would immediately change direction as fast as possible to get out of the firing line. The Trail Ranger would now allow the 'charging' elephant to come within 40 m of him and would then have to hit the moving target with a brain shot to kill the elephant bull. The Trail Ranger was, however, not left to his own devices. On either side and to the rear of him, two experienced Section Rangers would be positioned to assist in the event that the Trail Ranger could not bring down the elephant bull with his first few shots. These two Section Rangers were referred to as the 'stopper group'. As an additional precaution, there was an armed Section Ranger in the helicopter as well, who would intervene should things go totally wrong on the ground. Radio communication between the two parties involved was crucial. Sounds easy, doesn't it?

During this time, Bruce Bryden was the Chief Ranger at Skukuza. He called me 'Old Wannie'. On one of these Trail Ranger evaluation exercises, he invited me to be one of the so-called stopper group with him. Elephant-bull culling was scheduled to take place on the Malelane Section where there were two or three 'habitual criminals' that crossed over the Crocodile River and raided citrus orchards to the great agitation of the neighbouring landowner. For the sake of good neighbourliness, it was decided to cull two of the transgressors. The helicopter pilot and airborne ranger sighted the two bulls and identified them as citrus raiders. Their dung was the giveaway as it contained many whole oranges. The ground crew moved into a suitable position identified by them. The ground crew then selected the most suitable culling site, taking the direction of the wind and sun into consideration. The helicopter came back to the site to determine exactly where everyone on the ground was placed before going back to start the elephant herding process of one of the bulls. The Trail Ranger didn't seem to have a lot of faith in the stopper group as he was tensed up and as white as a sheet when we pointed out the different beacons to him: 'You must stand opposite this Bush willow, and when the elephant reaches that fallen tree trunk, you can commence shooting. Be careful to allow the helicopter enough time to get out of the firing line,' was Bruce's last instruction. I could see that the Trail Ranger's mouth was dry from stress. Place yourself in his position. His whole career was dependant on the successful execution of the impeding stressful operation. Not very easy! Bruce indicated to the Trail Ranger where he was going to position himself obliquely behind him, and 'Old Wannie' would be standing there, pointing to my position.

All of us were prepared and at the ready, hearing the helicopter gradually approaching herding the elephant bull. We could now see the helicopter above the tree level, moving to the left and then to the right in the elephant-herding pattern. We still could not see the elephant due to the dense vegetation on the other side of the clearing. We, however, knew that it was there. Then we saw the elephant about 60 m before the clearing. The helicopter pilot then skilfully applied extra pressure on the bull, and it picked up speed directly towards the chosen clearing. When the elephant ran onto the clearing, the helicopter took evasive action to get out of the firing line. The occupants of the helicopter were in danger if the Trail Ranger were to shoot too soon. At the predetermined beacon, the first shot was fired. The elephant charged on. I saw the disappointment and fear in his body language. He quickly loaded the second round, aimed, and fired. The elephant was almost on top of him. Fortunately for him, the second shot made the elephant veer off direction, and it missed him. The elephant bull was now on a collision course with me. I heard Bruce's shot. He had an impossible shot at an angle from the rear. The elephant charged on. I heard Bruce's second shot. I couldn't shoot as the elephant was obscured by a tree. Nobody had anticipated that the change of direction of the elephant would be that great. Bruce's second shot made the elephant stumble. The elephant was now on top of me. I had an impossible shot, obliquely from the bottom and to the front, which most probably is the longest route to the elephant's brain. I instinctively realised that if I were to kill the elephant outright, it would fall on top of me. I corrected my aim slightly and pulled the trigger and simultaneously jumped backwards as far as I could. Fortunately for me, after the brain shot had hit home, the elephant settled on the exact spot where I had stood. 'Wannie, are you all right?' I heard Bruce shouting. I loaded a second round into the breech, walked to the front of the elephant bull, and gave it a sure brain shot. I used the rifle as a support and breathed for the first time in 30 seconds. 'Old Wannie, I thought you were dead!' he sighed with relief. We both walked over to the Trail Ranger who was ashen in colour and who leaned on the rifle for support.

'Don't worry,' said Bruce. 'The next one will be a piece of old takkie.' We calmed the Trail Ranger down and tried to convince him that these things sometimes happened. I silently hoped that it would not happen again soon.

We made radio contact with the helicopter pilot. 'The first one went off well. Bring the second one.' We had moved on to another sodic area for the second elephant bull. We again took up our various stations with new beacons and stood ready, waiting for the second bull. When the Trail Ranger delivered his first shot, the elephant died in its tracks with a perfectly delivered brain shot. What an anti-climax! The following morning, Bruce went and reported the happenings of the previous day. The door to Oom Johan's office was open, and as I walked by, by chance, I heard Bruce say, 'If ever I have to shoot an elephant again, I will take 'Old Wannie' as backup any day. I don't know whether he is stupid, but he hasn't got a scared hair on his bald head.'

'Thank you, Bruce, for my character analysis,' I said to myself and walked past.

*   *   *

Now for a more enjoyable elephant story. An old elephant bull frequented the Lower Sabie area. His one tusk was broken off at the lip. My pet name for him was 'Stompie' (the one with the short tusk). I don't want to speculate about the cause. The other tusk was also worn off halfway through years of usage. The old bull was very mischievous, and many tourists had suffered due to his pranks. Whenever it took his fancy, he would block the road and prevent them from passing. Every so often, I had to listen to the excuse of tourists who arrived late at the gate because the one tusked bull had blocked the road and charged at them. 'We would have been on time if the bull hadn't stopped us. Are you going to fine us for being late?' I just smiled and opened the gate for them. Old Stompie and I could have made lots of money by collecting fines from latecomers.

Stompie could identify my vehicle, and whenever we had the opportunity to meet on one of the roads surrounding Lower Sabie, the same ritual would be enacted. Stompie would calmly be standing next to the road, nibbling at a tasty morsel. When I was approximately 30 m away, he would walk into the road like a seasoned traffic policeman with widespread ears to indicate to me that I had to stop. I would comply with his request. He would then approach me, lifting his front legs in an exaggerated fashion with widespread ears, trunk half mast in the air, and slowly moving his head from side to side. Stompie would move to within 10 m of the vehicle. He would stop and, with an almighty shake of the head, flap his ears. This was my queue to slowly move forward towards Stompie. Stompie would then indignantly glare down at me from a height, with those watery eyes of his like someone looking down at something through bifocal specs. If I did not stop, he would slowly retreat. Stompie looked very comical. Elephants were not made to walk backwards. Having 'pushed' him back for a while, I would suddenly stop. Stompie would then come forward while I reversed. Stompie and I would then waltz forwards and backwards in this fashion. Never during any of these encounters did Stompie show any aggression. Then for some unknown reason, Stompie would walk off the road and continue nibbling at his morsel, allowing me to drive past without any further intervention. Normally, other elephants would have charged the passing vehicle. Not old Stompie. He just continued eating.

On one occasion just before gate-closing time, I was on my way to the tree house to see if everything was in order. Our minister, Reverend Chris Marais, and his wife, Dorothea, and their visitors would be spending the night at the tree house. Just before I had reached the LubyeLubye firebreak turn-off to the tree house, I met up with Stompie. I was in a hurry and did not have time to waltz with Stompie. Stompie, however, had other ideas. We hadn't seen one another for quite a while and dance we would dance. After a few shuffles, he let me by. On my way back to Lower Sabie, Stompie had regained his second breath, and again, we had to waltz. Just before the Lower Sabie Rest Camp, I encountered the group on its way to the tree house. I foresaw problems. Rev Chris might have had good connections, but I doubted his ability to communicate with an elephant bull named Stompie. 'Chris, you guys must follow me,' I warned. 'Up ahead, there is an elephant bull that is not going to let you pass.' 'I am dead scared of elephants!' exclaimed Dorothea. She shouldn't have said that. 'Come and get into my vehicle, and I will show you that there is nothing to be afraid of,' I said, holding thumbs that old Stompie would play along. Dorothea sat wide-eyed when she saw the elephant bull on her side of the road. She sank a bit lower into the seat of the vehicle. As arranged, Stompie started his shenanigans on queue. Dorothea gradually disappeared behind the dashboard. 'You must not distract me from the elephant,' I warned her. 'I need to watch his every movement.' Stompie and I began our dance, and Dorothea began to mumble a silent prayer with eyes wide open. Suddenly, Stompie executed a movement that we had not practised before. Stompie went down on his knees about 2 m in front of the bakkie. 'What now?' I wanted to know from Stompie. 'Where is the elephant?' Dorothea wanted to know. She could not see the elephant from her low seating position. She came slightly upright and gave a faint stifled yell. I gave her a false annoyed look and reprimanded her to be quiet and to enjoy the moment. Stompie threw his trunk in a forward motion, hitting the bulbar of the bakkie, scattering spittle across the windscreen. (I hoped that it was spittle; the trunk is actually a nose!) Stompie repeated the movement, got up, moved off the road, and continued eating. I indicated to Chris and the accompanying vehicle to follow me, and all of us drove past Stompie. About 100 m down the road, I stopped for Dorothea to get back into their vehicle. 'Was that enjoyable?' I wanted to know from her. 'Van Rooyen, you are mad!' was the only answer I got as she transferred from the bakkie to their vehicle. I turned around to go home, and again, I had to dance with Stompie before he would let me pass by. Four times during the past half an hour. Fortunately, Stompie was also becoming tired, especially after executing the new step. We only had to do one waltz, and then Stompie let me be. Up until now, Dorothea has not forgiven me for the once-in-a-lifetime elephant experience. With thanks to Stompie.

It was the selfsame Rev Chris who boasted that he was the only man who had had the privilege to kiss a Section Ranger on the forehead. Yuck! It had been a wet and salty one at that. It happened as follows: I was busy at the Nature Conservation Office at Skukuza when one of the receptionists called me and said that someone wanted to talk to me on the VHF radio. It was the Tshokwane Section Ranger. There was a threatening refugee fire in the Metsi Metsi Wilderness Area. At that same instant, the Section Ranger at Crocodile Bridge called telephonically with his problem. Elephants had exited the KNP and were on their way to the town of Komatipoort. The Tshokwane Section Ranger continued with his fire report. He was urgently looking for assistance. The Crocodile Bridge Section Ranger telephonically wanted to know whether a helicopter was available to chase the elephant herd back to the KNP. I continued with both emergencies, one moment on the telephone and then on the radio and back to the telephone etc. With the microphone in the one hand and the telephone in the other, I tried to handle both emergency situations simultaneously. With this, Chris entered through the office doors. He greeted me. I could not reciprocate as both my hands and my mouth were otherwise occupied. He walked around the reception counter to where I was battling away. He grabbed hold of my head between his hands and planted a kiss on my forehead. 'The bugger kissed me!' I yelled simultaneously into the microphone and telephone. Needless to say, I threw down both and chased after Chris. 'I am going to kill you!' I shouted at him as he disappeared down the passage. The Park Wardens Office was at the end of the passage. He came to a halt in front of the office door and calmly walked into the office for his appointment with the Park Warden. Hot under the collar, I walked back to Reception, with all the girls bursting out in laughter, to continue my double emergency conversation on the radio and telephone. 'What did you mean by, *The bugger kissed me?*' both of them wanted to know. 'Are you two looking for assistance or conversation?' I rebuked them. This story would in any event do the rounds, and at some stage, the mealy-mouthed version would be relayed to all. By the time that Chris had finished his appointment with the Park Warden, I had been able to address both emergencies, and fortunately for Chris, I had calmed down considerably.

*   *   *

The semi-habituated/spoilt baboons on the Lower Sabie tar road and I were not friends. When they saw or heard my vehicle approaching, they would hastily flee from the road. These baboons were spoilt by tourists feeding them, and more often than not, they caused innocent tourists big damages. I received many complaints from the Nkuhlu Picnic Site, that especially elderly people and children had been 'attacked' by baboons. These people, however, were not the target but the paper bag or cooler box they were carrying was. The big male baboon would charge at the unsuspecting person, who would do the most logical thing: drop what they were carrying and run for dear life. The baboon would then purposefully walk to the loot, picking it up while the rest of the troop came nearer for the feast of titbits and delicatessens. Whenever a bag carrier did not want to let go of the bounty, the male baboon would show aggression by bearing its teeth and attacking up to close quarters with the same result. Research by the Medical Institute had proven results that baboons that scrounged along the tourist roads and at picnic sites, and rubbish heaps near rest camps all had higher cholesterol levels than those living from the natural veldt only.

*　*　*

At one stage, there was a male baboon at the Satara Rest Camp that was so organised that he waited for the labourer who carted waste to the rubbish dump in a wheelbarrow, at the gate leading to the dump. As the wheelbarrow moved through the gate, he would calmly place his one hand on the wheelbarrow and would walk alongside it up to where the wheelbarrow would be tipped over for the sorting to begin. The baboon took whatever it wanted, and the labourer continued with the tins, plastic, cardboard, and bottles.

On the way back to Lower Sabie one day, I found a vehicle that had left the road on a straight stretch and come to rest against a tree. Here, I found two tourists frightened out of their wits. They were both ashen-faced from fright and foreigners to boot, not being able to express themselves in English. They used sign language to explain to me that they had been travelling very slowly because of a troop of baboons on the road. From nowhere, a baboon had jumped through the passenger's window and onto the lady's lap. She had been frightened into another blood group. The gentleman behind the steering wheel had then done the manly thing to protect the lady, leaving the steering wheel and grappling with the baboon. He had not taken into account how long it would take. The vehicle had still been in gear, and he had not applied the brakes. The vehicle had left the road and crashed into the tree, at which stage the baboon had thought it best to jump out of the vehicle. On top of the bruised egos, scratch and bruise marks on the arms and legs from the squabble with the baboon, and damage to the vehicle, they had also received head injuries when the vehicle had struck the tree. All of the above could have been prevented if 'good-hearted' or ignorant tourists had not fed the baboon.

*　　*　　*

Due to family needs and loading space, we at one stage had to drive a Combi. Late one Saturday afternoon, after a cricket game at Skukuza, the whole family was on the way home to Lower Sabie. In the vicinity of the episode described above, we also encountered a troop of baboons lying in or playing across the whole road. A very calm scene, so I went to great lengths to drive off the road so as not to disturb the baboon troop. Halfway past the troop, a big male baboon jumped through the passenger's window and onto Liza's lap. Consternation followed. The baboon grabbed at a paper bag lying on the floor of the Combi. The baboon sat facing me while rummaging through the paper bag. Without thinking, I let go with a right fist with all the might that I could muster within the confined space and hit the baboon in the stomach. Winded and with great surprise written all over its face, it let go of the paper bag and jumped out of the passenger-side window. In the rear-view mirror, I could see the baboon coughing to regain its breath. After this incident, it became a rule that all windows had to be closed in the vicinity of baboons on the road, irrespective of the heat of the day. Be warned!

What tourists don't realise is that they are signing the death warrant of these baboons and vervet monkeys by feeding them. I will most probably never progress past the baboon heaven. They will most definitely lock me up for all the grief that I had caused them in the KNP. That is, if it is possible to cause a baboon grief!

*　　*　　*

I always promised myself that I would start playing golf when I went on pension. I would then have plenty of time to try my hand at playing this so-called notorious game. If one was able to get on top of tennis, squash, cricket, etc. where one had to deal with a fast-moving ball, what could be so difficult about dealing with a ball that was lying still even though the playing equipment looked rather strange? However, we landed up at Skukuza sooner than expected, and with the golf course practically in the front garden, I had no excuse but to try the game. After acquiring a set of golf clubs (to me, they looked more like modified knob-kieries) and a sort of push-pull cart, I went and hit a few practise shots on my own. I did not want other people to see how easy the game actually was. I set the white ball up on top of a peg on the tee. I then lined the ball up as I had on many occasions seen Gary Player and company do on TV. I must admit that I felt a slight tinge of nervousness, and my throat was dry. I took out the driver (knob-kierie with the largest head) and gripped it like a baseball bat, swung back, and let fly. The white ball that should have absorbed all my force was still stationary on the peg. I had completely missed the ball, or as they say in golfing parlance, I had hit a 'freshy'. I now knew how a boxer felt when he wanted to plant the knockout punch and completely missed the target. I looked around sheepishly to see if anyone had seen the freshy – no one! I again lined up the ball. 'Don't force it,' I heard a faint voice saying. I struck the ball, and it went flying down the centre of the fairway. It looked as if the most difficult part of the game was making connection with the ball. I was proud of myself, and on the way home, I kept repeating, 'Just concentrate on the ball and don't force it.'

Golf never frustrated me. Whether I had hit the golf ball 3 or 300 m far didn't matter. I would walk up to it and give it another wallop. I often heard players using foul language having hit a shot. Others would take the club and with an axe-motion hit the ground. Others threw the club away, then had to go and retrieve it again; others kicked the golf bag or golf cart as if that would have helped. Others talked to the ball in flight, 'dip-dip' or 'left-left' or 'fly-fly'. How stupid! A golf ball cannot hear and cannot alter course once one has put it on its course. I played most of my golf in the rough, more so than anyone I know. The advantage was that I went back home with more balls than what I had started off with. I was convinced that most of the golfers were too scared to go and look for their golf ball because the golf course at Skukuza was not fenced off and actually part of the Reserve. The scared and cautious golfers thought that an elephant, lion, or snake could be lying waiting for anyone wanting to retrieve a golf ball that had been hit into the Game Reserve.

*   *   *

I executed a few remarkable shots on the Skukuza Golf Course. One of them was hit from the first tee. The vehicle parking area was about 60 m away at 90° to the tee. I had addressed the ball, taken a deep breath, and let fly. I wanted to show the crowd of onlookers how it should or shouldn't be done. On impact, the ball ran along the ground at right angles towards the car park and found refuge under a yellow motorcar. I could have sworn the ball poked out its tongue and said, 'Wee! You can't get at me now!'

On another occasion, I had to play a nearing shot to the green on hole number 7. It was a perfect tee shot that came to rest in the middle of the fairway. I could be lying on the green for two shots, and with a good putt, a birdie was a distinct possibility. I played the next shots in my mind's eye, instead of concentrating and playing one shot at a time. The second shot was hopelessly too far and to the left of the green. Fortunately, it struck a Fever tree that was planted next to the squash courts, and the ball came to rest on the roof of the lean-to cool drink store. There was no other way out. I would have to climb onto the roof and hit the third shot from there. I wasn't going to accept defeat and settle for a penalty shot! As far as I know, I was the only guy at the Skukuza Golf Club who had played across three different fairways to come home with a par five. My ideal design for a golf course would be one with the rough straight down the middle, with two fairways one on either side of the rough.

I was always first in line for a 06.00 tee off for any competition. Playing golf, to me, was similar to a foot patrol of old. I concentrated more on the beauty of the morning and bird calls than on the golf at hand. One evening, during prize-giving, I had won the prize for the golfer who had played the most golf (most shots recorded) for the eighteen-hole course. As I was going to accept my prize, an envious golfer shouted from the crowd, 'He can't get a prize! He must pay R300 for being on a wilderness trail for the whole day.'

*　　*　　*

One of our Engineering colleagues took his golf bag one afternoon after work to go and play a few shots. It was already getting dark when Frans teed off from no. 3. A group of Impalas were grazing on the fairway, and his tee shot hit one of the young rams against the head. The Impala dropped down for dead. Frans walked closer to inspect the situation. When he was about 10 m from the 'carcass', he froze. He saw a young female lion charge out of the rough next to the fairway; she straddles the 'carcass' and growled at him, as if saying: 'This is my carcass. Come any closer, and you will be dealt with!' Frans obeyed the command and stood dead still until the lioness had dragged the carcass into the rough (my usual playing field). Frans stood still for a while longer and left fairway no. 3 in a hurry, without playing another shot. Frans must have got a big fright because we did not see him on the golf course for the next 6 months or so.

*　　*　　*

A young newlywed couple started working in Skukuza. He was a sturdy big guy who played lock for the Skukuza rugby club. His wife was a small, petite girl. Late one afternoon, they went to the golf course to hit a few golf balls. A pack of wild dogs appeared from nowhere and came running onto the fairway. The dogs noticed the couple and ran straight to them and surrounded the two of them. They swung their arms and golf clubs while shouting for help. The wild dogs with their tails in the air uttered their typical 'bark-twitter' sound while jumping up and down on the forelegs and running in a circle around the couple. In the commotion, the whole group moved closer to a tree on the fairway. The big guy took his gap and clambered up the tree as fast as he could, leaving his petite young wife on the ground to fend for herself. He now shouted from the treetop while she fended off the wild dogs by waving her hands and golf club. After a while, the wild dogs lost interest and jogged off. This young man never heard the end of how he had left his young wife on the ground to fend for herself. Shame on him. They very soon resigned and left to be rid of the continuous scorn of fellow Skukuza inhabitants.

*　　*　　*

Talking about wild dogs, there were a few long-distance runners in Skukuza, who practised for, ran, and completed the Comrades Marathon. The whole community was very proud of the achievements of these long-winded athletes. For them to be able to compete, they had to be members of an athletic club. Initially, all of them joined the Nelspruit Athletic Club. After a while, the long-winded ones decided to start their own club at Skukuza. However, to be acknowledged as a club, they had to organise at least one event per year. This was the beginning of the well-liked (and later known) Skukuza Half Marathon. Once every year, the Chairperson of the Skukuza Athletic Club had to come to my office to discuss possible dates, a route, entrance permits, etc. for the Half Marathon. Each year, I gave him hell. I stressed the point that the human body was not designed to run 26 km, let alone 100 km. In the design of the human body, a maximum of 4 or 5 km was an acceptable flight distance. If a person (our ancestors) could not escape a dangerous situation within that distance, it would have been 'tickets' anyway.

'Gus, in your learned opinion, has the design of the human body changed that much that it can now absorb the pounding of a 100 km run without any negative side effects?' 'Van Rooyen, you are wasting my time,' was his learned answer.

'Why did you choose the wild dog as your emblem?' I teased.

'What's wrong with that? The wild dog epitomises endurance,' he retaliated.

'I would have chosen the guinea-fowl,' I continued pulling his leg.

'A guinea-fowl!? Are you nuts?'

I motivated my choice of guinea-fowl to him. Late one afternoon, I had been on my way back to Skukuza from the airstrip. On exiting the gate, I had met up with five guinea-fowl that had obviously been on their way somewhere. I had decided to stay behind them to see where their destination was. The guinea-fowl had 'jogged' down the road 30 m in front of my vehicle, and I had patiently followed them at their 'jogging' speed. After about 2 km, we had reached the T-junction with the Tshokwane/Skukuza tar road. The guinea-fowl had turned right towards Skukuza and kept on 'jogging'. Just before the Sabie low water bridge, there was quite a steep descent onto the bridge. The guinea-fowl had one by one flown up over the Sabie River and into the big trees alongside the river to roost for the evening.

'What's your point?' Gus wanted to know.

'Gus, those guinea-fowl had the ability to fly from the airstrip directly to the trees. They, however, chose to "jog" for almost 3 km and to fly for approximately 100 m, just like you joggers. There are much easier and faster ways to get from point A to point B, but no, you would rather jog. Is that where you Souties got the phrase "birdbrained" from?'

'Ja, Van Rooyen, you will never understand, will you?' Gus knew that I also jogged to keep fit, of course, within reason. Even 26 km to me was excessive.

*　　*　　*

To be bitten by a Black mamba and to survive to tell the tale is a miracle. One of our colleagues, Danie, was a case in point. He was busy with scientific fieldwork on the Pretoriuskop Section. He had travelled by vehicle up to a certain point and continued his fieldwork on foot further and further from the vehicle. Concentrating on his fieldwork, he inadvertently trod on a Black mamba. The mamba retaliated and in self-defence struck Danie high up and to the back of his upper leg. Danie immediately recognised the snake. 'Just be calm,' was his first thought. He took off his uniform belt and used it as a tourniquet as high up as he could tie it above the bite mark. 'You must release the tourniquet every 20 minutes,' he reminded himself as he walked to the closest tourist road. It was closer than having to walk back to his own vehicle. The good researcher that he was, he decided to keep notes of the symptoms and the effect that the Black mamba poison was having on his system. If he didn't make it, someone would find the notes on the effect of the poison and the symptoms that he was experiencing useful.

Already seriously affected, he reached the tourist road hoping that someone would be able to give him a lift to Pretoriuskop. After a few minutes, someone pitched, and after listening to Danie's plight, the merciful Samaritan picked him up. Fortunately for Danie, cell phones had just hit the market, and this guy had one. Initially, they did not have reception. Pretoriuskop, at that stage, was one of the few stations that had landline telephonic communication to the outside world. Every so often, the tourist unsuccessfully tried to make communication. At one spot, the tourist road went across a high watershed, and reception was received. At that stage, Danie's speech was heavily impaired. The tourist had to stop to be able to make contact, wasting life-saving time. Eventually, the message was relayed to Pretoriuskop Reception after several repetitions. The tourist raced to Pretoriuskop. Reception contacted the Section Ranger in the meantime. At that stage, Tom drove a Combi with the middle seat removed to create space for his two small sons to play while travelling. Tom covered the play space in the Combi with a couple of blankets. He also notified the Nelspruit Hospital about the impending emergency and requested traffic-police escort to the hospital. The traffic police would meet up with them somewhere along the Bushman Rock road. Everything possible was arranged to get Danie to expert medical attention as quickly as possible.

By the time that the tourist got Danie to Pretoriuskop, the mamba venom had paralysed his voluntary muscles, and he could no longer move by himself. He was transferred to the Combi, and Tom set off as fast as the Combi could go. Approximately 15 km outside Numbi Gate, the traffic police met up with them and escorted them to the Nelspruit Hospital as fast as was humanly safe to all road users. On the way, Danie lost control of all his body functions. Thank goodness for all the blankets! At the hospital, Danie was placed on a heart-lung apparatus. He was already too far gone to receive antiserum. Danie spent 5 days in the ICU on the heart-lung machine. We formed a huge prayer chain. Danie was artificially kept alive while the Black mamba venom biologically broke down in his body.

Danie miraculously recovered completely and, after his enforced recuperation period, came back to work. I paid him a visit and questioned him on his fearful and wondrous experience with the Black mamba. He related in detail the symptoms and the effect of the venom on his body until he had lost consciousness. What a frightful experience!

* * *

About a month later, Pretoria Head Office, through the Head of Southern Parks (all National Parks excluding the KNP), requested me to go and divine water at the Marakele National Park where they were planning to construct a big rest camp, and they wanted sufficient water before they could commence with anything. Liza and I accompanied Willem to Marakele. Piet and Assie, previously the Section Ranger couple at Shangoni in the KNP, were now the Park Manager couple at Marakele. Piet was presently busy with his MSc thesis on the plant ecology of the Marakele National Park, and Willem was one of his external promoters. The visit to Marakele was, therefore, a combined effort.

In between the water-divining efforts, Piet and Willem made time for their academic discussions. On the first day, the search for a possible drilling site was conducted over a large area. There were several possibilities. These were all too far from the chosen site for the rest camp – again an example of choosing the site first and then having to find sufficient water. The correct way was to find water first and then finalise the site for the rest camp. That evening, we made an intensive study of aerial photographs of Marakele but more specifically those depicting the basin between the mountains where the camp was planned. We identified a number of potential drilling sites that would be thoroughly investigated the following day. At about midday, I indicated to Piet to stop. I 'saw' something that attracted my attention. About 100 m from the road, there was a clump of trees that were growing extremely luxuriantly. I wanted to go and 'see' with the divining rods whether I could determine the cause of the phenomenon. Liza remained in the vehicle while Piet, Willem, and I went to investigate.

I walked in front, concentrating on the divining rods. As we were moving through a patch of knee-high grass, I felt a prick on my left shin. It felt completely as if I was walking second in line, and the first in line had pulled a twig with thorns forward, and on release, it had struck back and hit me on the shin. I didn't take any more notice of it and kept on concentrating on the divining rods. These were indicating that I was walking over an activity line. When the divining rods stopped their movement, I stopped and looked down at my shin and saw three punctured areas close together with blood clots on them. These were not due to a twig with thorns! 'I was walking in front!' flashed through my mind. 'Piet, I think something has bitten me.' 'What?' asked Piet. 'I don't know. Let me just sit on this rock for a while,' I said, pointing at the rock in the clearing in the grass. Within a couple of seconds, I experienced a metallic taste in my mouth. 'I think a Black mamba has bitten me.' I again inspected the three puncture marks on my shin. Black mambas are known to strike twice in quick succession. The three blood clots confirmed my fears: one full strike and one at an angle. The distance between the puncture marks indicated that it wasn't a large snake. 'What now?' Piet and Willem asked. 'Don't get excited,' I said more to myself than to them. 'Let us slowly move towards the vehicle, but please don't tell Liza.' When we got to the double cab, I got in behind Liza, who was sitting up front, next to Piet. 'Where are we going now?' she questioned Piet. 'There is a slight change of plan. We need to go to Thabazimbi quickly!' At the back, I used my overall as a tourniquet on my upper leg. Liza was none the wiser. I started experiencing the second symptom—tunnel vision. In the middle of the 'eye, the image was sharp. The rest of the image was blurred by circles moving around the sharp middle section, blurring the whole image. By means of hand signs, I indicated to Willem that I was convinced that a Black mamba had bitten me. In the front of the vehicle, Liza and Piet continued with their conversation while Piet tried to make haste, driving as quickly as the road conditions allowed. Willem and I joined in the conversation, and then I experienced the third symptom. My speech was becoming impaired. I felt like I was talking with a swollen tongue. I now could not take part in the conversation any longer. I started perspiring involuntary; Symptom no. 4 had kicked in. I could feel my stomach muscles beginning to relax: symptom no. 5. One had to realise that the different symptoms didn't necessarily follow one another chronologically, and these became more intense with the progression of time. We were now in Thabazimbi, and Piet took a shortcut to the Thabazimbi Hospital. 'Why are we at the hospital?' Liza wanted to know. 'We have come to visit a colleague,' was Piet's white lie. Piet escorted Liza to the hospital reception while Willem assisted me to the Emergency Ward. After Willem's explanation, the nurse directed us to a room, saying that we were very fortunate because Dr Van der Merwe was presently at the hospital. At that stage, I couldn't climb onto the hospital bed unassisted. After 10 minutes, the nurses had to change the sheets on the bed as these were soaked with perspiration. I could not pull myself erect. All my muscles, but especially my stomach muscles, were non-functional and not reacting to messages from my brain. Then, Liza entered the room very upset. 'Has a mamba bitten you?' she wanted to know. 'Where did you hear that?' Willem wanted to know. 'A nurse wanted to know whether I was the wife of the man that was bitten by a Black mamba!' We most probably could not have kept it from her for much longer. Now there were four of us who could worry.

Dr van der Merwe entered the room. 'Were you bitten by the Black mamba?' he asked, looking at me. I nodded my head in a positive direction. 'Did you see the snake?' was his next routine question. Now my head moved in the negative direction. 'How can you be certain that it was a Black mamba?' I started telling him in a slurred speech the different symptoms that I had experienced. When I got to number three, he indicated to me to stop and said, 'A Black mamba did bite you!' The Thabazimbi bush veldt is known for its Black mamba, and Dr Van der Merwe had to treat at least four cases per year and, therefore, was an expert on the topic. With a bottle of adrenaline on hand, he administered the antiserum. After a couple of minutes, I could feel the effects of the Black-mamba venom abating. After about an hour, I was again my normal self and wanted to get up. 'You are going to spend at least the evening in bed. Doctor's instructions!' Who was I to ignore an expert's instruction?

I didn't go down the same road as Danie only because, first, I had got immediate assistance, second, the bite marks were on my shin, where there is very limited blood supply, and third, within just less than half an hour, I was in a hospital with expert medical assistance.

The following day, around midmorning, Dr Van der Merwe came to check on me and said I could be discharged at midday. Although I was still a bit under the weather, we commenced our journey back to Skukuza. We would return to continue divining for water at a later stage. A week later, I became very ill, with a rash very similar to German measles all over my body. I visited the medical doctor in Skukuza, who admitted that he did not know what the matter was. 'I can treat the symptoms, but I don't know what the cause is.' Skukuza is a small secluded community, and everyone knew of everyone else's problems and ailments. My symptoms were, therefore, also discussed at the State Veterinary Offices at Skukuza. Roy, the State Veterinarian, phoned and requested to come and see me after work. When Roy came into the bedroom, he was carrying a thick book under his arm. After the usual formalities, he opened the book at a book mark and started to read from the book.

After he had finished reading, he asked, 'Are these the symptoms you are experiencing?' Roy had read the symptoms better than I would have described them. 'I thought so,' said Roy. 'You are allergic to snakebite serum.' There you have it. A veterinarian making a snakebite-related diagnosis on a water diviner. I was again dumbfounded by the expertise that was abundant in Skukuza. My future, under similar circumstances, would have been to be put onto a heart-lung apparatus to survive a snakebite.

* * *

Towards the end of 1995, we received very disconcerting news. I received a letter from Pretoria Head Office that stated that I had been transferred to the Kimberley Office for operational reasons. My own career planning, however, indicated that I would spend all my working days in the KNP. Now this! I tried everything to have the transfer cancelled by the internal Human Resource Dept procedures. I even went so far as to initiate a grievance procedure against the Chief Executive Officer of SANParks. During January 1996, I received a final letter informing me that if I had not transferred to Kimberley by April 1996, SANParks Management would have no other option but to give me a severance package of 3 months' salary.

* * *

The first weekend of November was usually spent participating in the so-called Birding Big Day. The aim was for a team of four people to identify as many bird species during a 24-hour period, starting at midnight on the Saturday and ending at 24.00 of the same day. This was going to be my farewell Birding Big Day from the KNP.

Peter, Willem, Freek, and I were the designated team, and Louis was the driver of the vehicle. We started off from Lower Sabie at 00.00. For us, this occasion wasn't to break records. We just wanted to spend quality time together, reflecting on the past, present, and future and trying to make sense of the news that I had received. Don't worry, the birds were not neglected. During the 24-hour period, we managed to record just over 190 different species. Just before sunset, we were between the Nkuhlu Picnic Site and Lower Sabie on our way towards Lower Sabie. Up ahead, we encountered four big elephant bulls sauntering down the road in the same direction we were travelling in. Louis kept his distance, and the bulls were seemingly unaware of our presence. The procession moved slowly down the road, and we enjoyed the elephants, the surroundings, and the late-afternoon atmosphere. The elephants suddenly moved off the road and started eating on the tree and shrubs next to the road. Louis continued slowly and drove past the feeding elephants without any interference from them. As we were passing the elephants, Freek said, 'Ou Bles,' that was his nickname for me (old bald one), 'these four great ones have come to bid you farewell.' I pretended that a gnat had flown into my eye and, under this cover, wiped a tear from my eyes. I saw that the other team members also looked teary eyed. Most probably also got gnats in their eyes . . . Something that I really felt bad about was the many 'things' that we had promised one another that we would still do together if and when more time allowed for it. The reality, however, was that the more time became less and less. So much so that most of the promises and good intentions never materialised, to our own detriment.

*   *   *

The Makhohlola Dam was built in the drainage line (spruit/small river) of the same name. The spruit was one of the very few drainage lines of the Gomondwane bush situated between Lower Sabie and Crocodile Bridge. Louis, the incumbent Section Ranger at Crocodile Bridge, had built a camping terrain almost 300 m from the water's edge of the dam. For safety reasons, he built a branch enclosure around the facility with an entrance almost 4 m wide that gave access to the branched enclosure. One moonlit evening, I had the privilege of staying over at the campsite in my caravan. The enjoyment of the unique atmosphere of the Gomondwane bush before sleep time was very special. During the course of the evening, I was awakened by a strange puffing, snorting sound. I opened the caravan door and went and sat on the caravan step to enjoy the show. Just outside of the opening to the branched enclosure, a big White rhino bull milled around, kicking up dust and making his discontent known for the strange object within the bushed enclosure by these strange puffing, snorting sounds. At one stage, the rhino was so worked up that it made peculiar 'buck jumps' or rather 'rhino jumps' in the opening to the branched enclosure. What surprised me was that the rhino honoured the opening to the branched enclosure and at no stage breeched it. On one occasion, the rhino walked away from the opening, suddenly turned around, and charged at full speed. 'What now?' I thought, getting ready to seek safety in the caravan . . . absolutely unnecessary. The charge stopped in a big cloud of dust at the opening. After unsuccessfully trying for almost half an hour to intimidate the caravan, the rhino gave up in despair and ran off into the bush.

*   *   *

After this incident, I promised myself that I would return again to experience the unique Gomondwane atmosphere and more particularly the atmosphere at the Makhohlola Dam during a full-moon period. My time in the KNP was, however, slowly running out. I convinced Liza, Merle, and Ian to come and enjoy a farewell experience at the Makhohlola Dam with me. At sunset, we were already at the dam, and I parked the vehicle parallel to and 5 m from the water's edge on the western side of the dam. We parked the camping chairs alongside the length of the vehicle and took up our stations to enjoy the reflection of the rising moon over the dam. On the opposite side of the dam, three White rhinos came sauntering down to the water's edge to drink. Suddenly, there was an unearthly sound coming from the upper reaches of the dam. The two wives wanted to flee to the safety of the vehicles, but Ian and I calmed them down. Again, the sound reverberated through the bush. 'What is it?' they wanted to know. Fortunately, I had heard these sounds before during many foot patrols in the Gomondwane bush. At closer inspection, I had encountered two White rhino bulls battling it out for supremacy. These were their battle cries. 'Those are two rhinos battling for supremacy,' I reassured them. We were focussed on the social interaction of the three rhinos on the opposite side of the dam. The battle cries of the fighting rhinos did not bother them at all. I suddenly became aware of movement right next to me. Approximately 5 m from the rear end of the vehicle, a White rhino cow and calf were moving towards the water's edge to drink. I drew the others' attention to the cow and calf and indicated with a '*shhh*', finger in front of my mouth, that we should remain silent. I had not expected the rhinos to pass the vehicle at such close range, but they did. Then Ian saw two big male White rhinos moving past the front end of the vehicle, towards the water's edge, even closer than the cow and calf. In awed silence, we drank in the scene. Wonderful! The smell of the vehicle must have overpowered our human 'smells'. This was my only explanation for the fearlessness of the rhinos in such close proximity to us. We did not mind at all. We enjoyed the exceptional experience for another hour or so and then decided that it was time to leave the Gomondwane drama to play itself out. When we bade our friends goodbye at Lower Sabie, I reiterated it to Whytie that he had to make more time for these kinds of experiences before it was too late. Time was running out.

*   *   *

One of my honoured colleagues, John Mnisi, came into my office and asked, 'Mbazo, why does Pretoria want to transfer you?' To him, the Head Office in Pretoria was 'Pretoria', in all probability a place that he had never seen. 'John, I really don't know!' The two of us tried to rationalise the Head Office's decision from every angle, without any success. 'Mbazo,' said John, 'the people in Pretoria are flying too high!' 'What do you mean by that, John?' 'Mbazo, it is similar to when you have to fly somewhere with an aircraft. When one crosses the apron to get to the aircraft, one can still see everything very clearly. One can see an individual, ant, a toktokkie, fine grains of sand, and even individual grass seeds. When one sits in the aircraft looking out the window, some detail is lost. The ants, toktokkies, sand, and grass seeds are not visible anymore. However, one can still clearly see the leaves on the trees, grass blades, Warthogs, and Impalas along the runway and even the birds. As the aircraft moves down the runway and starts to get airborne, the individual leaves and blades of grass disappear as well as the birds. The Warthogs and Impalas can still be distinguished. These also quickly disappear. Giraffes and elephants and individual trees are still distinguishable. A while later, these disappear, and the trees and grass become a mass of green below the aircraft. Even elephant herds cannot be seen anymore. The different stone hillocks lose their height, and everything seems to become flat. The people in "Pretoria" fly too high.

They have completely lost contact with the realities on the ground and what is important at ground level. We must forgive them for flying too high.'

'John, thank you for your wise words,' I said, giving him a big bear hug. I could not help feeling like an outcast. The high flyers had banned me from the KNP. In due course, I made peace with the transfer. Had I not, at a very early age, requested a Higher Hand to be the 'Skipper' of my life's boat?

As in the KNP, I now also had the opportunity to rub shoulders with many wonderful people working in the rest of the SANParks organisation. After 2 years in Kimberley, I was transferred to the Pretoria Head Office until the end of February 2006 when I went on pension. One thing that I was very proud of was that I never neglected what was happening at ground level.

*   *   *

During 2010, out of the blue, I received a very appreciated phone call from a special old colleague, Louis Olivier (even though he was a Blue Bull supporter), the incumbent Regional Ranger stationed at Phalaborwa: 'Would you mind if we named one of the new-generation big ivory carriers in the KNP after you? We would like to honour ex-colleagues of the KNP who left their mark in the Kruger in this way.'

I gasped for breath. I was very moved by what I had just heard and could not utter another word.

'Hello, Lynn, can you hear me?'

'Yes, Louis, I can hear you. I am just totally taken aback. Are you serious about what you have just said?' was my reaction. 'Of course,' said Louis.

'How does one spell "Mbazo"?' Louis wanted to know. 'We would also appreciate a synopsis of your career in the KNP.'

'Louis, thank you very much for the great honour, and it will be my privilege to send you the info as soon as possible.' 'Oh yes, we also need a KNP photo of you!' Louis concluded.

I could not contain my excitement and immediately phoned Liza and the kids. 'I hope it is a young elephant bull that can still spend many years in the KNP,' was Magnus's comment.

Reflecting on what had just happened, I could not suppress a broad smile. Mbazo was banned from the KNP, but now he is back again; even though it is in the form of an elephant, he is back. Mbazo, the elephant, and I most probably walked on the same elephant footpaths criss-crossing the KNP at some stage or another during our dual tenure of the KNP. I knew that, Mbazo, the elephant, was going to give pleasure to many a KNP visitor. Most probably just as must pleasure as my stay in the KNP had provided me.

'Mbazo, you must thoroughly enjoy that big wonderful place that lies so close to my heart. I am spiritually there with you.'

*   *   *

LYNN 'MBAZO' VAN ROOYEN

Lynn 'Mbazo' van Rooyen started his extensive career on 1 October 1967 when he was appointed in Skukuza as the first full-time game-capture staff member with the job title of Ranger/Game Capturer. He remained in this position until 1970 when he resigned in order to study further at the Stellenbosch University. During this time, he spent every July and December back in Kruger, filling in for Section Rangers who were on leave at the time.

After finishing his studies in December 1972, as planned, Mr Don Louw retired from the Kruger National Parks, and Lynn was appointed in the vacant position as Section Ranger Shangoni from 1 January 1973 and remained there until end 1974. In 1975, the then National Parks Board sponsored Lynn to complete his Honours degree full-time in Wildlife Management at the Pretoria University. During this absence, Louis Olivier acted as Relief Ranger at Shangoni.

In 1976, upon returning to the Kruger National Park, Lynn was moved to Tshokwane as a District Ranger until 1977, when he was moved to the 'great north' as District Ranger based at Punda Maria (before the name change to Maria). At this time, no tourists were permitted in the summer months, and Lynn enjoyed many years there until April 1980, when he was transferred to Lower Sabie as the Regional Ranger for the south of the Kruger National Park, which, at that time, spanned from Crocodile Bridge to the Olifants River, and he remained there until December 1991.

Lynn was later transferred to the 'head office' in Skukuza in 1992 as Manager of Nature Conservation for the Kruger National Park and continued in this position until March 1996, after which he was moved to the Kimberly offices, in the position of Manager of Conservation/Head of the Northern Parks.

In January 1998, Lynn made his last move within SANParks to 'Groenkloof', Pretoria's head office, still as Head of Northern Parks, and was temporarily in the position of Director of Parks for 9 months and lastly was the Head of Biodiversity for all Parks (except the Kruger National Park) as well as Head of the Poverty Relief Unit.

MBAZO:

Origin of Name: Named after Lynn van Rooyen who served in conservation for South African National Parks for 39 years. (Mbazo meaning 'hatchet' refers to Lynn's early years as a ranger where he was known to lead field patrols armed only with a hatchet.) Range: This bull holds in the Orpen Gate area and is also known to frequent the area around Satara and N'wanetsi and slightly north of there, towards Balule.

Special Features: This bull has very unusually shaped ivory that makes him easily recognisable, with the right tusk fairly straight and the left considerably curved. Two areas of thickening on the trunk between the tusks are visible in all footage of this bull. No ear notches are easily visible; although, a u-shaped notch exists at the extreme bottom of the right lobe alongside the neck area.

General: This bull was first recorded in December 2008 by Nicole Cordes as part of the emerging tuskers' competition in 2009 and was noted as unusual. Several submissions followed, clearly identifying this bull's stomping grounds. He was recently named, confirming his 'status' amongst the 'new' era.

Courtesy: Ronnie & Nicole Rogoff

'Only "Mbazo", the elephant, will know what the Kruger National Park has meant to me. He has the privilege of spending his entire life within the boundaries of the Kruger National Park, a privilege that has eluded me, despite the fact that it was a lifelong ambition.'

BREAKDOWN OF CONTENTS:

Footprints through the Kruger National Park

Lynn van Rooyen.

18. Lynn had to be reasonably fit mentally and physically to be able to enjoy his work.
19. Studies in Stellenbosch and then appointed as Section Ranger at Shangoni.
20. Catching poachers.
21. Alone on foot patrol and enchanted by a very restful and contended elephant bull.
22. Further studies in Pretoria.
23. Klaas Prinsloo's homestead to track a wounded lioness.
24. The bush had a story of its own to tell.
25. Identifying the trees and shrubs in the Kruger National Park and discovering the *Suregada africana*.
26. Simeon attacked by a lioness.
27. Transferred to Punda Maria as District Ranger with the Sections Shangoni, Shingwedzi, and Pafuri reporting to Lynn.
28. 'Poisoned' water.
29. The mystical Xantangalani cave with Bushman rock art discovered by Lynn.
30. Cobra underneath the motorbike at Dzundwini hill.
31. Elephant bull at midnight.
32. Geologists from the Department of Geological Surveys at Punda Maria, speculating about mining in the Kruger National Park for Coking coal used by the iron industry.
33. The culling of buffaloes and elephants requires the most dangerous helicopter flying imaginable.
34. In need of water for the Mopane Rest Camp.
35. Transferred from Punda Maria to Lower Sabie during April 1980 with the following sections in the Southern Region: Houtboschrandt, Kingfisherspruit, Satara, N'wanetsi, Tshokwane, Skukuza, Pretoriuskop, Stolznek, Malane, Crocodile Bridge, and Lower Sabie.
36. Building of roads in the Kruger National Park.
37. A number of elephant carcasses were spotted from the air with tusks removed.
38. A 5-year-old kid, a true hero who was prepared, against all odds, to give up his life for his folks. And he did.
39. The KNP Commando.
40. Wilkie's encounter with the devil.
41. Awie de Qlerq and 'Your Honour'.

42. Building a tree house in the KNP bush.

43. SANParks imported Black rhinos from Kwa-Zulu Natal Parks to the KNP and the *Scope* photographer almost killed by a rhino. With every offload of Black rhinos, there was some sort of drama.

44. Law enforcement in the KNP. What has happened to: I went to the bush to find spiritual rest?

45. Rescuing a small elephant that was stuck in the mud while the Matriarch cow and the whole herd charged at Lynn on his motorbike.

46. Three hyenas and a kudu bull in a death battle at Msimuku Spruit.

47. Trail Rangers get the best possible training to ensure the safety of hikers on a wilderness trail, but sometimes the elephant charged on.

48. 'Stompie!' (the elephant with the short tusk). The old bull was very mischievous, and many tourists had suffered due to his pranks.

49. Baboons help themselves to tourists' food whenever they want.

50. Playing golf in KNP with wild animals receiving a tee shot! Enough reason for a lion to feed on the rough.

51. To be bitten by a Black mamba and to survive to tell the tale is a miracle.

52. In 1995, Lynn had been transferred to the Kimberley Office for operational reasons. His own career planning, however, indicated that he would spend all his working days in the KNP!

53. Lynn's farewell Birding Big Day from the KNP.

54. A last moonlit night at the Makhohlola Dam, with a big White rhino bull milling around and kicking up dust.

55. An honoured colleague's, John Mnisi's wise words to Lynn: 'Mbazo, the people in Pretoria are flying too high!'

56. During 2010, Lynn received the honour of a new-generation big ivory carrier in the KNP (there are only seven of the big tuskers) named after him. Mbazo was banned from the KNP, but now he is back again!

*   *   *